HODDER SCIENCE

GOLD

Pupil's Book

C

Nigel Heslop David Brodie
George Snape James Williams
Marguerite Hall

Hodder & Stoughton

Photo acknowledgements

The publishers would like to thank the following individuals, institutions and companies for permission to reproduce photographs in this book. Every effort has been made to trace ownership of copyright. The publishers would be happy to make arrangements with any copyright holder whom it has not been possible to contact:

Action Plus (45 right, 114, 115 all, 132 top left); Ampthill Photographic Services (1); Andrew Lambert (20 all, 22 all, 23 all, 27 all, 29 left, 30 bottom right, 31 right, 32 all, 35, 59, 95 top left and bottom right, 98 both, 100 left, 103, 139 middle and right, 140 top two and bottom left, 150 both); Associated Press (132); BBC Natural History Unit/ Wendy Darke (111); British Alcan (31 top left, 101 middle left); British Museum (26 bottom); Bruce Coleman Limited (90 all, 93 all, 118 bottom left, 124); Centre for Alternative Technology (42 all, 43 bottom); Corbis (3, 4 left, 6, 16a, 16e, 26 top, 28 top, 30 top left, 34 right, 45 left, 49 left, 77 top left, 95 bottom left, 99, 121 all, 132 right, 140, 155 both, 157, 165); Elizabeth Whiting (16b); Hodder & Stoughton (16d, 53, 63, 100 right, 156 all); Holt Studios (9, 86, 87, 89, 90 all, 91 all); Hulton Getty (16f); Life File (67, 101 top left, 106 top left)/ Dave Thompson (154)/ Emma Lee (34 left, 62 left, 65, 139 left, 153)/ Jeremy Hoare (107 bottom right)/ Nicola Sutton (95 top right)/ Nigel Sitwell (62); Moviestore Collection (112); Mrs E B Carpenter (4 right); NASA (79 bottom); New Media (29 right); Nigel Heslop (101 right); Oxford Scientific Films/ Jen and Des Bartlett (145)/ Mike Birkhead (158 bottom)/ Tony Bomford (118 top left); Peter Scoones (11 right); Radio Times/Hulton Picture Library (85); Reinhold Rau (10 right, 11 left); Ruth Hughes (16c, 50 top two, 54 both, 88, 106 two on right, 129, 152 all, 164); Science Photo Library (2 (sperm cell)), 12, 21, 55 both, 64, 76, 77, 79, 84 all, 101, 138 top left, 161)/ Carlos Munoz-Yague, Eurelios (137 left)/ Custom Medical Stock Photo (158 top)/ David Parker (137 right)/ Dept of Clinical Radiology, Salisbury District Hospital (138 top right)/ Dr E Walker (51)/ Dr Jeremy Burgess (2 (ovules))/ Dr Yorgos Nikas (2 (egg cell))/ European Space Agency (78 left)/ Eye of Science (2 (pollen))/ Ken Eward (14)/ L Willatt, East Anglian Regional Genetics Service (2 (chromosomes))/ Martin Dohrn (162)/ Matt Meadows, Peter Arnold Inc. (50 bottom left)/ Mehau Kulyk (28 bottom)/ NASA (64 left, 159)/ Schleichkorn, Custom Medical Stock Photo (50 bottom right)/ Science Source (138 bottom right)/ Space Telescope Science Institute, NASA (77 bottom, 126)/ Takeshi Takahara (120)/ Tek Image (49 right)/ University of Dundee (78 right); Still Pictures/ Mark Edwards (58)/ J P Vantighem (60 top); The Ronald Grant Archive/ Ron Batzdorff (72); The Zoological Society of London (10 left); Wellcome Trust (52 both); Chapter of Wells Cathedral (61 right); Weston Point Studios Ltd (106 bottom left); Zanussi (43 top).

The publishers would also like to thank the British Library for permission to use the pictures of the heliocentric and geocentric universe (page 76) from *A perfit description of the Caelestiall Orbes 718g52* and *Cosmographia 1007.g.24*, respectively.

Orders: please contact Bookpoint Ltd, 130 Milton Park, Abingdon, Oxon OX14 4SB. Telephone: (44) 01235 827720. Fax: (44) 01235 400454. Lines are open from 9.00 – 6.00, Monday to Saturday, with a 24 hour message answering service. You can also order through our website www.hodderheadline.co.uk

British Library Cataloguing in Publication Data
A catalogue record for this title is available from the British Library

ISBN 0 340 80440 8

First Published 2002

Impression number 10 9 8 7 6 5 4 3
Year 2008 2007 2006 2005 2004

Cover photo from Science Photo Library
Typeset by Fakenham Photosetting.
Printed in Italy for Hodder & Stoughton Educational, a division of Hodder Headline Ltd, 338 Euston Road, London NW1 3BH.

Contents

Preface

Hodder Science is a collection of resources designed to match exactly the QCA exemplar Scheme of Work for KS3. The core material of the series is suitable for the more able two-thirds of pupils. The scheme has successfully moved away from the minimalist approach of the past decade, is pupil-friendly and easy to read.

Hodder Science Gold has been written to extend the range of the *Hodder Science* series, specifically catering for the lower 30–35% of the ability range. These books will progressively target levels 2 to 4/5 of the National Curriculum.

Hodder Science Gold takes a new attitude to producing books for the lower attainer. It does far more than just present the same learning material at a slightly lower reading age. Marguerite Hall, a well-known learning methods consultant, has lent her expertise to increase the friendliness of the text and the accessibility of the way the ideas are presented. We have taken an integrated approach to producing material aimed at low attainers for the 21st Century.

- Key words boxes highlight and define target vocabulary on the spread where the terms are first used.
- Concepts are introduced at a level and rate more suitable for slower learners.
- Progression, through the concepts and models used, is tailored to the needs of a slower learner.
- There is no compromise on essential learning vocabulary, but peripheral vocabulary is kept to a simple reading level.
- Reading level concentrates on good sentence structure to make the flow of reading easier.
- Sometimes a few more simple words are used to explain a difficult concept rather than rigidly cutting word count.
- Generally word count per page is one half to two thirds of the parallel *Hodder Science* books.
- The number and style of questions has been altered to enable slower pupils to keep pace.
- Essential summary tasks contain a high level of prompt to ensure accuracy and success.
- To aid parallel use of the books, the spread by spread structure exactly mirrors the higher level books.
- To avoid stigmatisation of the lower attainer, many illustrations are the same and the book colour is the same. The gold trim signifies that these books are special.

Nigel Heslop 2002

Inheritance and selection

Starter Activity
Variation

In what ways are we different from each other and in what ways are we the same? Scientists call the differences between us **variation**. Can you remember the work you have done on the features we inherit from our natural parents?

Look at the picture of this family party. Try to pick out who is part of the family and who might just be a guest.

Questions

1 Variation can be caused by two things:

- Inheritance – the features we get from our natural parents.
- The environment – such as where we live and how we are brought up.

a) Which of the features in the boxes opposite are examples of inherited variation?

b) Which are examples of environmental variation?

c) Which could be examples of both?

hair colour | weight | nose shape | height | ability to draw | eye colour | hand size | ability to sing | being good at maths | foot size | mouth shape | skin colour

Why are we all similar, but not identical?

Key words

chromosomes Threads of DNA, a human has 46 chromosomes in 23 pairs

DNA The chemical in the nucleus of every cell, it controls what we look like and who we are

fertilisation The joining of an egg cell and a sperm cell

fraternal twins Twins that develop from two separate eggs and two separate sperm

genes Small bits of DNA that control how we look

identical twins Twins that develop from one egg splitting into two

Question

1 What are the two types of sex cells found in
a) Humans?
b) Plants?

We aren't identical to our parents. We may share some features like the shape of our nose, or the shape of our chin, or our hair colour, but there are differences between parents and their children.

For a new life to begin, a sperm cell from the father and an egg cell from the mother must join together. This process is called **fertilisation**. A similar thing happens in lots of plants. A pollen grain (the male cell) joins with an ovule (the female cell) and seeds are produced that can grow into new plants. This type of reproduction is known as sexual reproduction. In animals and plants it produces new plants and animals that are similar, but not identical to the parent plant or animal.

What we look like and how we grow is controlled by the nucleus of the cell. The nucleus of a cell contains a chemical called **DNA**. Our features are controlled by small sections of DNA called **genes**. Every nucleus contains many thousands of genes. Genes control the colour of your eyes and hair, the shape of your nose, they tell muscle cells to grow and many other things.

The genes are found on threads of DNA called **chromosomes**. The chromosomes occur in pairs. Each one of our cells contains 23 pairs of chromosomes, like the ones shown in the Figure 2.

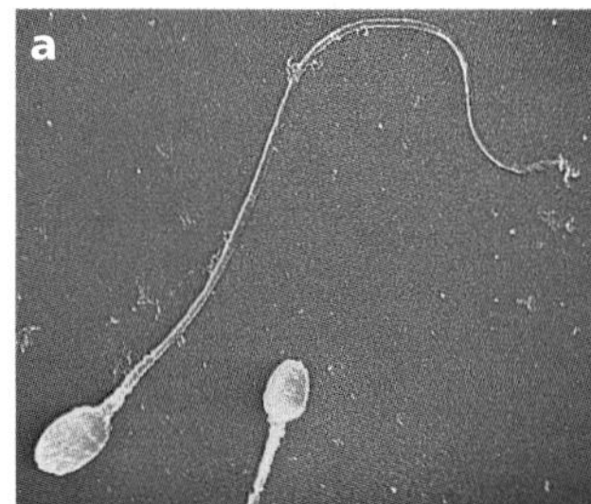

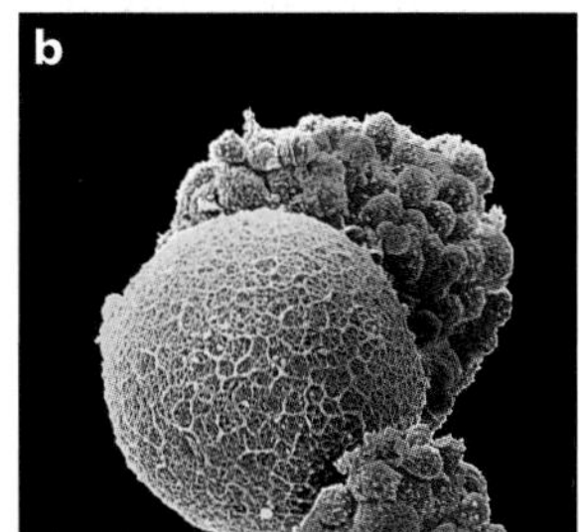

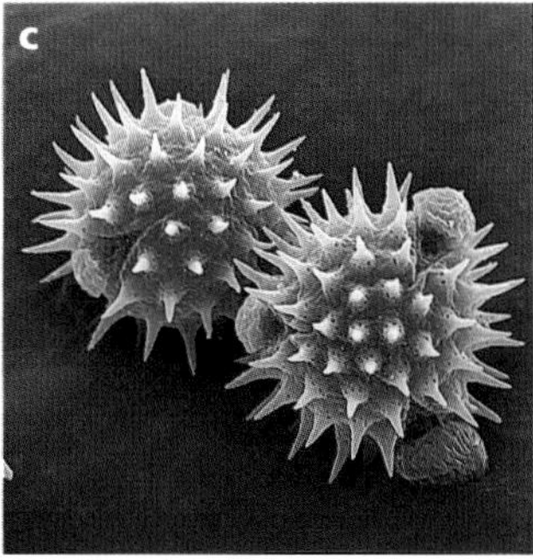

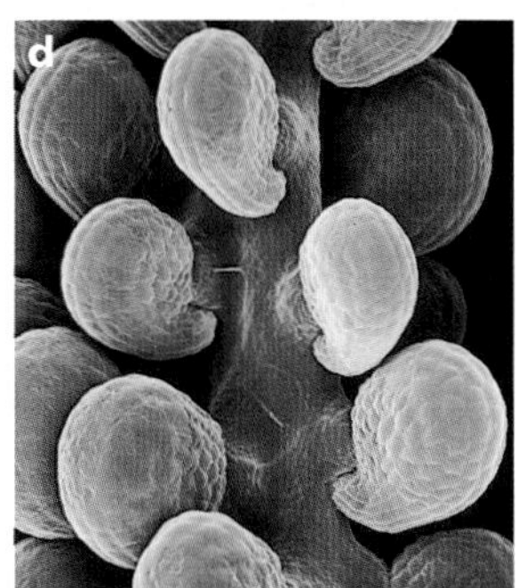

Figure 1 Sex cells: a) sperm cells, b) an egg cell, c) pollen grains, d) ovules.

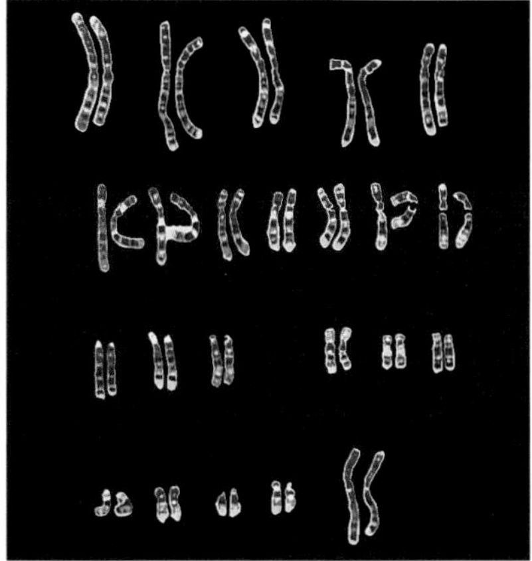

Figure 2 Humans have 46 chromosomes in 23 pairs.

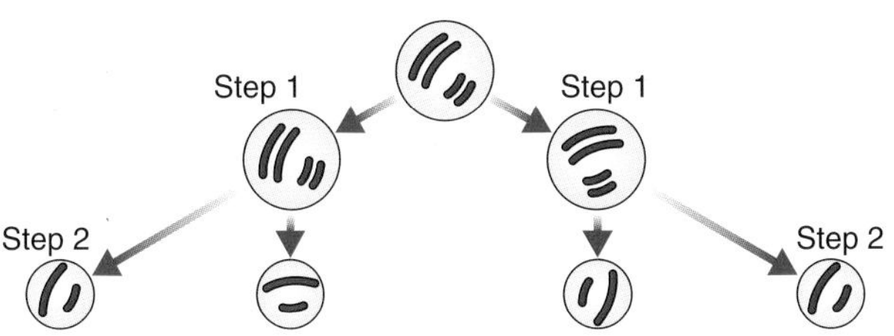

Figure 3 Producing sex cells from an animal with only four chromosomes

Egg cells and sperm cells are specialised cells. They only have 23 single chromosomes, half the number of a normal cell. Figure 3 shows how sperm cells would be produced in an animal with only four chromosomes (two pairs). In step 1 the cell divides just like a normal cell. This makes two cells each with four chromosomes. In step 2 the cell divides again. This time one chromosome from each pair ends up in each new cell. This makes four cells, each with two chromosomes.

After fertilisation the chromosomes pair up again. So a fertilized egg in this animal would have four chromosomes, two from the father and two from the mother.

Because there is a mixture of genes and chromosomes from the mother and father, the offspring would have a mixture of features from the mother and father.

Questions

2 Where are the chromosomes found in the cells of plants and animals?

3 What is a gene?

4 Why are children similar, but not identical to their natural parents?

Twins

When two babies are born on the same day to the same mother, we call them twins. There may be some pairs of twins in your school. There are two types of twins – **identical** and **fraternal**.

Identical twins can look exactly the same, or there may be small differences. Just after the egg is fertilised inside the mother, it begins to divide and grow. Before it gets too big, the egg splits completely into two. Because the DNA in each is identical, two identical babies develop.

Figure 4 Eng and Chan, conjoined or Siamese twins, born in Siam in 1811.

If the egg doesn't completely split then conjoined twins can develop. These are often called Siamese twins after the most famous pair Eng and Chang, born in Siam (now Thailand).

Fraternal twins happen when two different eggs in the mother are fertilised at the same time, by two separate sperm. Because the DNA is not identical, two different babies develop. They can even be of different sexes.

Question

5 Can identical twins be brother and sister? Explain your answer.

Remember

In small groups choose the correct word from each pair given, then copy the paragraphs into your exercise book.

Children are often **similar/identical** to their natural parents. Things like the shape of your nose, or the colour of your hair are inherited.

The DNA in the nucleus makes up threads called **genes/chromosomes**. Small sections of these are called **chromosomes/genes**. These control many of our features such as hair colour.

The male sex cell in humans is a **sperm/cheek** cell. In females it is an egg. In plants the male sex cell is **nectar/pollen** and the female sex cell is an ovule.

Identical twins happen when one fertilised egg completely splits in two. Fraternal twins happen when two different eggs are fertilised by two different sperm.

Sheepdogs

Key words

artificial selection Selecting two plants or two animals with specific traits to breed together

traits Features or behaviour

Sheepdogs are a good example of how we have bred animals with specific **traits**. We have done this to produce breeds of animals that are useful to us. The Romans brought sheep and sheepdogs to Britain when they invaded over 2000 years ago.

Figure 1 A Border Collie like this one is the breed of dog specially created to herd sheep. Crouching is one of the traits of a good sheepdog.

Shepherds needed dogs to help them control large flocks of sheep in the countryside. The trick was to find dogs that had the traits that shepherds needed, such as being able to herd sheep and to move them without attacking them. Over 120 years ago a Northumbrian farmer called Adam Telfer mated two collie dogs called Roy and Meg. Roy was a gentle dog, but not very good at herding. Meg was a good herding dog. She gave birth to a puppy on the 15th September 1893. The farmer called the puppy 'Old Hemp'.

The Border Collie, or sheepdog as we know it today, is descended from Old Hemp who fathered over 200 puppies until his death in 1901.

Questions

1 What do we mean by the word 'trait'?

2 What traits do you think humans have bred into the following animals:
a) a racehorse?
b) a dairy cow?

Figure 2 Old Hemp, the first true Border Collie.

Questions

3 The Border Collie is a working dog. It is used to being active in the countryside. What do you think you would have to do about the following things if you kept a Border Collie as a pet?
a) Exercise
b) Meals
c) Training

Traits in The Border Collie	Why the trait is important
A Eye	Border Collies control sheep with 'eye'.The dog concentrates on the sheep by staring at it. The sheep are 'held' by the dog's eye. Dogs that can do this well are called 'strong-eyed'.
B Crouch or Clapping	A Border Collie will often 'clap' or go down and face the sheep with its stomach close to the ground. This, along with 'eye', makes the dog look like it might attack. Dogs were bred for clapping and strong eye for many years. Now some are being bred or trained not to crouch down flat to the ground so they are ready to move quickly.
C Balance	Border Collies need to work quickly and often have to change direction suddenly to stop sheep from straying. To do this they need good balance. For newer breeds of Border Collie, where crouching is done more on their feet, balance is even more important.
D Power	Border Collies often need to run up a mountainside to round up the sheep. Powerful leg muscles are needed.
E Speed and agility	Sheep can scatter very fast if they are startled or frightened. The Border Collie needs to move quickly and be able to turn and twist.
F Interest in moving targets	Border Collies need to be quick to spot the sheep that wander off. If the dog didn't take any interest in moving targets they could easily miss a stray sheep.

Table 1 Behaviour traits which make up the Border Collie

Every dog has its day

Dogs have been pets and working animals for hundreds of years. We use dogs in lots of different ways, to help the blind and the deaf as guard dogs and just as friends and companions.

People use the different traits of dogs in some interesting ways. Small dogs were used by hunters to scare animals out of their burrows. Larger dogs were used to frighten people. Dogs that are easy to train are used as seeing dogs for the blind and hearing dogs for the deaf. Some dogs can be trained to sniff out drugs or explosives. Other dogs can be trained to perform tricks for television or film. When dogs are picked to breed with other dogs so that they pass their good traits on, we call this **artificial selection**.

Remember

Copy the following paragraph into your exercise book and write down the meaning of the words in bold underneath.

Animals can be bred specially to do a job. Sheepdogs are a good example of this. Sheepdogs have **traits** that make them good at their job. Some of the traits are **eye**, **crouch**, **agility**, speed, power and balance. Humans have used dogs to do different jobs for hundreds of years. Breeding animals to improve their traits is called **artificial selection**. Dogs are used for many things, such as guide dogs for the blind or hearing dogs for the deaf. They can also help the police find drugs and explosives.

1.3 Farmer's beef

Key words

breed A particular group of animals that have the same characteristics

If you visited a farm a thousand years ago, you would see animals that look similar to the ones we have today. You would recognise a cow, a sheep, a chicken and a pig. You would also notice a lot of differences. Over hundreds of years farmers have selected certain animals for breeding that contain the traits that the farmer and their customers want. This is a type of artificial selection.

Where's the beef?

Almost 250 years ago, the Tomkins family of Herefordshire, wanted to create a **breed** of cattle that could quickly produce high quality beef. After years of selecting the best Hereford cattle for breeding they produced a herd. All modern day Hereford cattle are descended from this herd.

Figure 1 A modern day Hereford cow.

300 years ago, Hereford cattle were much larger than they are today. Many weighed 1360 kg or more. Gradually, they were bred smaller and smaller so they had more meat and less fat. Today's Miniature Herefords weigh between 450 and 550 kg.

Question

1 Copy and complete this table and think of the traits or features that the following common farm plants and animals need in order to be useful to us as food.

Plant/animal	Most desirable traits or features
Potato	
Strawberry	
Dairy Cow	
Pig	
Chicken (egg laying)	
Chicken (meat)	
Sheep (wool producer)	
Lamb (meat)	
Beef cattle	

Hereford Cattle Changes

Hereford cattle are very common in America. Following World War II, the smaller, fatter type of cattle were still the most popular in cattle shows, but there was a change taking place in the meat industry and in the American diet. Beef fat (or tallow), was not used so much for making wax. People did not want to buy fatty joints of meat. So beef packers paid less for cattle that were too fat. The meat industry wanted a different type of cattle. People wanted a trimmer, leaner kind of cattle with lots of muscle. The over fattened cattle didn't fetch a high price in the market anymore.

Figure 2 The beef is very lean

This change in market meant two things had to happen:

1 The cattle needed to gain weight quicker each day, but this needed to cost less.
2 The cattle needed a food that increased muscle and not fat.

This gave breeders a big challenge to change the breed and turn it into a new kind of Hereford.

In the late 1960s breeders found that some of the European breeds were better. They imported cattle from Europe to improve the Hereford breed. They produce a new breed of cattle called the Miniature Hereford. This breed successfully turns its feed into muscle, grows quickly and has meat with the taste and look that people want to buy in the supermarket.

Questions

2 What can beef tallow be used for?

3 Why were people unhappy about the type of meat being sold after World War II?

4 What two things did the farmers have to do to meet their customers demands?

5 Where did the farmers find cattle with the traits that they wanted?

Remember

In small groups choose the correct word from each pair given, then copy the paragraph into your exercise book.

For many years farmers have been using **natural selection/artificial selection** to breed cattle that produce good quality **meat/fur**. As well as cattle, many other plants and animals have been bred to produce better quality food. People know that having too much fat in their diet can be unhealthy. As a result cattle that have **less/more** fat are produced.

How do you grow a seedless grape?

Key words

hormones Chemicals that make plants grow, produce fruit or roots

ovule The female sex cell in plants, found in the ovary

pollen The male sex cell in plants, found in the anthers

pollen tube A tube that delivers the nucleus from a pollen grain to an ovule

rhizome An underground stem

Next time you eat a seedless grape, think about how it grew. Seedless grapes, oranges, and other fruits are nice to eat and do not taste any different to fruits with seeds. You know that plants grow from seeds, so, just how do you grow a seedless grape?

First of all we need to understand what happens when plants produce seeds.

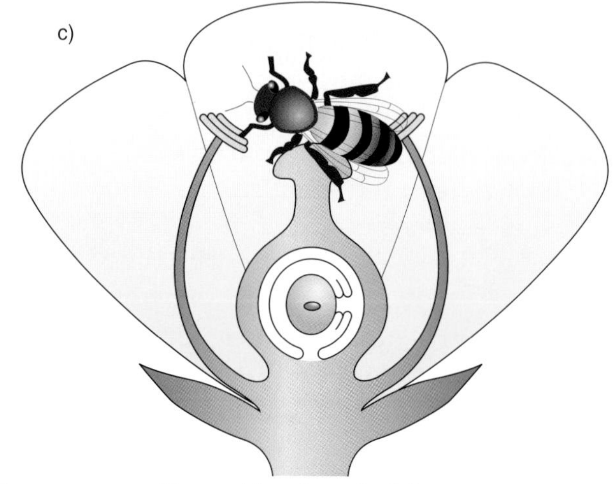

Flowers are pollinated by the wind, insects or pollinate themselves

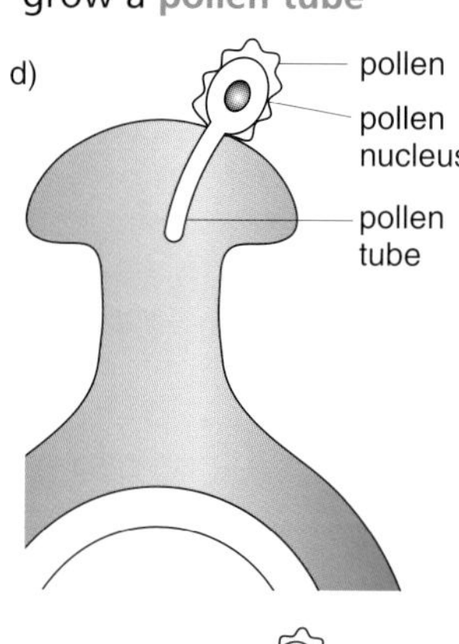

The pollen cells stick to the stigma and begin to grow a **pollen tube**

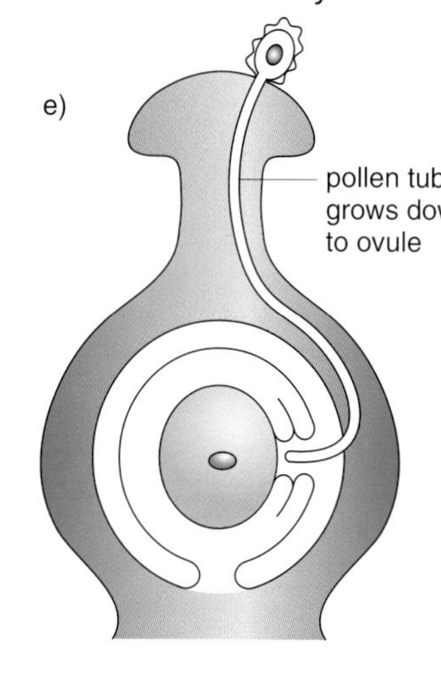

The pollen tube grows down the inside of the style, towards the egg cells in the ovary

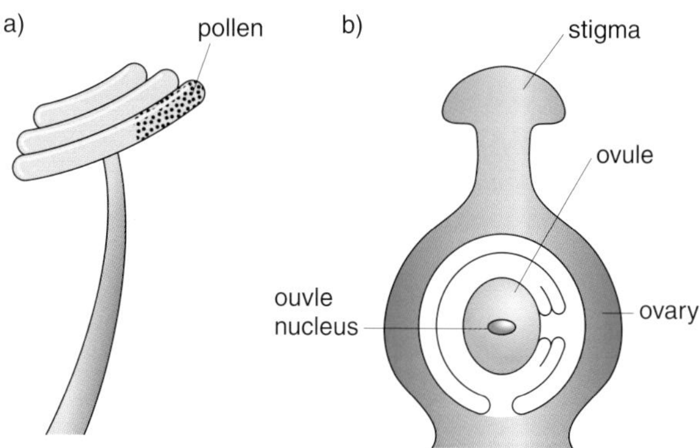

Male sex cells or **pollen** are made in the anthers

Female sex cells or **ovules** are made in the ovary

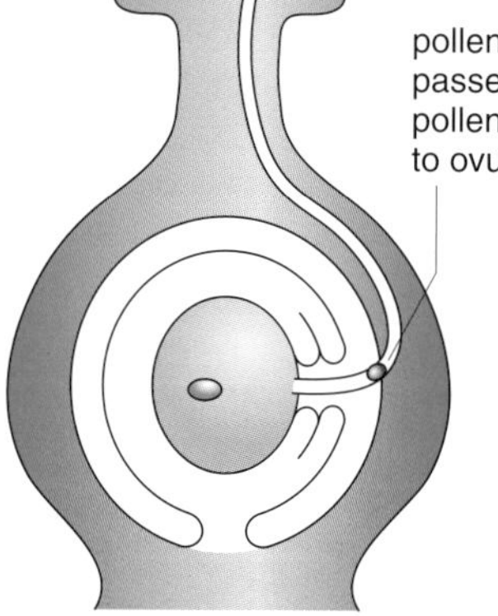

Once an ovule has been reached, the nucleus of the pollen grain travels down the pollen tube and joins together with the ovum

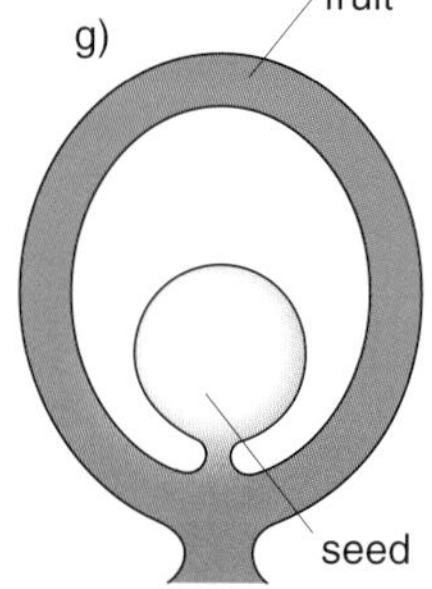

A seed grows, which can then develop into a new plant

Figure 1 Producing seeds.

Plants only normally produce seeds after an ovule has been fertilised. The seeds are found in fruits, such as grapes, oranges, and lemons. The fruits can be eaten by animals, who scatter the seeds in their droppings.

Questions

1 Draw a simple strip cartoon to show how a pollen tube travels down the stigma and style to reach the ovules. (You might want to turn this into a flick book. Ask your teacher if you are unsure of what a flick book is and how to make one.)

2 What do the ovules normally develop into after they are fertilised?

Seeds are a nuisance to us as we normally have to spit them out. So, just how do you grow a seedless grape, or orange? The answer is really quite simple. Plants have special chemicals called **hormones** that control how they grow, produce fruit, grow roots, and drop leaves and fruit at the right time of year. By spraying grapevines with the hormone that controls fruiting, the plant can be forced to produce grapes even though these normally only grow after the flower has been pollinated and is ready to produce a seed.

Not all plants produce fruits with seeds. Bananas are naturally seedless. The male flowers cannot produce the male sex cell or pollen. The female flowers produce the fruit.

Bananas don't grow on trees. The banana plant has no wood and is really the world's largest herb. The plant grows from an underground stem called a **rhizome**. New shoots grow up and clumps of bananas called 'hands' grow where the female flowers were. Banana plants only live for one year and produce one crop of bananas, then they die.

Figure 2 The banana plant may look like a tree, but it is in fact a flowering plant.

Questions

3 What evidence do we have that bananas are not trees?

4 What is a rhizome?

5 What type of chemical do you think rooting powder contains to help cuttings from plants grow?

Remember

Copy and complete the sentences. Use these words:

hormones bananas style pollen pollen tube seedless ovules

Seeds develop once the female sex cells, the **o**________, have been fertilised by the male sex cells, the **p**________. Once the right type of pollen lands on the sticky stigma of a plant, the pollen develops a **p**________ **t**________ that travels down the **s**________ to the ovary.

In order to grow **s**________ fruits, you have to spray the plants with special chemicals called **h**________. These chemicals make the plant grow fruit without being pollinated. Some plants naturally grow fruit without seeds, such as **b**________.

1.5 Bringing the quagga back to life

Key words

extinct When every animal of one particular type dies out

fossil The remains of plants and animals preserved in rocks millions of years old

species All the animals of one type that can breed and produce offspring

taxidermist A person that stuffs animals for display

Once a **species** is **extinct** we have lost it forever. In the film Jurassic Park, science was supposed to be able to recreate dinosaurs from their DNA found inside insects trapped in amber. The truth is that the methods they used in the film are just not possible. But one man believes he can bring back an extinct animal using selective breeding.

Figure 1 The only live quagga ever photographed lived in London Zoo in 1870.

Horses and zebras are very close cousins. The quagga is actually a variety of zebra. Figure 1 shows one of the last known quaggas.

Quaggas fed mainly on grasses growing on the plains of Southern Africa. Early settlers in the 1800s saw them eating the food they needed for their sheep, goats and horses. Quaggas were hunted by the settlers for food and their skins were exported or turned into leather for bags. Nobody worried that the quagga might become extinct.

By the 1860s there were very few, if any, quaggas left in the wild. Some quaggas were kept in zoos, but unfortunately zoos in those days did not do much work on saving animals from extinction. The last quagga died on the 12th August 1883 in a zoo in Amsterdam.

In 1967, Reinhold Rau, now Head **Taxidermist** at the South Africa National Museum, found a badly stuffed quagga foal. Looking at it, he was convinced that the quagga was a variety of the living plains zebra.

Question

1 How are zoos today different from zoos in the 1860s?

Figure 2 Reinhold Rau (far right) with the quagga foal he found.

What is a species?

For two plants or animals to be the same species they must be able to breed with each other. For example all cats belong to the same species. No matter what the variety of cat, Siamese, Persian etc., they can mate with each another and produce kittens that can also mate with other cats and have kittens.

Rau decided to prove that the quagga was a variety of the plains zebra. He noticed that some plains zebras had light stripes and were a similar brown colour to the quagga.

Reinhold Rau had a piece of evidence that he couldn't use in 1967. When he looked carefully at the quagga foal in the museum he found small pieces of quagga flesh stuck to the inside of the skin. When the quagga DNA in this flesh was tested in the 1980s it was found that it was almost identical to the DNA of the plains zebra. That meant that quagga genes were still around in the DNA of the plains zebra.

Figure 3 This specially bred zebra foal has few stripes on its hind legs.

Rau began recreating the quagga in 1987. By carefully choosing zebras that had features similar to quaggas, such as light striping or hind legs with no stripes, he has managed to breed zebra that are beginning to look like quaggas.

Questions

2 What is a species?

3 How would we know that two plants or animals came from the same species?

The Coelacanth

Figure 4 A coelocanth – a genuine 'living fossil'.

An animal that we thought was extinct was found less than 100 years ago. Just before Christmas in 1938 a large fish was caught off the coast of South Africa. Scientists had never seen such a strange looking fish. One scientist, J L B Smith, remembered seeing similar fossilised fishes. He eventually identified it as a coelacanth. Coelacanths had only been found as **fossils** and were thought to have died out 70 million years ago. The coelocanth lives deep in the oceans and only comes out from underwater caves at night.

Remember

Copy and complete the sentences. Use these words:

species fossil extinct breed

Once a species is **e**_________ it is lost forever. For two plants or animals to be the same **s**_________ they must be able to **b**_________ with each other. The Coelocanth is a 'living **f**_________'.

The Forgotten Evolutionist

Alfred Russel Wallace.

You might remember the name of Charles Darwin. Most people know of him because of what is called Darwin's theory of evolution. But most people do not know the name of Alfred Russel Wallace. He also came up with a theory of evolution. This is the story of Wallace and how a theory of evolution was published on 1st July 1858 to explain how plants and animals survived and changed over time.

Alfred Russel Wallace was born on 8th January 1823 in the village of Llanbadoc, near Usk in Monmouthshire. He was the seventh of eight children. When he was five his family moved to Hertford, and Wallace went to the local grammar school. After leaving school he worked with his older brother William and trained as a **surveyor**. He eventually ended up in the market town of Neath in South Wales, after William died. For a short time Wallace worked as a teacher in Leicester. He planned a trip to South America in order to discover the origin of **species**. He had read the books of many travellers, including Charles Darwin's '*The Voyage of the Beagle*', and decided that South America looked like the most interesting place to **explore**. He went there in 1848 and spent four years travelling and collecting plants and animals.

In 1852 Wallace decided to return to England and set sail from South America, but 25 days later the ship he was on caught fire and sank. Wallace's belongings and all of his **specimens** sank with the ship. All he had left was a box of notes on palm trees and some drawings of fishes. After 10 days in a lifeboat, the crew and passengers were **rescued** and returned to England. Wallace spent some time writing about his travels and produced a book on the palm trees of the Amazon.

In 1854 Wallace set off again, this time to the other side of the world – the Malay Archipelago in the Pacific Ocean. It was here that he came up with his theory of evolution by natural selection. He spent time collecting birds, mammals, insects and plants, and sent them back to England to be sold to fund his trip.

In 1858 Wallace had an attack of what was probably malaria, a tropical **disease** spread by mosquitoes. While he lay sick in his bed he remembered an essay written by Thomas Malthus that he had read 10 years earlier. Malthus had said that the human population was kept down by war, disease and **famine**. Wallace realised that some of these would also affect animals. The weak animals would die, but the strong ones would survive. When he had recovered enough from his attack of malaria he wrote an essay, outlining his theory of evolution by natural selection.

Questions

1 Why did Wallace decide to go to South America to look for the origin of species?

2 What disease did Wallace have that caused him to have a fever?

Wallace was not a well-known scientist. He needed someone to help him publish his ideas. He sent his essay to Charles Darwin in February 1858. When Darwin received Wallace's letter and essay in June 1858 and read it, he was very upset. He could see that Wallace had exactly the same explanation for how evolution took place as he did. In fact Darwin had also read Malthus's essay on population and had come to the same conclusion as Wallace. So Darwin asked two friends, the geologist Charles Lyell and the botanist Joseph Dalton Hooker, what he should do about Wallace's essay. They decided that they should publish a letter and a short essay by Darwin, and Wallace's essay. On 1st July 1858 Wallace's essay and Darwin's letters were read to a scientific society by Lyell and Hooker.

Lyell and Hooker persuaded Darwin to write his now famous book '*On the Origin of Species by means of Natural Selection*' the following year. Wallace didn't know what had happened until he received a letter in September 1858. Wallace never questioned Darwin's claim to be the man who thought of the theory of evolution.

Alfred Russel Wallace died on 7th November 1913 at Broadstone in Dorset, where his grave is marked by a large fossilised tree trunk. Charles Darwin is buried along with many other famous scientists, poets and authors in Westminster Abbey.

Questions

3 Make a list of the words in bold and write down what they mean.

4 If Wallace's letter was sent in February 1858, why might Darwin not have received it until June 1858?

5 Why do you think Wallace didn't know what was happening to his theory during July 1858?

6 How old was Wallace when he died?

7 Who do you think should be given the credit for the theory of evolution by natural selection, Darwin, Wallace or both? Write down the reasons for your choice.

Finishing off!

Remember

What we look like is controlled by our DNA. The DNA is found in the nucleus of almost every cell we have, except red blood cells. The DNA is found as long thread like structures called chromosomes. Humans have 23 pairs of chromosomes. The chromosomes contain genes. Genes are small pieces of DNA and our genes control how we look.

Plants and animals can be bred so that useful characteristics or traits are passed on. For example, cows that produce large amounts of milk are also used for breeding so that they pass this characteristic on.

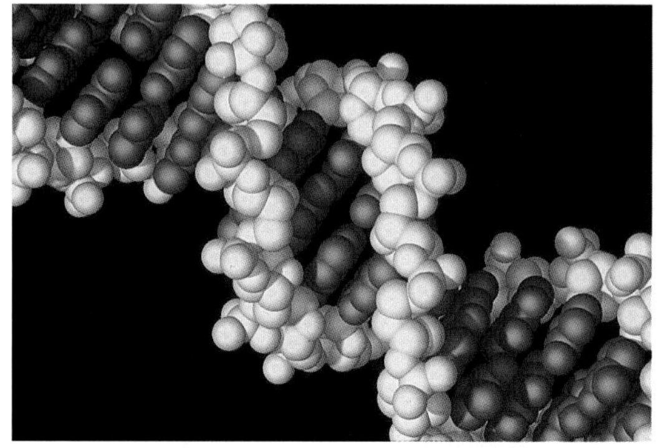

A computer image of a DNA molecule.

Questions

1 Take a new page in your exercise book. Make a list of all the Key Words from the boxes in this chapter down the side. Take two lines per word. Try to write the meaning of each word without looking. Then go back and fill in any you did not know or got wrong.

Now learn to spell them by the Look – Say – Cover – Write method.

2 When a farmer breeds a type of cattle to improve the quality and amount of meat is this an example of natural selection or selective breeding?

3 What is another name for selective breeding?

4 Which of the following are examples of inherited features?

natural hair colour **weight**
shape of nose
skin colour after sunbathing

5 What chemical needs to be added to plants to make them produce seedless fruit?

6 Explain in your own words how Reinhold Rau is trying to recreate the quagga.

Web sites to visit:

The Quagga Project
http://www.museums.org/za/sam/quagga/quagga.htm

The Story of the Coelocanth
http://www.dinofish.com/

Reactions of metals and the reactivity series

Starter Activity
Periodic Table Quiz

			H														He
Li	Be											B	C	N	O	F	Ne
Na	Mg											Al	Si	P	S	Cl	Ar
K	Ca	Sc	Ti	V	Cr	Mn	Fe	Co	Ni	Cu	Zn	Ga	Ge	As	Se	Br	Kr
Rb	Sr	Y	Zr	Nb	Mo	Tc	Ru	Rh	Pd	Ag	Cd	In	Sn	Sb	Te	I	Xe
Cs	Ba	La	Hf	Ta	W	Re	Os	Ir	Pt	Au	Hg	Tl	Pb	Bi	Po	At	Rn
Fr	Ra	Ac	Unq	Unp													

Ce	Pr	Nd	Pm	Sm	Eu	Gd	Tb	Dy	Ho	Er	Tm	Yb	Lu
Th	Pa	U	Np	Pu	Am	Cm	Bk	Cf	Es	Fm	Md	No	Lr

Is this just a list?

Questions

1 Why is air *never* pure?

2 Salt is a compound in sea water. What is a compound?

3 How could you get pure water from sea water?

4 What is the correct name for the salt in sea water?

5 Oxygen is an element in the air. What is an element?

6 Many metals are elements. Write down the names of four metal elements.

7 Oxygen is a non-metallic element. Write down the names of four more non-metal elements.

8 What is the Periodic Table?

9 What elements have these chemical symbols? H, O, N, Mg, S, Al, C , Ca? (*Hint*: the letters are parts of the elements' names.)

10 What is an atom?

11 Often atoms of different elements join together in small identical groups. What are these groups called? (*Hint*: begins with an 'm'.)

12 What is the chemical formula (symbol) for water and for carbon dioxide?

We Need Metals

Key words

alloy A mixture of metals

brittle A material that does not bend, it snaps apart

conduct Let energy pass through them easily

hardness Sugar is hard but not strong, it crushes easily

non-metal An element that does not have the properties of a metal

a) Iron is used to make steel.

b) Manganese is used in stainless steel.

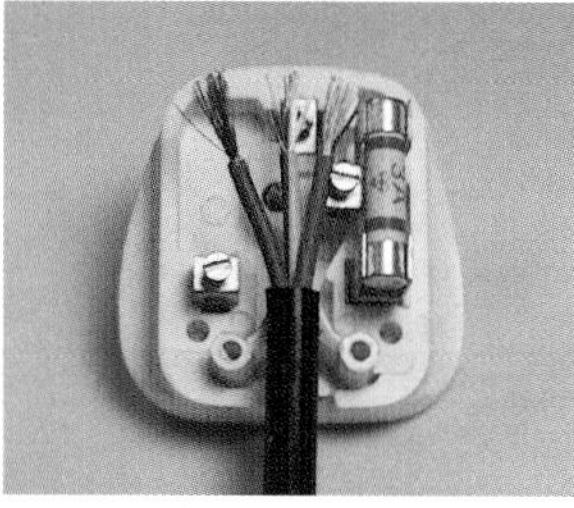

c) Copper is used for electrical wiring.

d) Aluminium is used for airframes.

e) Silver is used to make expensive ornaments.

f) Gold stays shiny, so is used for jewellery.

Figure 1

Metals are very important to us. Iron, in the form of steel, holds up most of our buildings, bridges and roadways. It is also used for trains, videos, dishwashers, forks, and bedsprings. Iron is strong, hard and tough.

Other metals, like copper, can be drawn out into wires. Shiny metals such as silver and gold can be bent into decorative shapes for jewellery.

Alloys are mixtures of metals. One metal dissolves in the other when they are both melted. When the mixture is cooled down, the new mixed metal often has better properties. Alloys such as brass make a nice noise when hit.

Magnetic materials are needed for motors and loudspeakers. **Conducting** metals are used for lighting, heating and making music happen.

Remember

Iron is 100% iron atoms. Steel is 99.6% iron atoms and 0.4% carbon atoms. Steel is much harder than iron.

Non-metals

There may be not very many **non-metals**, but they are important for keeping us alive.

The human body is mainly made from carbon, oxygen, hydrogen, and nitrogen. Chlorine, sulphur and iodine keep us healthy. Silicon is also the main element in most rocks on the surface of the earth.

Comparing Metals and non-metals

	Metals	Non-Metals
Surface	All metals are shiny	Most non-metals have a dull surface
Melting point	Most metals have high melting temperatures	Most non-metals melt at low temperatures
Hardness	Metals are mostly hard materials	Non-metals are soft and easy to cut
Strength	Many metals are strong	Most non-metals have a weak structure, so they are not very strong
Brittleness	Metals do not break, they bend (flexibility). They can be pulled into wires and hammered into flat sheets	Non-metals break very easily
Sound	Metals ring like a bell when hit	Solid non-metals make a dull thud when hit
Magnetism	Iron (steel), nickel and cobalt are the *only* magnetic materials	No non-metals are magnetic
Electrical conductivity	*All* metals conduct electricity well	Non-metals do not conduct electricity well, except carbon in the form of graphite
Heat conductivity	Metals allow energy to flow through them, causing heating	Non-metals are poor at conducting energy to cause heating

Questions

1 What are the properties of metals mentioned in the text? (There are nine properties. Look at the underlined words).

2 Explain what alloys are.

3 Make a list of the non-metal elements from the text.

Remember

Copy the diagram below. Put these property words into the correct place in the diagram:

brittle shiny yellow colour gas electrical conductor useful tough hard make a nice sound bendy

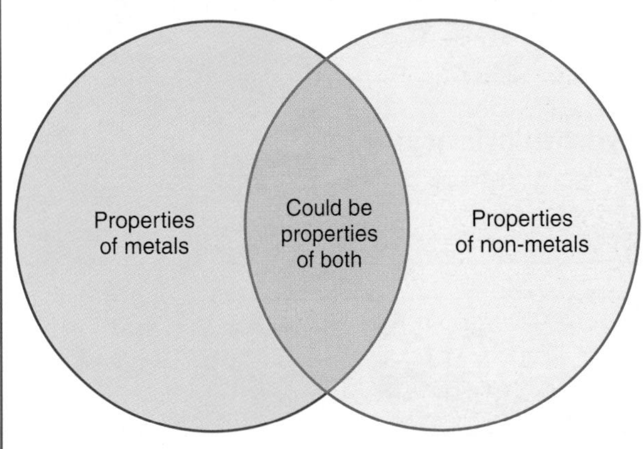

Acid patterns

Key words

acid Substances that can have dangerous reactions

alkali A different set of substances that can also have dangerous reactions

ion When some compounds dissolve they split into particles called ions

neutralisation Acids and alkalis can cancel each other out to make new substances

salt Formed by the spectator ions left over after neutralisation

spectator ions The part of the acid or alkali that just looks on

Acid

All **acids** react in the same way. This is because only the hydrogen atom in the acid does the reacting.

When acids dissolve in water, they all split up to make hydrogen **ions**. These hydrogen ions are the 'acid particles.' The other part of the acid is the '**spectator ion**'.

Hydrochloric acid
HCl splits into H^+ (hydrogen ion) and Cl^- (chloride ion)

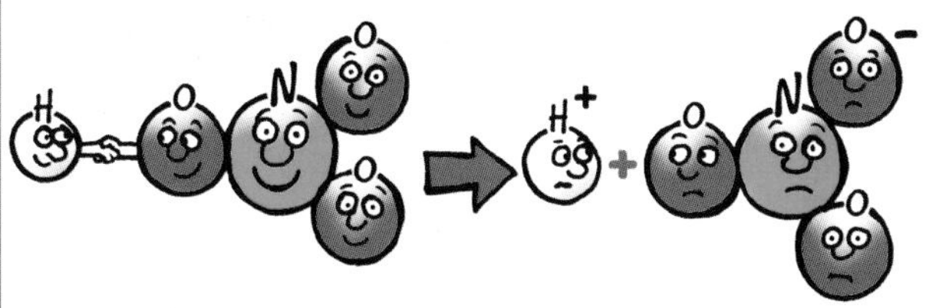

Nitric acid
HNO_3 splits into H^+ (hydrogen ion) and NO_3^- (nitrate ions)

Alkali

When an **alkali** dissolves it also splits into different particles. The hydroxide ion is the 'alkali particle.' The other part of the alkali is the 'spectator ion'.

Sodium hydroxide
NaOH splits into Na^+ (sodium ions) and OH^- (hydroxide ions)

Neutralisation

When **neutralisation** takes place the spectator ions take no part. They stay dissolved in the solution. They just look on.

Neutralisation: example A

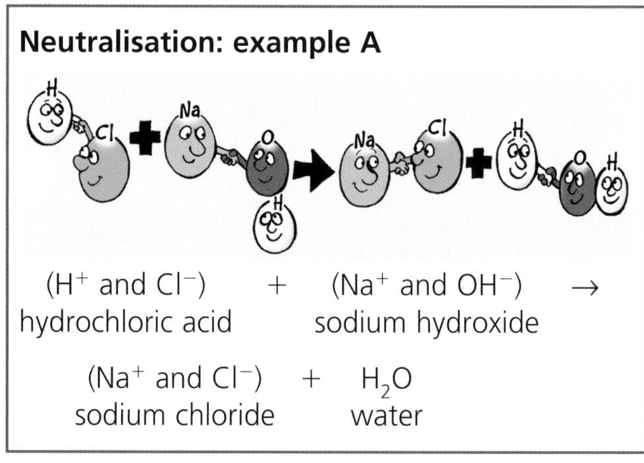

(H^+ and Cl^-) + (Na^+ and OH^-) →
hydrochloric acid + sodium hydroxide

(Na^+ and Cl^-) + H_2O
sodium chloride + water

Neutralisation: example B

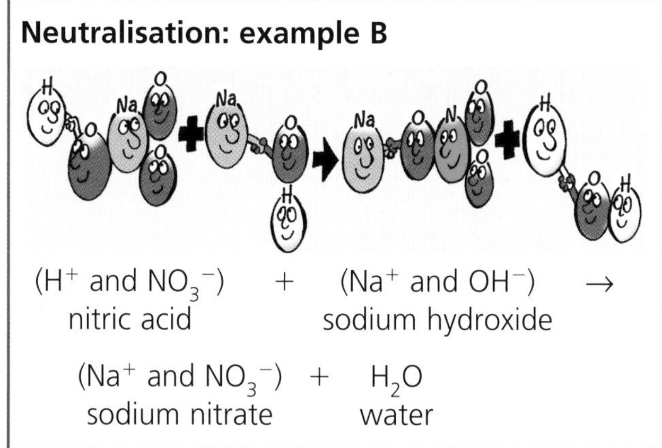

(H^+ and NO_3^-) + (Na^+ and OH^-) →
nitric acid + sodium hydroxide

(Na^+ and NO_3^-) + H_2O
sodium nitrate + water

Note

- Remove the **spectator ions** and both neutralisation equations become exactly the same:

$$H^+ + OH^- = H_2O$$

- Only one change happens in any acid–alkali reaction: hydrogen ions join with hydroxide ions to make water molecules.
- The spectator ions are left over. They form the **salt** in the reaction.

Making Salts

When the water is evaporated from the solution, only the spectator ions are left behind. They pack together to make solid crystals of salt.

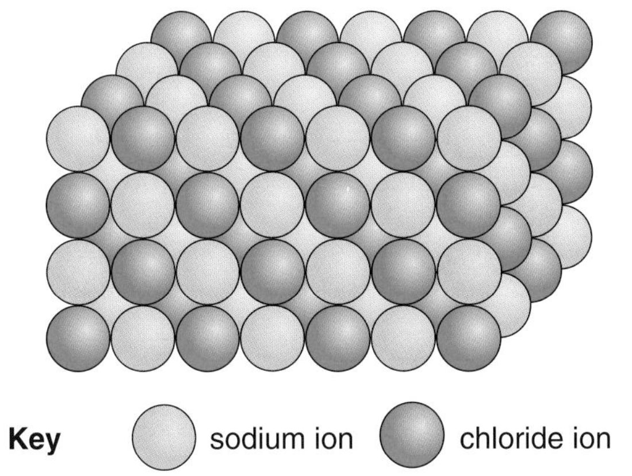

Key sodium ion chloride ion

Figure 1 Ions packed together to make salt crystals.

Remember

You can work out the name of the salt from the names of the acid and alkali that made it.

Questions

1 What particle is present in all acid reactions?

2 What particle is present in all alkali reactions?

3 What is a spectator ion?

4 Copy and complete this table about neutralisation and salts (see Table 1 for help).

Name of alkali	Name of acid	Name of salt
Potassium hydroxide	Nitric acid	
Magnesium hydroxide	Sulphuric acid	
		Potassium sulphate
		Lithium chloride
Calcium hydroxide	Phosphoric acid	

Remember

Copy and complete the sentences. Use these words:

looks on alkali spectator different hydrogen hydroxide

When acids react only the **h**________ ion particles take part in the change. The other part of the acid particle just **l**________ **o**________. It is often called a **s**________ ion. This is why **d**________ acids have the same type of reaction. The same general rule applies to **a**________ reactions.

First part of name from alkali		Second part of name from acid
sodium hydroxide makes a 'sodium' salt	with	hydrochloric acid makes a 'chloride' salt
potassium hydroxide makes a 'potassium' salt	with	sulphuric acid makes a 'sulphate' salt
calcium hydroxide makes a 'calcium' salt	with	nitric acid makes a 'nitrate' salt
magnesium hydroxide makes a 'magnesium' salt	with	ethanoic acid makes an 'ethanoate' salt

Table 1 Naming salts.

2.3 Acid treatment

Key words

base In chemistry, this is a substance that neutralises an acid

displace Take something's place

reactive Changes quickly or releases lots of energy.

Substances that neutralise acids are called **bases**. Alkalis are a special sort of chemical base. They are soluble bases. This means they dissolve in water to form a solution.

1 Acid plus metal oxide

acid + metal oxide (base) = salt + water

Alkalis are metal oxides that dissolve in water. Other metal oxides don't dissolve, but they all react with acids in the same way. All metal oxides are called bases because they neutralise acids.

Figure 1 Rust remover.

Weak acid is used to dissolve rust off iron and steel. Rust is iron oxide. The acid is exactly the right strength to work. The iron oxide is dissolved quickly by the acid, but the acid is weak and only dissolves the iron metal slowly. When all the rust has gone the acid is washed off with lots of water, leaving clean metal.

2 Acid plus carbonate

Acid + carbonate (base) = salt + water + carbon dioxide

When a carbonate neutralises any acid, carbon dioxide gas gets made. A carbonate compound is a base.

a)

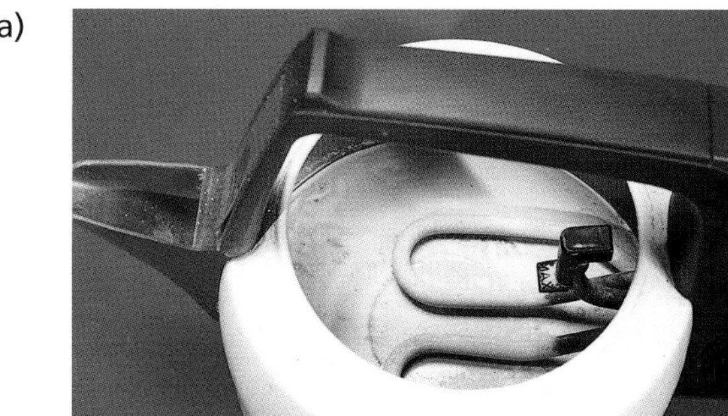

b)

Figure 2 a) Limescale in a kettle b) acids are used to dissolve the limescale.

The limescale on kettle elements is calcium carbonate (like chalk). You can use tartaric acid to dissolve it. There is a fizz as carbon dioxide is made by the reaction. The acid dissolves the limescale, but doesn't attack the metal and doesn't make the tea taste nasty.

Questions

1 Coke, the drink, is a weak acid. If you put a piece of rusty iron in coke for a few hours, what would happen to the rust?

2 Why do we use weak acids to get rid of limescale in coffee machines?

3 What is the fizzy gas given off when acids are used to remove limescale?

3 Acid plus metal – a less predictable reaction

acid + metal oxide (base) = salt + water

Only some metals react with acids. Metals are not called bases because no water molecules are made.

Magnesium reacts quickly and makes lots of fizz. Zinc reacts less quickly, and copper and gold do not react at all. **Reactive** metals **displace** hydrogen from the acid and a new salt is made.

Figure 3 The fizz this time is hydrogen gas.

Remember

The test for carbon dioxide gas is it turns lime water cloudy.

The test for hydrogen gas is it burns with a squeaky pop.

Questions

4 What gas is given off when an acid reacts with a metal?

5 Would anything happen if pieces of gold were put into acid?

Remember

You have some rusty bike parts, a kettle with lime scale, half a bottle of flat coke and a packet of tartaric acid (used in cooking).

Explain:

1 How to make the rust go away.

2 How to make the kettle clean.

Use this writing frame for both questions:

What I want to do is . . .
What I will use is . . .
What I will see is . . .
What will happen in the end is . .

Metal and non-metal oxides

Key words

corrodes Metal reacts to become a brittle material and flakes break off the surface

hydrogen peroxide A substance used to make pure oxygen in the lab

oxide Simple compounds made by oxygen

oxidises Reacts with oxygen to produce an oxide

oxygen A very reactive non-metal

Favourite partner

It is easy to recognise the metals. They are shiny solids that conduct electricity and heat well. The shininess is true for sodium when it is freshly made, but it **corrodes** in seconds when water or air gets to it. That's why it's normally stored in oil.

The non-metals are on the right in Figure 1. The non-metals are gases or dull coloured solids that melt easily.

Phosphorus should be stored in water. If it is exposed to air for too long it **oxidises** so easily that it bursts into flame. Silicon is a puzzle. It is a shiny non-metal with a high melting point.

Every element's favourite reaction partner is **oxygen**. Oxygen will react with both metals and non-metals. The new substances produced by the reaction can be acids or bases. Non-metal **oxides** are acidic. Metal oxides are bases, some dissolve so they are alkaline.

Questions

1 How can you tell if a substance is a metal?

2 What is a typical property of a non-metal?

Making acids and alkalis

Figure 1 shows the elements in the third row of the Periodic Table. All of them, except argon, will easily react with oxygen. Argon is a very unreactive element and forms no compounds at all. Because it is so unreactive it is used to fill light bulbs.

Figure 2 The oxides are rather dull looking, but put an indicator in the solution and you get a rainbow of colours.

Figure 1

Metal oxides are bases so they make the blue colours with the indicator. Non-metal oxides are acids. These are the red, orange and yellow colours.

Phosphorus oxide and sulphur dioxide dissolve to produce strongly acidic solutions. Chlorine oxide is also an acid. Silicon dioxide will react like an acidic oxide. So non-metal oxides act like acids

Testing a gas: oxygen

Figure 3 To make a little bit of oxygen, heat some potassium manganate (VII) crystals in a test tube.

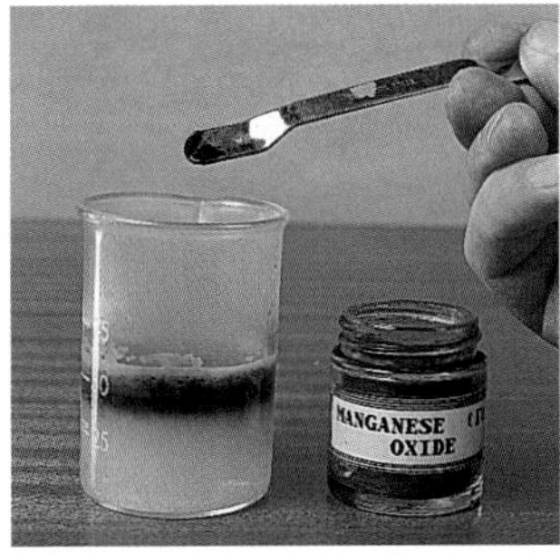

Figure 4 To make lots of oxygen add manganese dioxide to **hydrogen peroxide**.

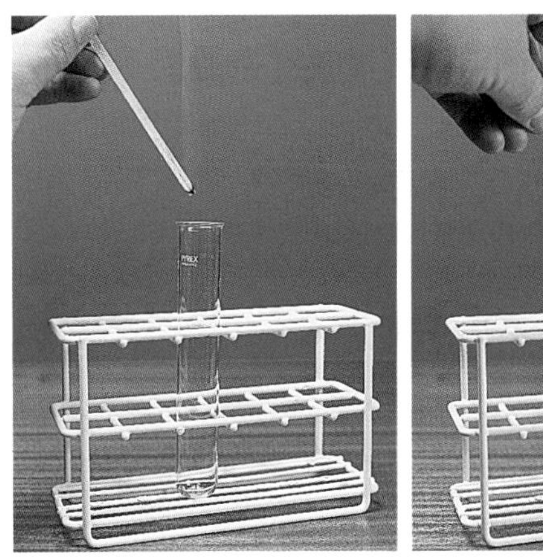

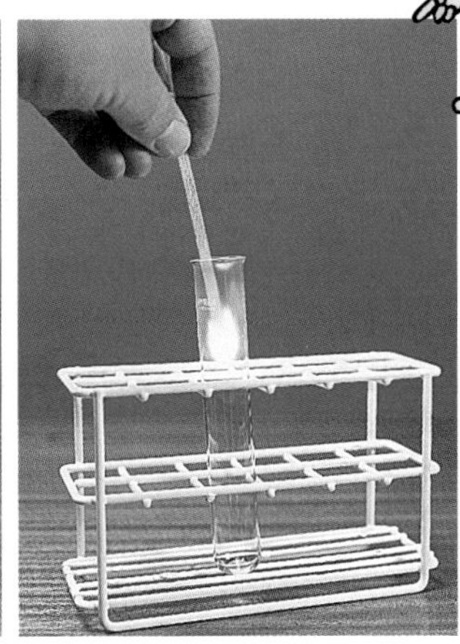

Figure 5 Set light to a wooden splint. Blow it out so it is just glowing. Put it in oxygen gas and it burns so well that it bursts into flame again.

Questions

3 How do you test the oxide solutions to see if they are acidic or alkaline?

4 Which sort of oxides are acidic?

5 What crystals give off oxygen gas when heated?

Remember

Copy and complete the sentences. Use these words:

neutralise glowing oxygen alkaline metals

Shiny **m**________ react with **o**________ to make substances called metal oxides. A metal oxide will **n**________ an acid. Some metal oxides dissolve to make **a**________ solutions.

The test for oxygen gas is that it will relight a **g**________ splint.

Metals: a short history

Key words

bronze A mixture of copper and tin metals

metal ore Rocks containing metal compounds, usually metal oxides

smelting Heating metal ore with charcoal to get the metal from it

Some rocks contain metal atoms, usually in the form of metal compounds. This sort of rock is called a **metal ore**. The compounds are chemically changed to give us useful pure metals.

Over millions of years all the metals in the earth, except gold, reacted with oxygen. These metal oxides are no use to us, but the metals are very useful. Gold is rare and precious.

Ten thousand years ago every home, big or small, cave or palace, had a fire. Man built his fire on rocks to keep it under control. When he cleaned out the fire he found shiny blobs of copper metal. He made a necklace out of them.

Seven thousand years ago the Afghan people were deliberately **smelting** rocks with charcoal to get copper. The carbon is more reactive than the copper. It steals the oxygen away from it.

Copper oxide + carbon = carbon dioxide + copper metal

Five thousand years ago people found out about **bronze**. Mixing rocks containing copper and tin made a metal that was much harder than either copper or tin.

Reactions of metals and the reactivity series

Three thousand years ago people could make iron. Making iron needs high temperatures. They blew a blast of air through the charcoal to increase the temperature. People used iron to make tools and weapons. Iron was very much harder than bronze.

2000 years ago the Romans used the copper and tin mines in Britain. They also made lead metal. Lead pipes have been found in Roman remains.

The more reactive metals are produced by ripping compounds apart with electricity. Aluminium is made like this. Aluminium was a precious metal in the times of Napoleon in the early 1800s.

Now we know about seventy or more metals. Most have been discovered in the last 150 years.

Questions

1. What metal is found naturally as an element?
2. How are the other types of metals found naturally?
3. What were people doing when they accidentally made metal?
4. Which metals were discovered first?
5. What substance was used to remove the oxygen from metal compounds?
6. Why was iron more difficult to make?
7. How are the more reactive metals like aluminium made?

Remember

Copy and complete the sentences. Use these words:

heating ore rocks oxygen metals gold

Most **m**________ are man-made materials. Only **g**________ is found naturally as a metal element.

Metals are found in **r**________as compounds with **o**________.

The metal **o**________ is made into metal by removing the oxygen. To do this you **h**________ the ore with charcoal.

2.6 Treasure

Key words

corrosion Damage to metals by reacting with water and air

displaced When a more reactive metal takes the place of another one in a compound

pitted Little dents in the surface of a metal caused by corrosion

reactivity series League table for which metal reacts fastest

tarnish Dull oxide layer forms on the surface of the metal

I brought a treasure chest back from my travels and I have hidden it deep in the cellars below the house. It was full of objects made from valuable metals.
There was gold and silver.
There was the finest ironware we had ever seen.
There were beautiful copper drinking vessels.
There were plates of a strange new metal.
This metal was very light in colour and weight.
But I am badly ill and will not survive the winter. . .

Figure 1 The treasure chest.

Two sisters discovered this note when they were staying with their aunt in her old seaside house. So they went exploring in the deep cellars and found the treasure chest.

Sea water had got into the treasure chest. The chest was covered in lead sheeting to protect the wood, but it had been badly **corroded** by the sea.

Figure 2 These gold ornaments are still in good condition.

The gold ornaments were in perfect condition. Their surface was as shiny and beautiful as the day they were made.

The silver helmet was very fine. The silver metal was dark and black, but only on the surface.

Figure 3

The copper goblets were heavily **pitted** by the sea water, but they could still be used, and they cleaned up well.

The iron sword with a fine handle was useless. It was a mess of crumbly rust. Worst of all were the metal plates. The sea water had completely corroded them away. All that was left was white powder.

The girls' aunt explained what had happened.

'Metals have different reactivities. Gold is the least reactive of the metals. It stays shiny for centuries.

Silver reacts very slowly. Usually it only **tarnishes** on the surface. Copper and lead corrode slowly. Iron is a reactive metal and corrodes quickly. Aluminium was the light metal used for the plates. The aluminium has reacted quickly with the sea water.'

Questions

1 Make a list of all the metals mentioned in the passage.
2 Which metal has reacted least with the sea water?
3 Which metal must have reacted fastest?
4 Which two metal objects became useless in sea water?

A League table

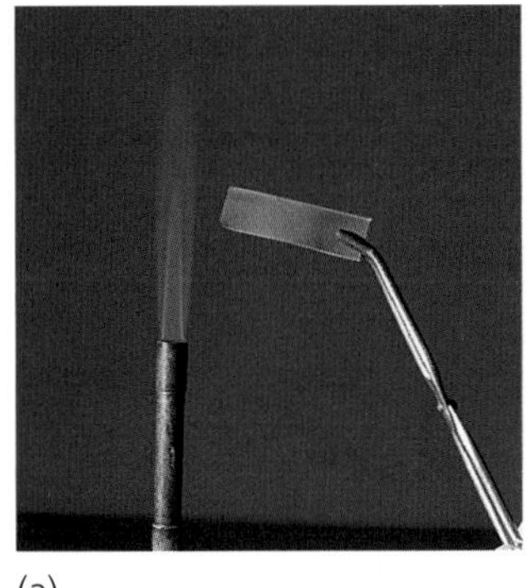

(a)

(b)

Figure 4 Copper just goes black when heated, magnesium burns.

Magnesium reacts quicker than copper and iron. There is a league table of reactivity for metals – it is called the **reactivity series**.

Magnesium
Aluminium
Zinc
Iron
Lead
Copper
Silver
Gold

(a)

(b)

Figure 5 Iron fizzes slowly in acid, magnesium fizzes quickly.

Figure 6 Zinc has displaced copper from copper carbonate solution.

Metals that are higher in the reactivity series will **displace** metals that are lower than them from their compounds.

Remember

Copy and complete the sentences. Use these words:

sea metals faster reactivity Corrosion

C________ makes metals useless. Most **m**________ will react with **s**________ water. Some react **f**________ than others.

There is a league table of how strongly metals react. It is called the **r**________ series.

Reactivity to order

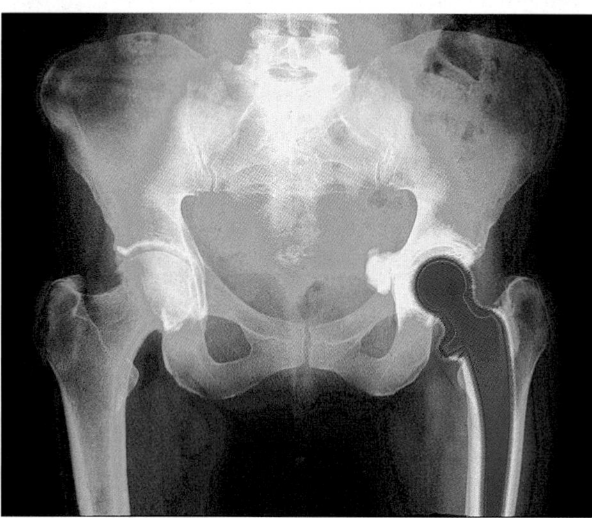

Figure 1 Titanium is used for these things.

Titanium is an important metal. It's expensive, but very strong and light. It resists corrosion very well. Titanium is used in aeroplane parts and it's an ideal material for replacement hip joints.

Titanium metal is made in the following reaction. It works because sodium is more reactive than titanium. Sodium is one of the most reactive metals. Sodium is an **alkali metal**.

titanium chloride + sodium metal → titanium metal + sodium chloride

Questions

1 Why is titanium used in aeroplanes?

2 Why is titanium used in replacement hip joints?

3 Why is sodium used to make titanium?

Key words

alkali metals A family of similar metals, very reactive

caustic This means the substance will damage flesh and skin

titanium A very strong, light metal

The Alkali metals

Beware: The alkali metals are **caustic**. They will attack and damage flesh.

The alkali metals are:
Lithium
Sodium
Potassium
Rubidium
Caesium
Francium (this one is very rare and radioactive)

Alkali metals are the most reactive of all. They occupy the top places in the reactivity series for metals.

These are a really spectacular set of elements. They react rapidly with the oxygen in the air – so rapidly that they must be stored in oil.

Figure 2 Lithium reacts rapidly with water, producing hydrogen gas. The lithium dissolves and becomes lithium hydroxide solution.

Figure 3 Sodium gets melted by the heat released as it reacts with the water. The molten blob races round the surface on a cushion of hydrogen gas.

Figure 4 Potassium reacts so rapidly with water that it bursts into flame.

Questions

4 Why are alkali metals dangerous?

5 Finish this word equation for sodium reacting with water:

s_____ (metal) + water = hy______ (gas) + sodium hydroxide (solution)

6 Look at the alkali metal reactions in Figures 2, 3, 4, 5 and 6. Put them in order of reactivity.

Figure 5 Rubidium reacts rapidly. The heat from the burning hydrogen makes the metal explode and fly about the room. Rubidium is very caustic, so this is far too dangerous to do in a school laboratory. People would be blinded.

Figure 6 WOW!! The reaction between caesium and water is even more explosive.

Remember

Draw up a new safety sign warning about the dangers of the alkali metals. Use images and not words. Be creative!

Unspoilt Antarctic

Key words

Antarctic Continent round the South Pole – totally frozen

thermit Reaction used by rail workers to join steel rails

wilderness Out in the wilds, a long way from any towns

Metals will compete with each other. The ones that are more strongly reactive will win.

Figure 1 This hole in the ground used to be a mountain, but it was found to be a good place to get copper ore.

There are large amounts of metal ores in **Antarctica**. But should this unspoilt continent be mined for the good of mankind? To get the useful metals out of the ground makes a lot of waste material and mess. This would get dumped in the unspoilt **wilderness**.

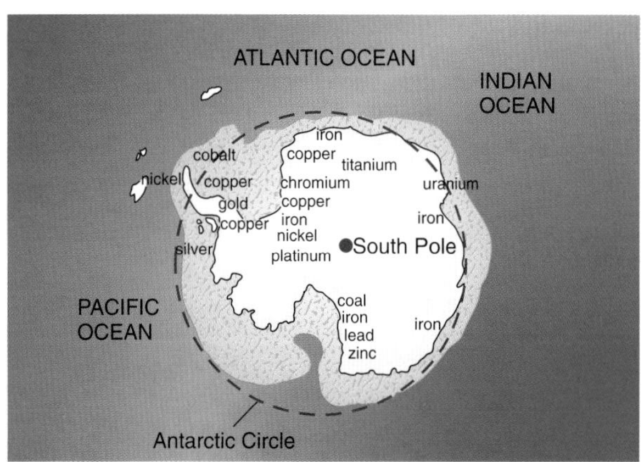

Figure 2 Leave it or use it.

Questions

1 What metals can be found in the Antarctic?

2 Write a short newspaper paragraph in favour of mining in the Antarctic.

3 Write a letter against mining in the Antarctic. You don't want to see the area spoiled by mining waste.

Reactivity series

Metals don't just compete with each other for oxygen. They will fight each other in any reaction. They compete even more easily in solutions.

Figure 3 Battling metal ions.

CuO powder Zn powder

Reacting mixture

A bit of heat gives the reaction between zinc and copper oxide a kick start. The zinc steals the oxygen away from the copper oxide. This makes copper metal. The zinc turns into zinc oxide. Energy is released as heat and light.

zinc (metal) + copper oxide = zinc oxide + copper (metal)

Railway workers use **Thermit** to weld rails together. Thermit is a mixture of iron oxide and fine aluminium powder. The aluminium steals the oxygen from the less reactive iron. A great deal of energy is released. This melts the rails. The iron metal produced fills the gap between the rails and joins them together.

aluminium (metal) + iron oxide = aluminium oxide + iron (metal)

Questions

4 Explain how you know a chemical reaction is happening between copper oxide and zinc metal.

5 How would railway workers know the thermit reaction had finished?

Remember

Here is a full reactivity series written as chemical symbols. Rewrite it as the names of the metals. Use a copy of the Periodic Table.

(Most reactive) K – Na – Li – Ca – Mg – Al – Zn – Fe – Cr – Pb – Cu – Ag – Au (least reactive)

Iron filings and copper sulphate solution before the reaction

Iron sulphate and copper metal is left

The iron atoms in the iron fillings displace the copper from the copper sulphate solution. The solution becomes iron sulphate and copper metal. Iron is more reactive than copper.

iron (metal) + copper sulphate (solution) = iron sulphate (solution) + copper (metal)

Finishing off!

Remember

Spectacular Change

Chemical changes take place in cooking, cleaning, burning fuels and making our bodies work. There are many different types of chemical changes.

In a **physical change** (melting, dissolving or boiling) the particles are not changed. But they do get arranged differently – as a liquid, or solution, or a gas. There is no change in mass.

In a **chemical change**, the particles are taken apart and recombined (put together again) into different particles. The total mass of the substances remains the same. And the total numbers of each different type of atom remains the same.

When any change takes place – chemical or physical – there has to be an energy transfer making it happen.

Most metals are made by a chemical change. Metal atoms are found combined with other elements in rock. There has to be energy put in to separate the atoms and leave just the metal.

a) Magnesium displacing lead from lead nitrate solution.

b) Ethanol burning.

c) Copper carbonate reacting with sulphuric acid.

Questions

1 Look at the three photos above which show chemical changes. How can you tell there is a change taking place?

2 Write word equations for each photo:

a) **M**_________ (metal) + **l**_________ nitrate (**s**_________) = magnesium **n**_________ (solution) + lead (**m**_________)

b) **E**_________ + oxygen = **c**_________ dioxide + **w**_________ vapour

c) **C**_________ **c**_________ + **s**_________ic acid = carbon **d**_________ + water + copper **s**_________ate (solution)

Web sites to visit:

School Chemistry – The Reactivity Series
http://www.schoolchem.com/xcontent.htm

Web Elements – The Periodic Table
http://www.webelements.com

Energy and Electricity

Starter Activity
Circuit predictions

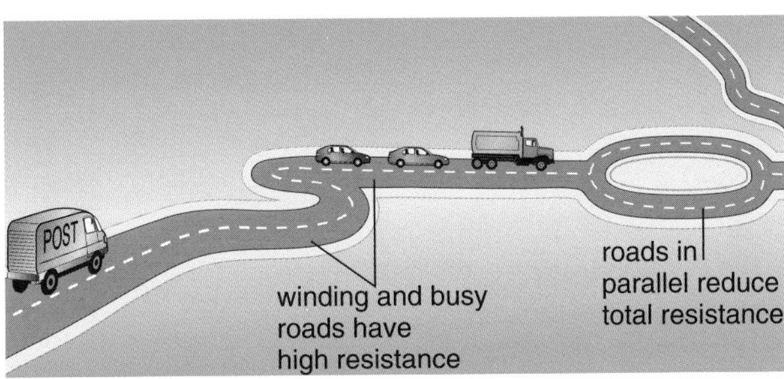

Think of a post van on its rounds. Sometimes it will meet resistance to its journey. It might have to travel along a narrow road, or a very busy one with traffic jams. This can make the journey difficult. Sometimes there will be two roads running parallel to each other, so the traffic has a choice of road. Traffic flow will be easier.

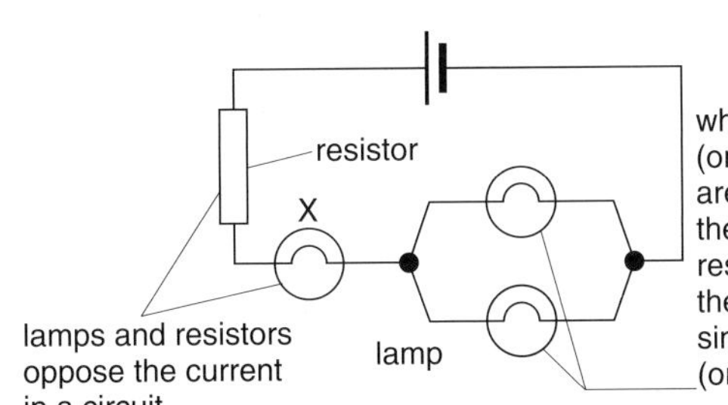

Electric circuits can have resistance too. It might be a lamp or a resistor causing the resistance. These components reduce the flow of current. If they come one after the other, **in series**, the total resistance is high, so the current is low.

If the components are side by side, **in parallel**, there is a choice of route. So the total resistance is not so high.

We use an ammeter to measure the current in a circuit. Current is measured in amps.

Current rules

Rule 1: In a circuit with resistors in series, the current is the same all the way round.

Rule 2: In a parallel circuit, when the current reaches a junction, it splits. When the circuit joins up again at another junction, the currents join up again. The current going into a junction always adds up to the same as the current coming out of a junction.

Questions

1 a) Draw a diagram of three resistors:
i) in series
ii) in parallel

b) Which arrangement has the most resistance to current in a circuit? Explain why.

2 In each of these circuits, use rules 1 and 2 from above to predict the value of the current in ammeter X.

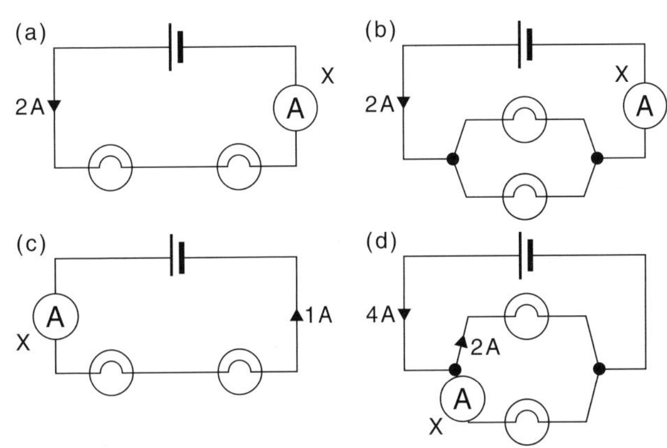

Energy transfer from circuits

Key words

dissipated Spread out into the surroundings
filament A very thin wire
terminals The ends of a battery or power supply
voltmeter Instrument to measure the voltage or strength of an electrical supply

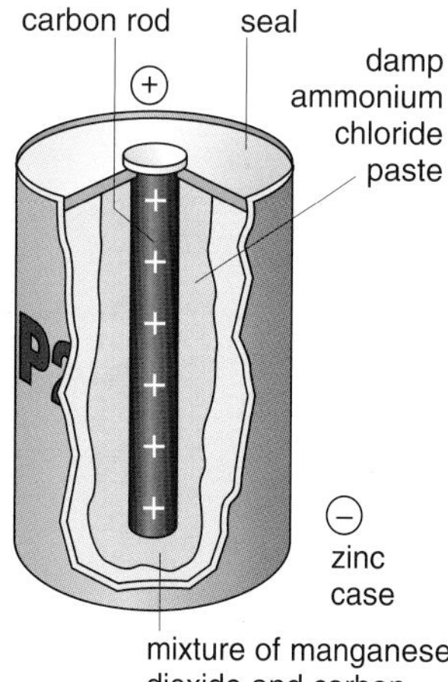

Figure 1 A cell (or 'battery') and the chemicals inside it.

A cell or battery has two **terminals**, one is positive (+) and the other negative (−). An electric current will flow between the terminals when a circuit connects the two together. The cell has chemical energy which is transformed into electrical energy.

Cell measurements

Every cell or battery has a measurement written on it. The unit of measurement is the volt (V). We use a **voltmeter** to measure the voltage. We measure the voltage difference across the terminals of a cell (or component). The bigger the voltage, the more energy the cell or battery can transfer. The large voltages used in the mains supply to our homes are dangerous.

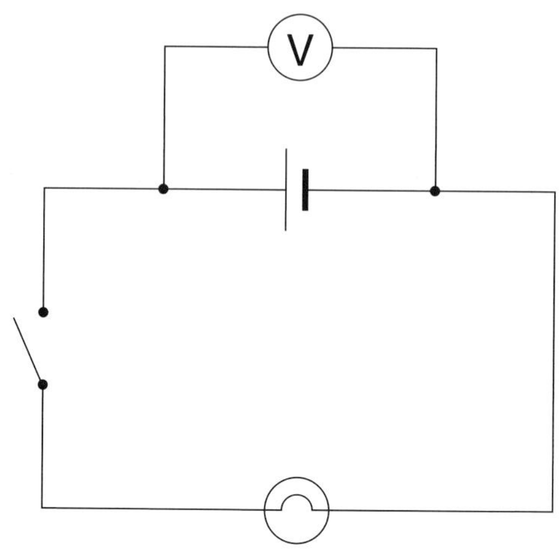

Figure 2 A voltmeter is connected across the cell or component.

Transforming electrical energy

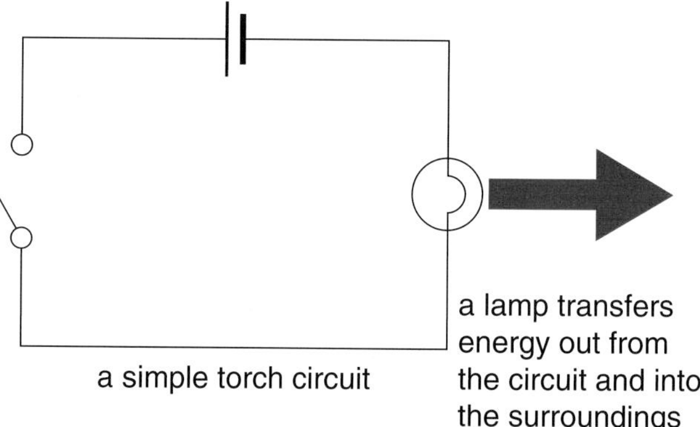

Figure 3 A torch and a torch circuit – where energy transfer takes place.

We use electricity for many things, in lamps, in heaters, in motors, in loudspeakers. We can transform the electrical energy into light, heat, movement, or sound energy.

The wire in the torch bulb gets hot. This wire, or **filament**, gets so hot it glows white. The battery provides the energy for this. The energy spreads to the surroundings so they are heated as well. The light from the bulb is very useful, but once the energy has spread into the surroundings we can't use it any more. We say that the energy has been **dissipated**.

Question

1 What would you expect to happen in a torch circuit if you added an extra battery?

Motors

Figure 4 This toy has an electric motor. The electric current turns the motor and transforms the energy to make the toy do work and move.

A motor in a toy needs a flow of electric current to make it work. The electric current makes the motor turn. The motor transfers energy to other things around it. It is this force that makes the toy travel. The motor does work. The battery provides the energy to make this happen. The battery can store energy. You can keep the battery for a long time, and use it whenever you want to.

Some energy spreads into the surroundings. The motor gets warm and heats the surroundings. The movement of the toy makes the air move. Friction of the wheels causes a little bit of heating. The energy becomes spread out or dissipated.

Question

2 An electric circuit can make a motor go round.
- a) What is needed apart from the circuit to make the motor go round?
- b) What has happened to the energy when the motor has stopped?

Remember

Copy and complete these sentences. Use these words:

work heat stores from surroundings dissipated positive current

Cells and batteries act as energy **s**_________. They have negative and **p**_________ terminals. When a wire is connected to the two terminals, a **c**_________ will flow in the wire.

Energy transfers out **f**_________ the circuit into the **s**_________. For example, the circuit can **h**_________ the surroundings, or the circuit can make a motor do **w**_________. The energy from the battery is eventually **d**_________. It spreads into the surroundings.

Circuit power

Key words

kinetic About movement
potential About position
potential difference Voltage

Batteries supply energy to components in circuits. A battery is measured by its voltage. The bigger the voltage, the more energy it can supply.

Lottie lives in the mountains. In winter when there is plenty of snow she goes up the mountain on a ski lift and then she speeds downhill. Sometimes she stops at a mountain café.

Figure 1 Lottie gaining position or potential energy.

To get up the mountain Lottie lets the ski lift do the work. As it goes higher it gives her position or **potential** energy.

Figure 2 Lottie losing potential energy and transferring energy to her surroundings.

On her way down she has the energy of movement – **kinetic** energy. Friction forces and air resistance also act on Lottie. She transfers energy to the snow and the air as she skis downhill. Her energy does not change when she stops at a café.

In an electric circuit, it's not the ski lift but the battery that can provide the energy. The higher the ski lift, the more position or potential energy the skiers will have. The battery doesn't provide a height difference, instead it provides voltage. Another name for voltage here is **potential difference**. It's the difference between the two terminals of a battery that makes the current flow.

Figure 3 Lottie having a rest from all that hectic energy transfer.

In an electric circuit, energy transfers take place in the resistors, such as lamps and motors. These components are like the slopes of the mountain.

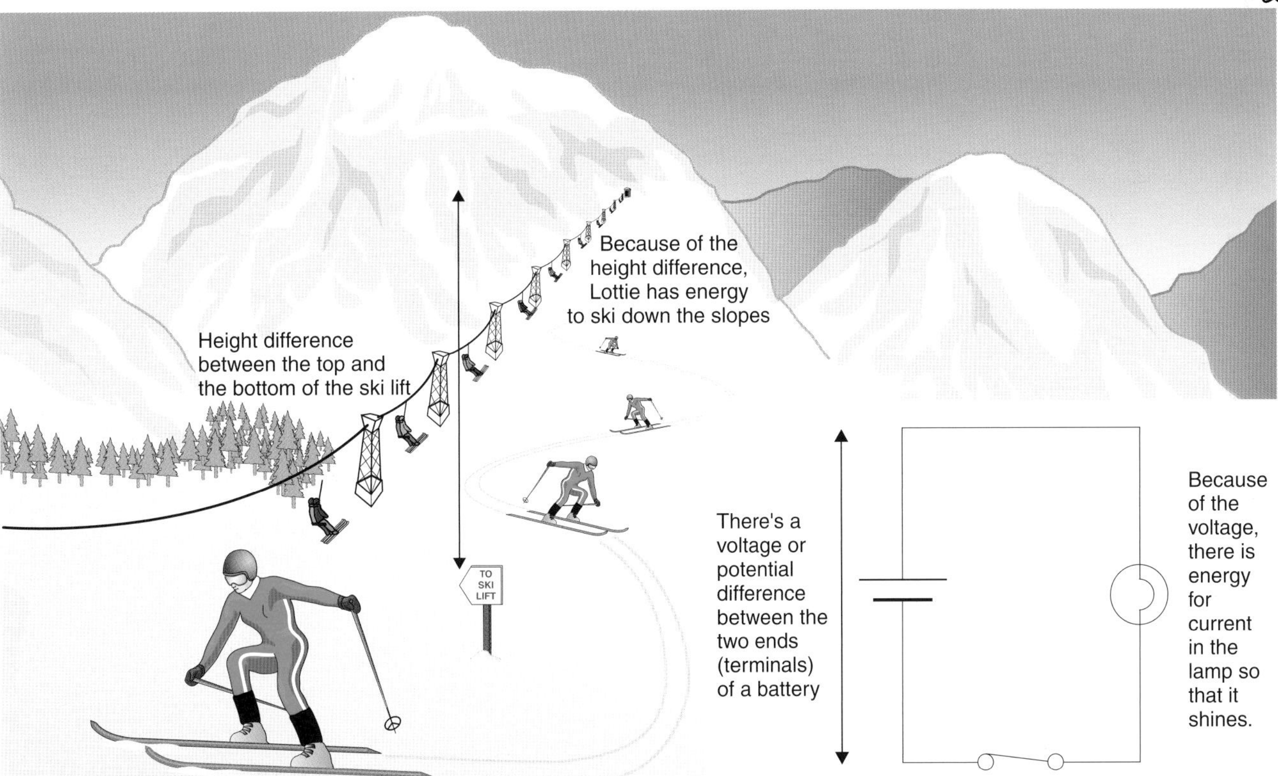

Figure 4 Look for similarities between the circuit and the skiing. The potential energy for the skiers comes from the difference in height between the top and the bottom of the ski lift. The potentlal difference or voltage of the cell provides energy for the current to flow through the lamp.

Lottie can go round and round the mountain circuit, time after time. A current can go round and round an electric circuit. There are energy changes in both kinds of circuit.

To find the voltage between the two ends of an electric component you use a voltmeter.

A voltmeter looks like an ammeter. An ammeter measures the current flowing through the component. Current is like a flow of skiers. The more skiers there are, the bigger the current is. But a voltmeter measures difference – the potential difference across the ends or terminals of a battery, or the difference between the ends of components. Voltmeters are connected in parallel to the component or cell.

Questions

1 What is the unit of
a) electric current?
b) electric voltage?

2 Which part of an electric circuit is most like the ski lift in Lottie's mountain circuit?

3 List the other similarities between an electric circuit and the mountain circuit.

Remember

Copy and complete the sentences. Use these words:

flow amps component height battery volts equal

Electric current is measured in units called **a**________. Current is like a **f**________ of skiers up a ski lift and down the mountain slopes.

Electric voltage is measured in **v**________. Voltage is a difference. It could be the difference between the ends of a **b**________ or the difference between the ends of a circuit **c**________.

The total height difference between the bottom and the top of the mountain slopes must be the same as the total **h**________ difference between the bottom and top of the ski lift. The voltages between the ends of the circuit components when added together must **e**________ the voltage of the battery.

Meeting the demand

Key words

generator A device which transforms movement energy into electrical energy

hydroelectric Using flowing water as an energy source

pumped storage A power station which uses the potential energy of water stored in an upper reservoir. At times of peak demand water flows from the upper reservoir into a lower reservoir generating electricity. When electricity demand is low, the water is pumped back to the upper reservoir

Motors and generators

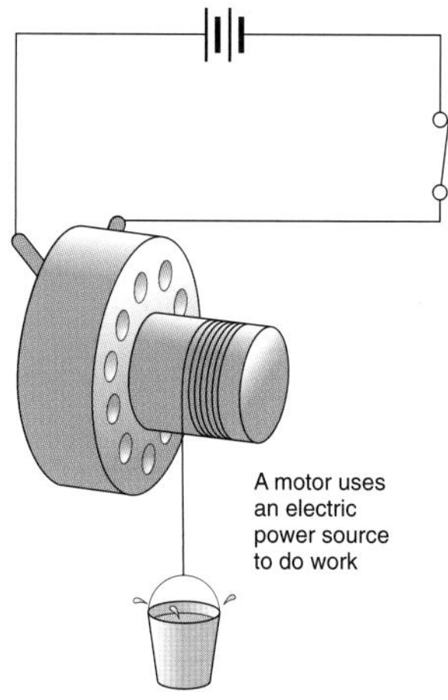

Figure 1 An electric motor.

Figure 2 An electric generator. We do work to turn the generator. It provides us with electricity.

An electric motor transforms electrical energy into work. Switch on, and the motor will turn.

In most power stations it is hot steam that transfers energy to the turbine blades. The blades are connected to the **generator**. The turbines make the generator turn very fast producing electrical energy. The energy then transfers through electric cables to our homes and factories.

Question

1 Explain the differences between a motor and a generator.

Always generating enough to meet demand

We cannot store mains electricity. Power stations take time to warm up to make hot steam to turn the turbines. So power stations must generate electricity all the time. But if we don't need much electricity the power stations must generate less. And when we need more electricity, power stations must generate a lot more. This happens on a cold night, or when the big match on TV finishes and everyone gets up and puts the kettle on.

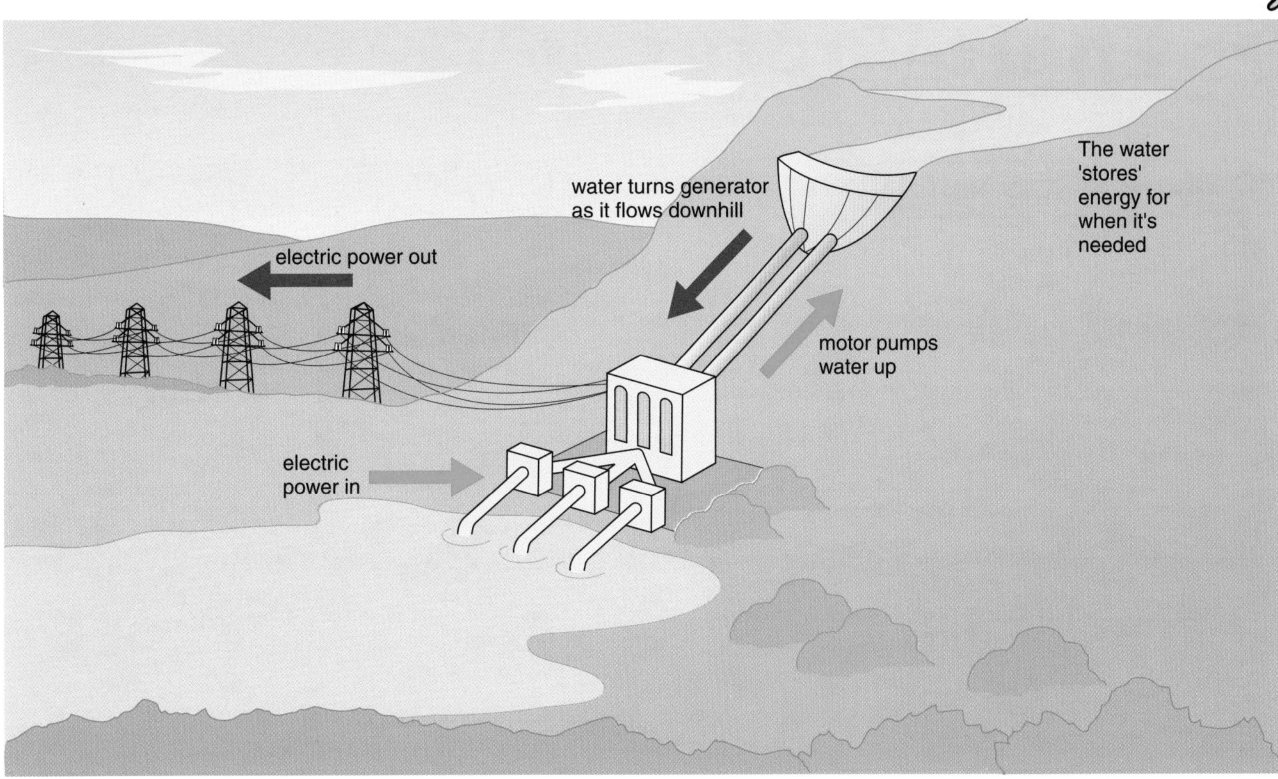

Figure 1 How a pump storage system works.

A pumped storage power station

A **pumped storage** power station can generate electricity quickly when demand is high. It has two reservoirs, one is high up and is connected to the lower reservoir with big water pipes. The power station itself is near the lower reservoir. As the water flows through the pipes it turns the turbines round very fast. The turbines are a bit like an old water wheel, only much faster. They turn the generator and provide electricity. The lower reservoir fills up with water. Using flowing water to generate electricity is called **hydroelectric** generation.

At night, when demand is much less, electricity from other power stations is used to pump water back up the mountain to the upper reservoir. The water has position or potential energy. The system acts as a store of energy. This system, unlike coal or oil has a quick start-up time. All the operator has to do is to open the tap or valve to let the water flow.

Questions

2 a) Why does demand for electricity change depending on the time of day?
b) Why is this a problem for the electricity company?
c) What can they do about it?

Remember

Copy and complete the sentences. Use these words:

changes turbines reservoir pumped storage water

People's demands for electricity **c**________ from summer to winter and from one time of day to another. One way to meet the demand is to use **p**________ **s**________ systems. They use spare energy to pump **w**________ up to a high **r**________ when demand is low. Then when demand is high, the water can flow down to turn the power station **t**________.

Energy rates

Key words

efficiency Producing a lot of useful energy with little wasted energy

power rating The rate at which an appliance transfers energy

watt The unit of measuring power. One watt is the transfer of one joule of energy per second. 1 kilowatt = 1000 watts

Figure 1 Power = 2400 watt. Energy cost for one hour is *about* 24p.

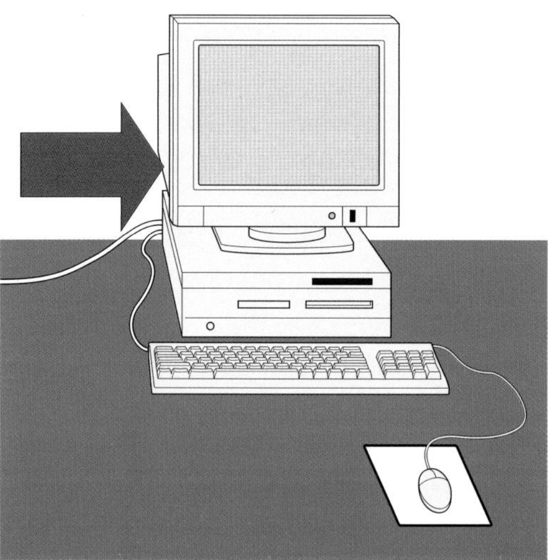

Figure 2 Power = 500 watt. Energy cost for one hour is *about* 5p.

Figure 3 Power = 400 watt. Energy cost for one hour is *about* 4p.

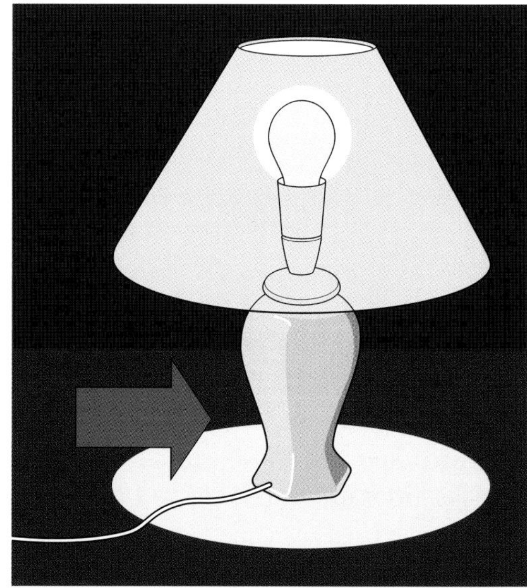

Figure 4 Power = 60 watt. Energy cost for one hour is *about* 0.6p.

Transferring energy

Different appliances have different **power ratings**. They transfer energy at different rates. A kettle has a high power rating and transfers a lot of energy in a short time. It has a strong heating effect.

Power is a measure of how quickly we transfer energy.

$$\text{Power} = \frac{\text{energy transferred (joules)}}{\text{time taken (seconds)}}$$

We measure power in **watts**.

When we transfer 1 joule of energy in 1 second our power is 1 watt. It is a very small unit. The kilowatt is a larger unit.

1 kilowatt (kW) = 1000 watts (W)

Costing electricity

The longer an appliance is used, the more we have to pay for the electricity. We can use this equation to work out the cost.

Cost of electricity = kilowatts × hours × cost of a unit of electricity

Example:

If a unit of electricity costs 10 p, how much will it cost to run a 2 kilowatt heater for 6 hours?

Cost = 2 kW × 6 hours × 10 p

Cost = 12 × 10 p

Cost = 120 p or £1.20

Question

1 If electricity costs 10 p a unit how much will it cost to run:

a) a 3 kW cooker for 1 hour?

b) a 0.25 kW TV for 8 hours?

Efficiency

All appliances transfer energy. A lamp shines and a kettle heats. We pay for all the electricity these appliances use. But the lamp gets hot. The electrical energy is transformed into heat as well.

Appliances transfer heat to their surroundings whether or not we want the heat. We want the lamp to light the room, not to heat it. All the energy we pay for dissipates. If only we could store it. We would save a lot of money. Unfortunately this is just not possible.

We can compare the useful energy we transfer with the amount 'wasted', by talking about **efficiency**. If the lamp transfers 10% of its energy as light, and the other 90% is 'useless' and 'lost' as heat, we say the lamp is 10% efficient. In the end all of the energy (100%) is dissipated.

Question

2 How does a hair drier transfer its energy to its surroundings?

Remember

Copy and complete the sentences. Use these words:

power   watts   energy   efficiency

Appliances transfer **e**_________. The rate of transfer of energy is called **p**_________. Power is measured in units called **w**_________. A kilowatt is a 1000 watts. **E**_________ is a measure of the 'useful' energy from an appliance compared with the energy that went into it.

Future homes

Key words

insulate Slowing down the process of transferring energy

passive heating Collecting heat from the Sun

renewable energy An energy source that will never run out

Figure 1 An energy-efficient house at the Centre for Alternative Technology.

Energy sources like coal and oil are being used up. We can't replace them. We have to think hard about how we use our energy.

Figure 2 These walls have insulation to reduce energy transfer.

Scientists at the Centre for Alternative Technology have built energy efficient houses.

These houses are designed to make careful use of energy. Energy cannot be created from nothing and it cannot be destroyed, but it can be transferred from place to place. When this happens the energy is dissipated.

To keep warm, we need to control these energy transfers. We need to **insulate** our houses.

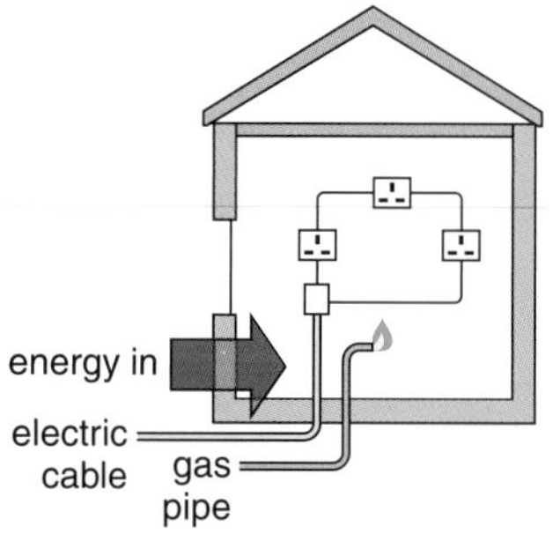

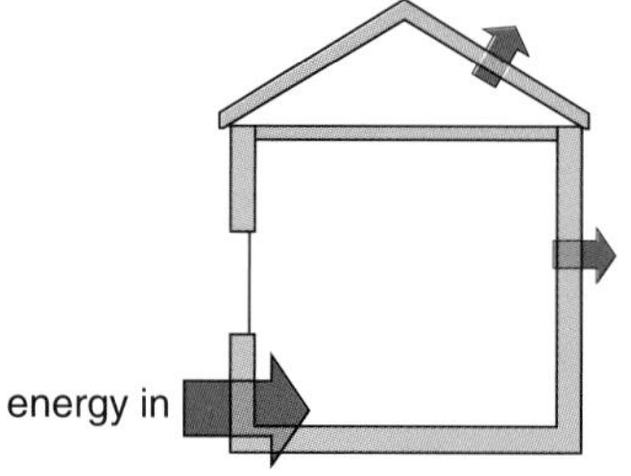

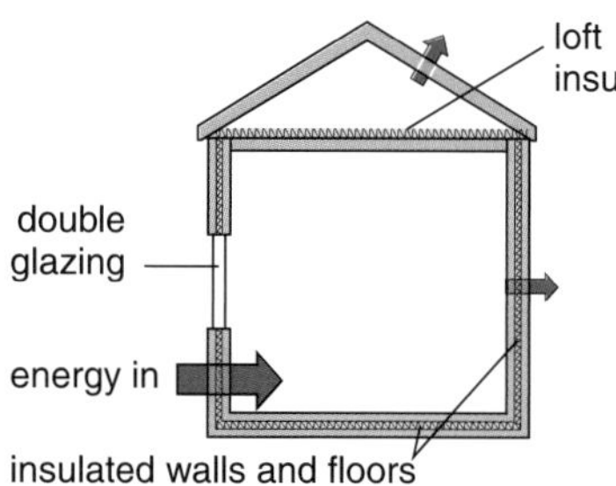

Figure 3 Comparing energy transfers with and without insulation.

We can insulate the roof space with rolls of glass fibre. We can use cavity wall insulation to reduce energy loss through the walls. Double glazing reduces heat transfer through the windows.

We can transfer less energy in our homes by using appliances that are very efficient. Fridge-freezers with thick walls use less electricity and save us money.

Figure 4 Thick insulating walls make this fridge-freezer very efficient.

Questions

1 Name three design features that make houses 'energy efficient'.

2 Do you think you should use an energy efficient fridge-freezer at home? Explain your answer.

Using renewable energy resources

Another answer to our energy problems is to use **renewable** energy resources. Sunlight on solar panels generates electricity.

Figure 5 Solar panels generate electricity on a house at the Centre for Alternative Technology.

Passive heating is one way to make maximum use of the warmth of the Sun. Large south-facing windows on a house will let the sunlight in and warm the house for free. In hot countries large solar heating panels can make the water very warm. So the water does not need much electricity to make it hot.

Questions

3 Name two ways in which houses can be designed to make maximum use of renewable energy resources.

4 Do you think you should have solar panels at home? Explain your answer.

Remember

Copy and complete the sentences. Use these words.

created renewable stored warmer transfers insulation destroyed dissipated colder

The Sun provides us with energy, including our **r**_________ energy resources.

Energy **t**_________ out from our homes in all directions. We have to replace the energy or the home will get **c**_________ while the air outside gets just slightly **w**_________. We can reduce the energy transfer out of our homes and still keep warm, by using good **i**_________.

Energy can't be **c**_________ from nowhere and it can't be **d**_________. But it can be transferred and **s**_________. It can be **d**_________, this means it is spread out uselessly.

Finishing off!

Remember

- ★ Current is the same all the way round a **series** circuit. In a **parallel** circuit there is a choice of routes.
- ★ Circuits transfer energy from the cell or battery to the surroundings. They can do this by heating or by doing work.
- ★ Batteries and power station **generators** are sources of energy for electric circuits.
- ★ A motor can transfer energy from the electric circuit. It can give objects **kinetic energy** by making them move. It can give objects position energy or **potential energy** by lifting them to a higher level.
- ★ Energy transfer takes place from a warm home to the colder surroundings. We can try to reduce this by **insulating** our homes.
- ★ Energy cannot be created from nowhere and it cannot be destroyed. But it can be **dissipated** and then is no longer useful to us as a resource.

Questions

1 Take a new page in your exercise book. Make a list of all the Key Words from the boxes in this chapter down the side.

Take two lines per word. Try to write the meaning of each word without looking. Then go back and fill in any you did not know or got wrong.

Now learn to spell them by the Look – Say – Cover – Write method.

2 Imagine a hot potato on a cold plate. Which gains energy and which loses energy?

Do a simple sketch to show the energy transfer.

3 An electric heater has four identical heating wires connected in parallel. The total current through the heater is 8 amps.

Draw a circuit diagram to show how the wires are connected. How much current flows in each one?

Web sites to visit:

The Centre for Alternative Technology
http://www.cat.org.uk

First Hydro Company – pumped storage power
http://www.fhc.co.uk/INTRO.htm

Fit and healthy

Starter Activity
What is fitness?

Your idea of fitness is not always the same as someone else's idea. A runner needs a different type of training from a weightlifter. If you look at a runner and a weightlifter, you can see the difference in their body shapes. Both of them are fit and do a lot of training.

Fitness means being able to do normal physical activity without getting exhausted. Your level of fitness depends on your strength, flexibility (how supple you are) and stamina (how long you can train or play a sport). In this chapter we will look at fitness. How you live, exercise and what you eat and drink can affect your fitness.

A weightlifter and a runner are both fit, but look completely different.

Questions

1 To run or do any exercise we need energy. Where do we get our energy from?

2 Which foods are a good fuel to produce energy in our bodies?

3 Describe the sort of exercises you might do in PE lessons to increase your level of fitness.

4 Think of a person in a wheelchair, who cannot use their legs to run and walk. Why is it important for them to exercise and keep fit?

Healthy systems

Key words

alveoli Small damp air sacs at the end of each bronchiole. Oxygen enters the body and carbon dioxide leaves the body through the alveoli

bronchi Two pipes that branch off the trachea, one pipe (bronchus) for each lung

bronchioles Small tubes that take air deep into the lungs

ligaments An elastic tissue that stops joints moving too far

oesophagus The food pipe or gullet leading from the mouth to the stomach

organ systems Groups of organs that work together

tendons Tissue that joins a muscle to a bone

trachea The wind pipe leading from the mouth and nose to the lungs

Figure 1 The respiratory system.

There are three **organ systems** that have to work together to keep us fit and healthy. These are the respiratory system, the digestive system and the circulatory system. Two other systems, the skeleton and muscle systems, are needed for support and movement.

The respiratory system

The respiratory system includes the **trachea** (wind pipe) and **bronchi**, pipes leading to each lung. The lungs contain the **bronchioles** and **alveoli**. The respiratory system also includes muscles in the chest and the diaphragm to control breathing. See Figure 1.

The digestive system

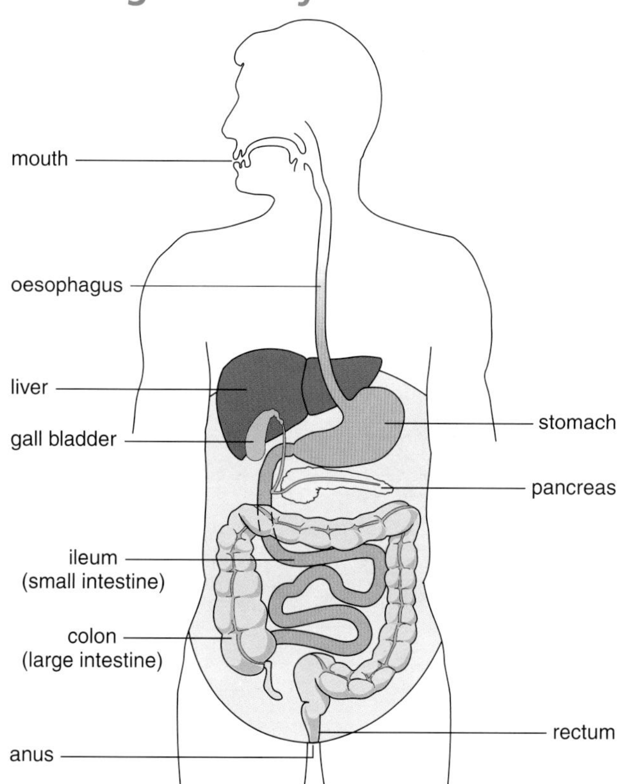

Figure 2 The digestive system.

The digestive system is the group of organs that break down food into its basic chemical parts so that they can be absorbed and used for energy and building new cells. This system includes the mouth, the **oesophagus** (gullet), stomach, small and large intestine and the rectum.

The circulatory system

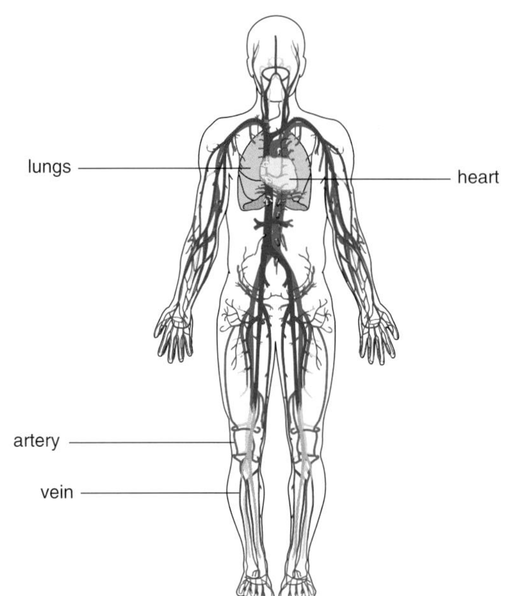

Figure 3 The circulatory system.

The circulatory system is made up of the heart and blood vessels. They provide a continuous flow of blood around the body. They carry oxygen and nutrients to all of our tissues and take away any waste products.

The skeletal system

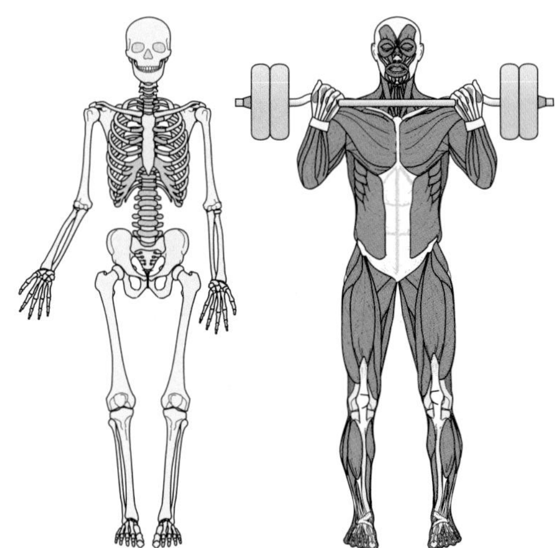

Figure 4 The skeletal and muscle systems.

The skeletal system gives us a body shape. It also works with our muscles to allow us to move or lift things. Our arms and legs act like levers. The skeletal system is made up of the bones of the skeleton and the different types of joints between the bones.

The muscle system

The muscle system is made up of all of the muscles of the body. The **tendons** that join the muscles to the bones are also part of this system.

Ligaments are like a tough band of elastic tissue that bind together the ends of bones. They help stop the joints moving too much during exercise.

Question

1 Match the first half of the sentence in column 1 to its correct tail in column 2, then copy the full sentence into your exercise book.

When I go to sleep my breathing rate ...	increases quickly then slows down.
When I suddenly run 20 metres for a bus my breathing rate ...	increases slightly.
When I get a sudden fright my heart rate	slows down.
When I sit down quietly in front of the television my heart rate ...	increases a lot.
When I go for a brisk walk my breathing rate...	doesn't change a lot.

Remember

The three main organ systems that keep us fit and healthy are:

★ the respiratory system
★ the digestive system
★ the circulatory system

Copy the table into your exercise book and put these words into the correct column.

trachea heart small intestine arteries stomach bronchi large intestine veins stomach lungs oesophagus bronchioles

Respiratory system	Digestive system	Circulatory system

Diet, exercise and fitness

Key words

arthritis A condition in which a person's joints become painful, swollen and stiff

ball and socket joint The type of joint you have in your shoulder and hips

hinge joint The type of joint found in your elbows and knees

Getting fit is not just about training and exercise. You must eat a balanced diet and exercise properly and safely. Adults should not drink too much alcohol or smoke. Nor should you take any drugs, other than those prescribed for you.

Very active people like athletes need lots of energy. People who are less active need less energy. Men usually need more energy than women, and adults need more energy than children.

People also need different amounts of nutrients as they get older. As a teenager you will need extra protein and minerals.

Top class athletes have their diet carefully worked out for them. They make sure that they have a diet that gives them all the energy they need. But even athletes' diets vary. A weightlifter and a runner need different diets.

Questions

1 What do you think might happen if a normal person ate a weightlifter's diet, but didn't do any weightlifting?

2 List the following workers in order of which one needs the most energy and which one needs the least energy from their diet.
  a) an international long distance runner
  b) a physical fitness trainer in a sports club
  c) an office worker using a computer
  d) a post office worker delivering mail on foot every day

Help prevent injuries

Exercise is important in keeping you fit and healthy. But any exercise must be done properly. It is easy to injure yourself if you don't know what you are doing, and how your skeleton and muscles work. The most common type of injury that happens when people exercise is an injury to the joints such as the elbow, ankle, shoulder, knee, back or neck.

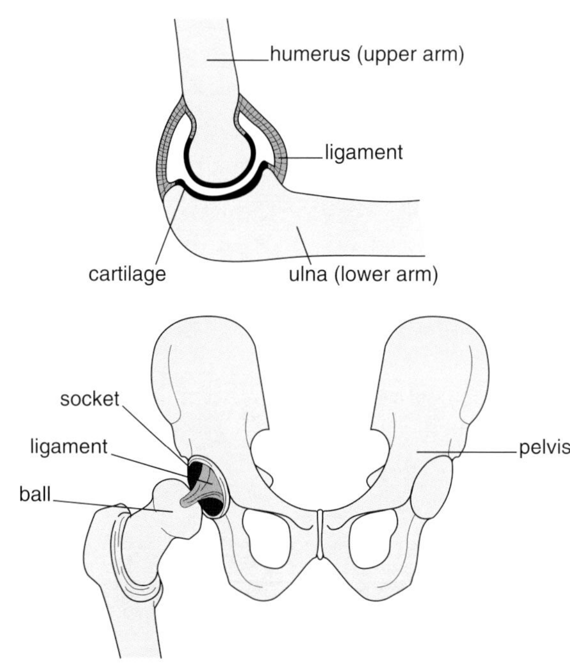

Figure 1 A hinge joint and a ball and socket joint.

Figure 1 shows the two main types of joints that we have. A **hinge joint** allows our arms and legs to bend. A **ball and socket joint** allows our arms to circle at the shoulder and the legs to circle at the hips.

Very often injuries happen when a muscle is stretched too far (a pulled muscle), or a joint is pushed further than it should go. Another common injury happens when ligaments are stretched too far (a pulled ligament).

	Heart and lungs	Joints	Muscles
Golf	★	★★	★
Swimming	★★★★	★★★★	★★★★
Jogging	★★★★	★★	★★
Brisk walking	★★	★	★★
Football	★★★	★★★	★★★
Tennis	★★★	★★★	★★

Table 1 The effects of different sports. (* = poor, **** = excellent)

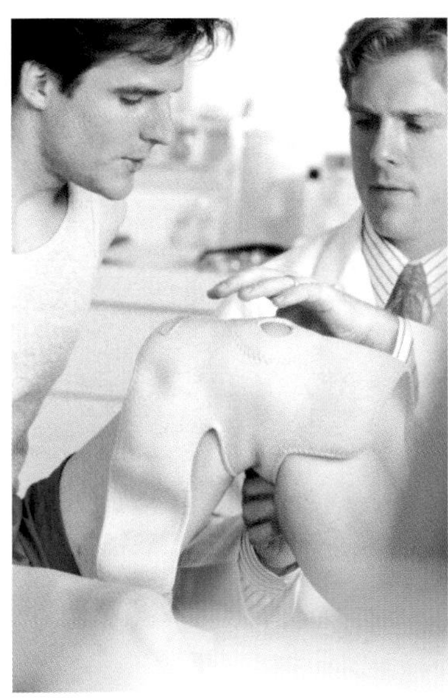

Figure 2 This physiotherapist is treating the sportman's injury.

If a muscle or ligament has been pulled or a joint injured it needs to be rested so that the body has time to repair the damage. Sometimes, if the damage is too great the body cannot repair the muscle or joint.

Question

3 Why do most athletes and teams have trainers. What else might the trainer do apart from advise them on exercise?

Not all injuries and joint problems are caused by exercise. Sometimes the joints just wear out. This happens in people that suffer from **arthritis**. It often happens to hip joints. Fortunately we can now replace hip joints by surgery.

Different sports exercise different muscles and parts of the body. Regular exercise is important even if you don't want to be a sportsperson. Table 1 shows the benefits of doing different sports.

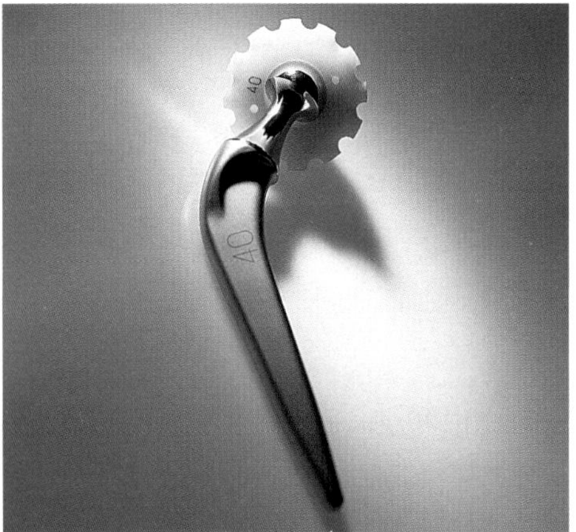

Figure 3 A replacement hip joint.

Question

4 Look at Table 1. Which would be the best sport to take up if you wanted to improve the fitness of your heart and lungs, the suppleness of your joints, and your muscle power?

Remember

Rearrange the sentences into a sensible paragraph. Copy the paragraph into your exercise book.

- You must eat enough energy giving foods for the sports you do.
- You must make sure that you eat a balanced diet.
- You need to exercise regularly even if you don't want to play in a team or be a sportsperson.
- Being fit and healthy means looking after lots of different systems in the body.
- One of the best ways to keep fit and healthy is to go swimming regularly.

4.3 Smoking and health

Key words

addictive Something you cannot stop taking once you've started

carbon monoxide A poisonous gas

emphysema An illness that stops you from breathing properly

nicotine A harmful chemical found in tobacco

passive smoking Breathing in harmful tobacco smoke in the air, but not actually smoking

tar Another harmful chemical found in tobacco

Smoking can cause serious health problems for people. Often the problems don't appear for many years, so some young people think smoking isn't harmful. The truth is that smoking can lead to all sorts of health problems and it can seriously affect your fitness.

Why is tobacco harmful?

There are three harmful chemicals in tobacco smoke. They are **nicotine**, **carbon monoxide** and **tar**.

Figure 1 Cigarettes are often smoked by young people. Some become addicted and get ill when they get older.

Nicotine is a powerful chemical that is **addictive**. This means that your body starts to need nicotine all the time. At first the amount of nicotine the body becomes addicted to is quite small. But the longer a person smokes, the more nicotine they need and they find it difficult to live without nicotine every day.

Carbon monoxide is a gas. It is similar to carbon dioxide, the gas we breathe out, but it is very dangerous. The gas is colourless and doesn't smell. It is poisonous and in large amounts can kill. People who smoke only take in small amounts of carbon monoxide. But over a long period of time the carbon monoxide stops oxygen reaching the tissues in the body.

Figure 2 Cigarette companies have to put health warnings on all packets of cigarettes.

The tar in cigarettes and cigarette smoke irritates the lungs and respiratory system. It leaves behind a layer of chemicals on the trachea, bronchi, bronchioles and alveoli. This can make it difficult to breathe. Because the layer of tar shouldn't be in the lungs, the body tries to get rid of it by producing mucus and trying to cough it up. This is the smoker's cough. The longer you smoke the worse it will get. The tar also contains chemicals that can cause cancer. Smokers are much more likely to develop mouth cancer, cheek cell cancer and lung cancer than non smokers.

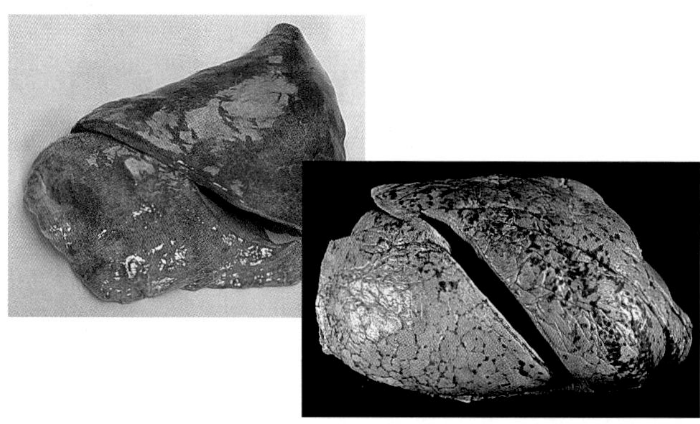

Figure 3 The smoker's lung on the right does not work very well. The tissue becomes hard and black because of the chemicals in the tobacco smoke.

Questions

1 What is the name of the addictive chemical found in tobacco smoke?

2 Low tar cigarettes are better than high tar ones, but why are these cigarettes still unhealthy?

Smoking and cancer

Ninety percent of lung cancer deaths are linked to smoking. Thirty percent of all deaths from cancer are caused by tobacco. Lung cancer is not the only type of cancer you can get from smoking. You can also get mouth cancer, lip cancer, bladder cancer and cervical cancer in women (the cervix is the entrance to the womb). Some smokers smoke pipes and cigars because they think that they are less dangerous. It is true that these people are less likely to develop lung cancer, but they are more likely to get lip, mouth and throat cancer.

Questions

3 If there were 20 000 deaths from lung cancer in a year, how many of these could be linked to smoking?

4 If there were 100 000 deaths from all types of cancer in a year, how many of these could be linked to tobacco?

Smoking and other diseases

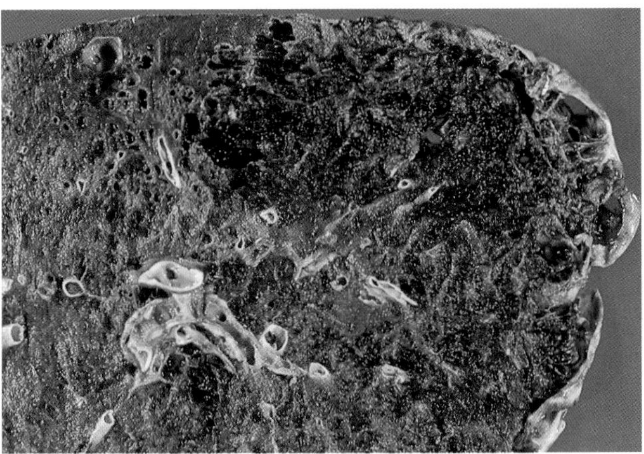

Figure 4 Emphysema means that not enough oxygen is getting to the tissues. This photo shows a lung from a smoker with emphysema.

Many people do not know that there are other diseases, apart from cancer, that are linked to tobacco and smoking. Tobacco smoke causes the tiny air sacs in the lungs (alveoli) to become hard. This stops them letting oxygen into the bloodstream and carbon dioxide out. This makes it difficult to breathe. We call this **emphysema**. Many heavy smokers die from this.

Smokers are more likely to suffer from blocked arteries. This reduces the blood flow around the heart and can cause chest pains and heart attacks. Smokers are also more likely to have a stroke. A stroke is where part of the brain is damaged because it doesn't get enough blood.

Women who smoke when they are pregnant also risk harming their unborn baby. The chemicals in tobacco smoke can pass into the mother's bloodstream, and then pass into the unborn baby's bloodstream. Because the baby is so much smaller, the chemicals have a much greater effect on the baby than on the mother.

Passive smoking

When you inhale the tobacco smoke of other people, but don't smoke yourself, it is called **passive smoking**. You may still be at risk from some diseases. The children of smokers often have more chest and ear infections than the children of non-smokers. Non-smokers who work in smoke filled rooms like pubs and bars are also at risk.

Question

5 Name four diseases that smokers are more likely to get.

Remember

Use the information on the problems and diseases linked to smoking to produce a leaflet on the dangers of smoking. The leaflets need to be suitable for year 7 pupils

Alcohol and health

Key words

alcohol A colourless chemical found in alcoholic drinks

units of alcohol A useful way of measuring how much alcohol you drink

How **alcohol** affects your health will change from person to person, it depends on how much they drink and how often they drink. Alcohol is a dangerous drug if too much is consumed for too long.

How much is too much?

To measure how much alcohol people drink we use a system of **units of alcohol**. One unit of alcohol is the same as ½ pint of ordinary beer or lager, one glass of wine or one pub measure of whisky or vodka.

The problem is that some drinks have more alcohol in them, so drinking these means that you are actually having more than one unit in a measure. Some drinks manufacturers now label their bottled drinks with the number of units it contains to help people. People who drink at home often give themselves and their guests more than a pub measure. Another problem happens when young people drink alcohol. The number of units that are recommended as safe limits are set for normal healthy adults. But alcohol has a much greater effect on children, so this recommended number of units would not be safe for children.

Figure 1 All these drinks contain one unit of alcohol.

Drinking and Health

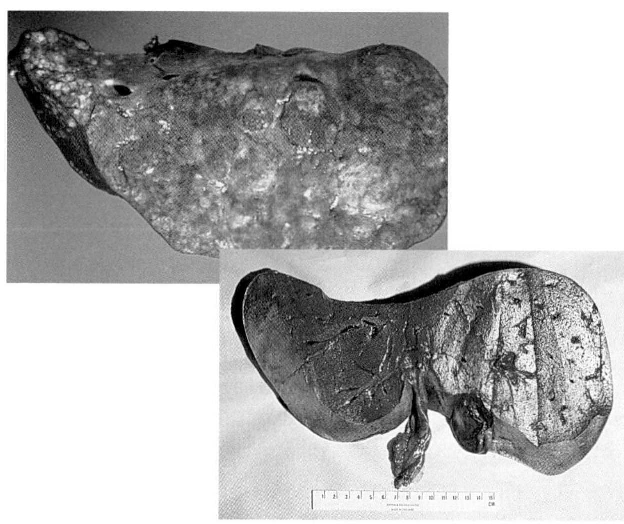

Figure 2 A badly damaged liver (top) compared with a healthy liver (below). The cause of the damage is alcohol.

Alcohol can affect many different cells, tissues and organs in your body. The organ most at risk is the liver. Heavy drinking destroys liver cells and eventually the liver can stop working.

Scientists have found that for adults, small amounts of alcohol can lower the risk of heart disease. A small amount of alcohol is no more than two units a day. Drinking more than this each day increases the risk of heart disease. Heavy drinkers also suffer from stomach problems, like stomach cancer, ulcers (where the lining of the stomach is being eaten away by the stomach acid), cancer of the mouth, tongue, throat and oesophagus. Heavy drinking can also lead to brain damage.

Women who drink when they are pregnant can also damage their unborn baby's health. The alcohol enters the mother's bloodstream and passes into the baby's bloodstream. Because the baby is much smaller and its cells, tissues and organs are still developing, the alcohol can seriously damage the baby's health.

Number of units a week for an adult male over 18 years of age	Too much or not?	Number of units in a week for an adult female over 18 years of age
Up to 21	This is normally a safe limit for healthy normal adults if spread over a week.	Up to 14
22–35	This level of drinking may not damage your health in the long term. But if you drink all of this in two or three sessions it will cause damage.	15–21
36–49	Regularly drinking this much in a week will cause long term damage to your health.	22–35
50 or more	Regularly drinking this much will definitely cause serious damage to your health. You may even become dependent on alcohol. This means it will be difficult for you to cut down or give up.	36 or more

Table 1 Guidelines for safe drinking

Question

1. What is the recommended safe number of units of alcohol that a normal healthy adult can drink over a week?

Alcohol and behaviour

Figure 3 The driver of this car had been drinking alcohol and lost control of the car, killing the motorcyclist in the crash.

Alcohol often causes silly or violent behaviour. Drinking alcohol can have different effects on different people. Some people feel tired and just want to fall asleep. This could be a problem if people have a few drinks at lunchtime and then have to operate machines after lunch. Other people get bad-tempered after drinking and this can often lead to fights and people being seriously injured.

Alcohol actually slows down our reactions. People who drink often think it speeds up their reactions, but they are wrong. Drinking and driving is wrong. To drive a car, a motorbike or a scooter you must be alert and ready to react quickly to other traffic and pedestrians. Scientists have shown that even drinking small amounts of alcohol can affect how safely you drive. The only safe way to drink and drive is to drink non-alcoholic drinks.

Questions

2. Lots of fights and arguments take place in town centres, when are they most likely to take place?
3. Alcohol must not be drunk in football grounds during a match. Why do you think that this law has been introduced?
4. Why is drinking alcohol and driving dangerous?

Remember

Use the information on this page to produce a leaflet for sixth formers telling them about alcohol and its effects.

Drugs and health

Key words

drug A chemical that can be manmade or natural that changes how the body works, or reacts to disease

illegal drugs Harmful drugs that cannot be bought or used legally

medicinal drug Drugs taken to prevent or cure illness

recreational drug Drugs taken for pleasure that can be bought legally

The word **drug** is used for any chemical that changes how the body works or that changes how a disease affects us. Drugs include any medicines prescribed to us and those you can buy 'over the counter' at a chemist shop. Many drugs are produced by drug companies, but others can be found naturally. Drugs can be placed into three groups, **recreational**, **medicinal** and **illegal**.

Recreational drugs

Figure 1 Recreational drugs.

Tea and coffee contain a drug that affects how our bodies work. This drug is called caffeine. It is found in coffee beans, tea-leaves and cocoa beans. Caffeine increases the nerve activity in the brain. When you drink a cup of coffee or tea it has the effect of 'waking you up'. If you take lots of caffeine it can make your hands tremble and your heart feels like it is racing. Caffeine is on the list of banned drugs for athletes, as it can help them perform better.

Other recreational drugs are more harmful than caffeine, but they are still legal for adults to buy and take. These include nicotine (found in tobacco) and alcohol.

Questions

1. How many groups can we put drugs into and what are they?
2. Which recreational drug(s) is it legal for you to buy and which recreational drugs is it illegal for you to buy?

Medicinal drugs

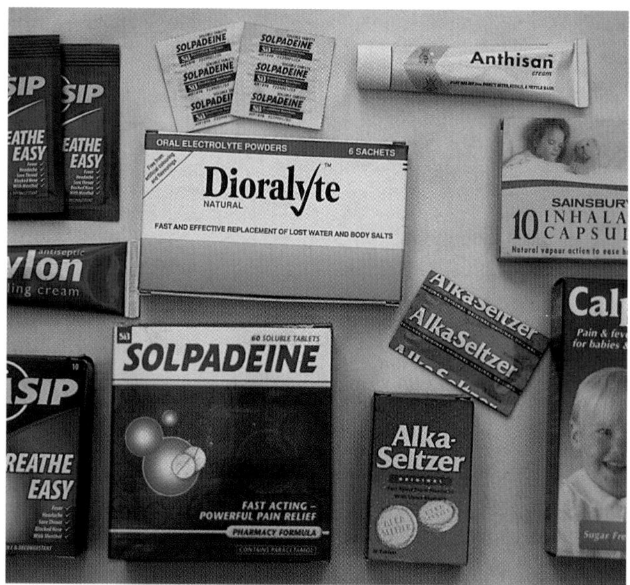

Figure 2 Medicinal drugs.

Lots of drugs can be bought over the counter at a chemist shop. But you still have to be careful when you take them and how you take them. You must carefully read and follow the instructions. Only take them when you really need them.

Paracetamol is a common pain killer, it could kill you if you take too many at once or if you don't follow the instructions carefully. Paracetamol can damage your liver if you take too many. You should always ask your parents or guardians before taking any type of drug or medicine.

Some drugs prescribed by your doctor are just as addictive and dangerous as illegal drugs. But doctors know how much to give you. They keep a check on patients to make sure that the drug is not causing any problems. All prescription and 'over the counter' drugs have also been carefully tested. Drugs and medicines prescribed for someone should never be taken by anyone else. Any drugs left over should be handed back to a chemist to prevent accidents.

Illegal drugs

a)

b)

Figure 3 Ecstasy (a) and marijuana (b) are both illegal grugs.

There are many different types of illegal drugs. These drugs all have one thing in common – they all change the way a person feels or thinks they feel.

The most common types of illegal drugs are cocaine, heroin, cannabis, acid and ecstasy. They all have street names and some have more than one name, like cocaine which can be called charlie, coke, snow, white and sniff.

Questions

3 Some prescription drugs can be as dangerous as illegal drugs. How does a doctor try to make sure that their patient isn't harmed by the drug?

4 Many illegal drugs are known as 'mind altering'. What do you think this means?

Remember

Using the information on the problems linked to drugs, produce a leaflet on drugs that would be suitable for pupils in your school.

Finishing off!

Remember

Sketch the outline of a running athlete on a page in your exercise book. Put as many of these words as you can around the figure with a ✓ if it is good for an athlete and a ✗ if it is bad. If you cannot put a tick or a cross describe what the word or words mean.

muscle system | smoking | skeletal system | alcohol | brain | diet | fitness | illegal drugs | reactions | joints | training | digestive system | exercise | health | tobacco | medicinal drugs | recreational drugs

Questions

1 Take a new page in your exercise book. Make a list of all the Key Words from the boxes in this chapter down the side. Take two lines per word. Try to write the meaning of each word without looking. Then go back and fill in any you did not know or got wrong.

Now learn to spell them by the Look – Say – Cover – Write method.

2 Make a list of all the exercise you have done in the last week. List them in three groups:
- a) exercise that was good for the heart and lungs (your breathing and heart rate increased)
- b) exercise that helped make your joints supple (knees, elbows, hips and shoulders)
- c) exercise that worked on your muscles (you were pushing or pulling something)

3 Make a list of what you ate last week. List the foods into the following groups:
- a) energy-giving foods
- b) fruits and vegetables
- c) meat and fish
- d) junk food
  - (i) Would you say that your diet was balanced?
  - (ii) Which food group do you eat too much or too little of?

4 Why do you think there is a law preventing young people from buying tobacco and alcohol?

5 What is the difference between the following groups of drugs:
- a) recreational
- b) medicinal or prescription
- c) illegal?

Web sites to visit:

ASH – Action on Smoking and Health
http://www.ash.org.uk

Institute of alcohol studies
http://www.ias.org.uk

Kids Health
http://www.kidshealth.org

Chemistry and the environment

Starter Activity
Rock revision

The Earth has existed for about 4 600 million years. Its surface has often changed. Mountains come and go. Mountains get pushed up as continents collide. Mount Everest in Tibet is the highest point on the Earth's surface at 8 848 metres high. Mount Everest is less than 20 million years old.

Over the last 200 years people have also changed the Earth and its atmosphere – not all of this change has been for the better.

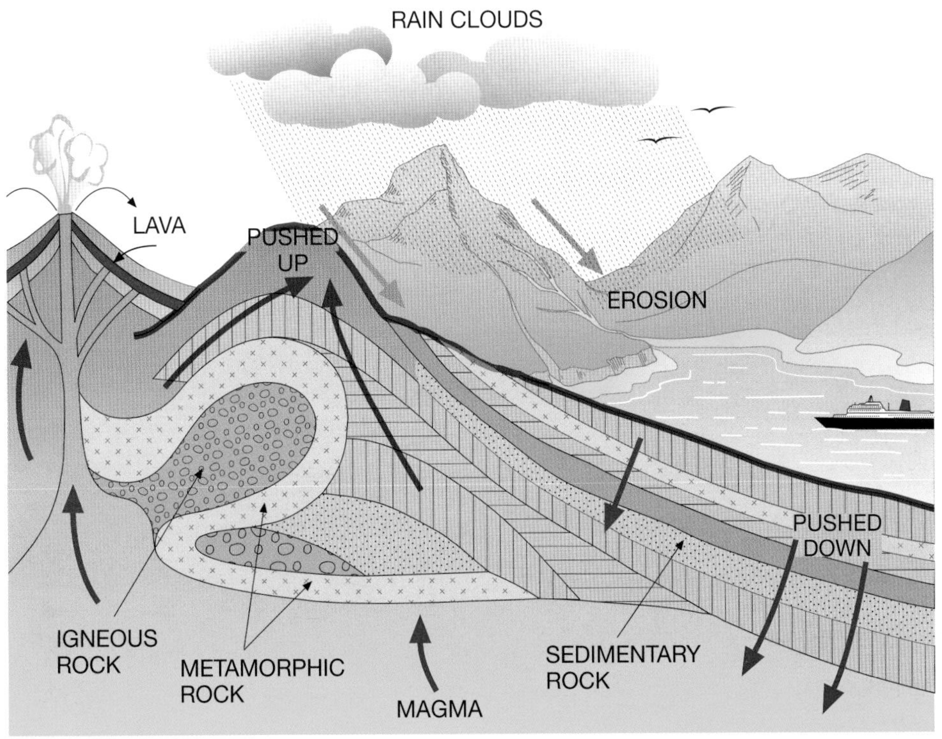

Questions

1. How are igneous rocks made?
2. What causes mountains to get pushed up?
3. What do you call liquid rock that comes out of volcanoes?
4. How does ice break up rocks on the surface of the Earth?
5. How do plant roots help to break-up rocks into smaller fragments?
6. What happens to the shape of rock fragments as they are moved down rivers?
7. How can you tell that a rock sample is sedimentary rock?
8. How is metamorphic rock made?

Acids in the air

Key words

acid rain Pollution dissolves in the water in clouds to make the rain more acid

lime This sort of lime is a white powder called calcium oxide. Do not confuse it with the sour green fruits called limes.

pH scale Number scale to measure acidity, neutral is 7

pollution Waste materials in the wrong place

Figure 1 Lime spraying is used to counteract acid rain because it is alkaline in solution. Lime is the compound calcium oxide.

Rain is naturally acidic. It always has been. Carbon dioxide from the atmosphere dissolves in the rain water to make it weakly acidic.

During the last 200 years the problem of acidic rain has got much worse. **Pollution** from homes and industry have made rain much more acidic. **Acid rain** attacks stonework. It also kills plants, and runs into rivers or lakes where it kills the water life.

Lime is alkaline. Lime can be sprayed on to trees or added to lakes to make them less acidic.

A sad story

I am a sad Swedish tree.

My friends around me look in an awful state.

We are not growing, we are dying.

The weather is killing us.

The rain used to be good for us. Now it is poison.

It is full of acid.

The acid gases in the air dissolve in the rain. Then the rain falls on us.

The acid gases come from burning coal and oil to make electricity.

The acid kills my leaves.

The acid poisons the fish in the lakes.

Just so people can watch television and use the microwave.

In a country called Britain.

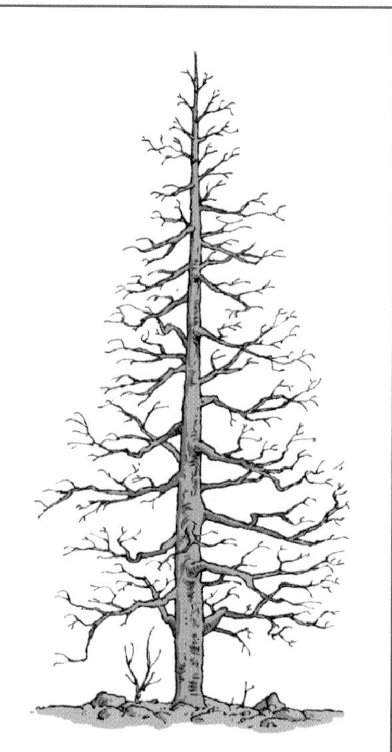

The pH scale

On the **pH scale** 7 means a neutral solution.

Acid solutions have a pH number of less than 7.

Alkali solutions have a pH of more than 7.

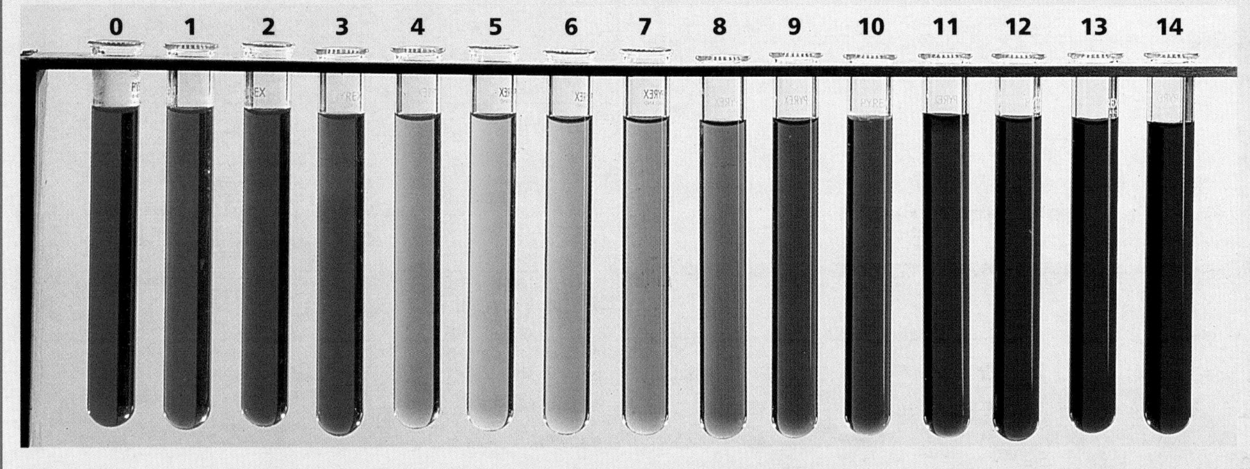

When coal and oil get burnt to produce electricity, sulphur oxides are made. These dissolve in rain to make sulphuric acid. When petrol and diesel fuel are burnt nitrogen oxides (NOx) are made. These dissolve in rain to make nitric acid. These are the acids in acid rain.

Acid rain never falls in the places that produce the pollution. It is carried by the wind to other places. Pollution from Britain causes acid rain which falls in Sweden.

Questions

4 What colour is Universal Indicator solution in a strong acid?

5 Draw a diagram to show where the pollution in acid rain comes from.

6 Catalytic converters in car exhausts turn NOx back into nitrogen gas. Explain why this reduces acid rain.

Remember

Copy and complete the sentences. Use these words:

fish neutralise lime trees acid rain

A_________ **r**_________ is produced when pollution gets dissolved in clouds. Acid rain can damage growing **t**_________ and kill **f**_________ in lakes.

L_________powder is used to **n**_________ the acid in acid rain.

Plants and rock

Key words

base This is any substance that neutralises an acid

erode Break up rock and carry it away

humus Dead plant remains, adds nutrients to the soil

stalactites These are rock points hanging from the roofs of caves. They are made when a slow drip leaves minerals behind.

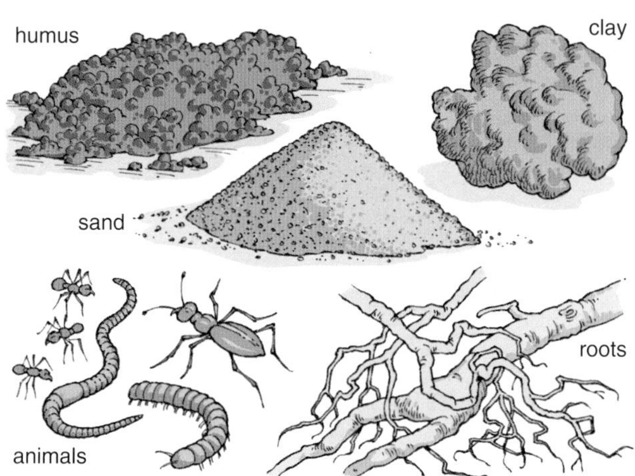

Figure 1 The components of soil.

From an early age, we know about soil or 'earth' from digging in it. We imagine that the soil goes deep down, but in fact it's really only a layer about 10 metres thick. Soil is made up of lots of different things. Plants grow and and die in soil. When plants die they become **humus**. Humus adds nutrients to the soil.

Acidity and pH

Most soils have a pH of between 6.0 and 7.0. This means that soil is weakly acidic. This is because roots add acid particles to the soil. Some plants need soils of a different pH to grow well. If the soil is too acidic, nutrients will not get into the soil.

Soil pH	How to fix it
Less than 4.0	Badly polluted. Add lots of lime and give time to recover
4.0 to 6.0	Add lime (calcium oxide)
6.0 to 7.0	NORMAL SOIL
7.0 to 9.0	Add gypsum (magnesium sulphate)
Above 9.0	Badly polluted. Add lots of gypsum and sulphur powder

Table 1 How to treat soils of different pH

Questions

1 What is pH and how is it measured?

2 What are the components you would find in a good healthy soil?

3 What is humus, and what does it add to soil?

4 What do you do to a soil if it is *too* acidic?

Rock wear

Figure 2 Cave roof stalactites.

Normal rain is acidic. As it flows down through rocks it dissolves some material to make huge caves. The caves have stalactites in them.

Figure 3 Acid damage on rocks.

Buildings made of limestone get damaged by acid rain. The rain dissolves the rock away.

What can wear away solid rock?

- The Sun – heating, expansion and contraction of rock causes it to flake.
- Frost – gets into cracks, and then expands the water in them as it turns to ice. This splits the rock up.
- Growing plants – continue the damage caused by frost.
- Rain – contains dissolved carbon dioxide which makes it weakly acidic.
- Running water – gradually beats at the rock and wears it away.
- Pollution – chemicals in the environment react with the minerals in the rocks, and pollution adds to acidity in the atmosphere making rain more acidic.

Remember

Rocks can be a mixture of many different minerals, but minerals are pure substances.

Most rocks contain many minerals. Some of these minerals are '**bases**'. A 'base' in chemistry is a material that neutralises an acid. Acids in the environment dissolve the grains of minerals out of the rock. This makes the rock weak and easy to **erode** away.

Figure 4 The Limestone carvings on Wells Cathedral have been badly damaged by acid rain, so they are now being replaced by new carvings like the one on the left.

Questions

5 Name six things that can damage rocks.

6 Why should a bridge over a polluted river *not* be built of limestone?

Remember

Copy and complete the sentences. Use these words:

weakens 6.0 soil plants rock 7.0 wrong

Both **p**________ and rocks suffer if the pH is **w**________. Normal **s**________ has a pH of between ________ and ________.

If acidic water gets onto **r**________ then it dissolves some of the minerals. This **w**________ the rock.

5.3 Global greenhouse

Key words

global warming The average temperature of the Earth's surface is getting hotter

greenhouse effect A greenhouse heats up because it lets light in and uses it to cause heating. Heat is being trapped in the Earth's atmosphere, like a greenhouse.

greenhouse gases Some gases trap energy in the atmosphere like the glass of a greenhouse traps energy

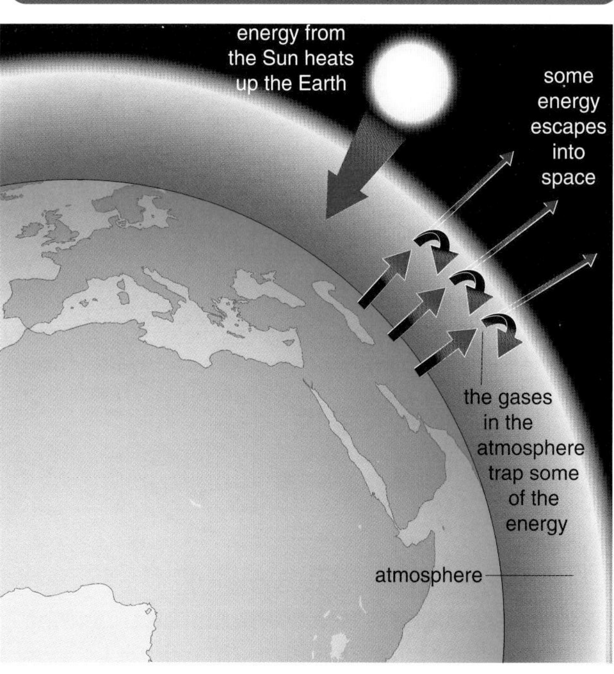

Figure 1

There are some gases in the Earth's atmosphere that trap energy. These gases cause **global warming**.

The Earth's atmosphere acts like a kind of greenhouse. It traps energy and keeps the Earth warm. Without the **greenhouse effect** the Earth would be a frozen planet with no life.

Not all the gases in the atmosphere absorb energy. Oxygen, argon and nitrogen in the air absorb very little energy. These make up 99.9 % of the air. The most significant **greenhouse gas** is carbon dioxide. Some natural and industrial processes put carbon dioxide into the atmosphere, and others take it out (see Table 1).

Questions

1 What causes the Greenhouse Effect?

2 What would happen to the temperature of the Earth if there was no greenhouse effect?

3 Name one gas that contributes to the Greenhouse Effect

Figure 2 This is slash and burn rainforest clearing. All the trees are cut down and then burnt. This puts lots of carbon dioxide into the air.

Human activity is increasing the amount of carbon dioxide in the atmosphere. We are disturbing the natural balance. The Earth's environment may be able to cope in the long run, but there will be severe problems caused by the extra energy.

These put carbon dioxide into the atmosphere	These take carbon dioxide out of the atmosphere
• Burning fossil fuels • Animal respiration • Rotting plants • Burning forests to create farmland • Volcanic eruptions	• Photosynthesis and growth in forests and jungles • Photosynthesis and growth of sea plankton

Table 1

Figure 3 Volcanic eruptions put lots of carbon dioxide into the air.

Global warming will cause:

- Higher temperatures, 2 °C to 5 °C higher during the next century.
- Melting of ice at the North and South poles.
- Rise in sea level of maybe between 20 and 30 cm.
- More flooding of low lying land.
- More violent weather.
- More cloud cover and heavy rain.
- Changes in sea currents.
- Deserts may move further north.
- More storms, hurricanes and floods causing human suffering.

Questions

4 How is human activity making global warming more of a problem?

5 What are the effects of global warming on human life?

Remember

Look at the list of effects of global warming.

Draw some illustrations to show these effects. Combine the drawings into a collage, warning about what will happen because of global warming.

5.4 A Tale of Two Ozones

Key words

CFCs Ozone destroying chemicals

ozone A particular type of oxygen molecule (O_3 instead of O_2) that is harmful to life at ground level

ozone layer A layer of ozone gas high up in the atmosphere that absorbs harmful radiation

The high atmosphere

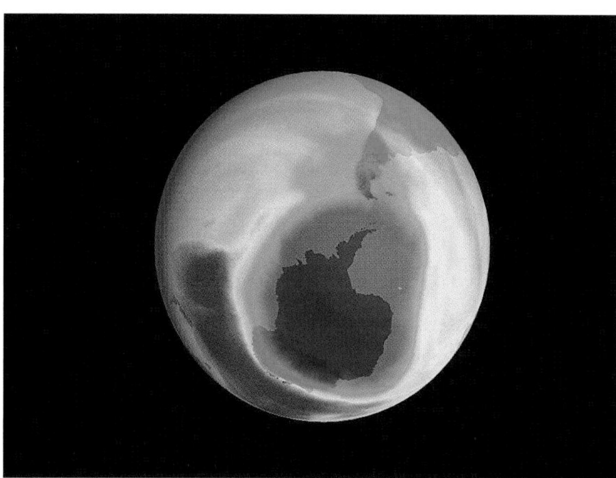

Figure 1 The thinning of the ozone layer is particularly bad over the Antarctic.

Man-made chemicals called **CFCs** come from fridges and aerosol sprays. They drift up to the high atmosphere (between 20 and 50 km above the Earth) and react with the **ozone** molecules there. The ozone molecules do a useful job absorbing harmful ultraviolet (UV) radiation from the Sun. Because of the CFCs there is less ozone up there. So more harmful radiation gets through. Without the **ozone layer**, life may never have evolved as we know it now. To protect us from ultraviolet radiation we use sun screen cream, or sun block cream.

UV radiation and skin

- Skin is 3 mm thick and UV radiation penetrates through it.
- UV light makes skin lose its elasticity.
- Then it makes skin furrowed and lumpy.
- Then it can damage the skin DNA.
- This causes cancers.
- These cancers have to be cut out leaving scars.
- There were 40 000 cases of skin cancer in the UK last year.
- The number of skin cancer cases doubles every ten years, as ozone layer damage gets worse.
- If left untreated, skin cancer can kill.

So make sure you wear high factor sun tan creams and sunglasses.

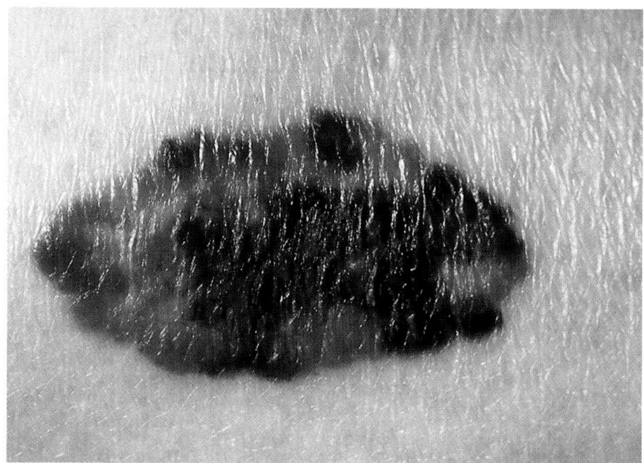

Figure 2 UV radiation can cause skin cancer.

Type of radiation	Ultraviolet A	Ultraviolet B	Ultraviolet C
Harm rating	Least harmful.	Does lots of damage.	Kills.
Effect	Tans skin. Can cause damage if skin is exposed to it for too long.	Burns and ages skin. Causes skin cancers and eye damage.	Kills small creatures. Rapidly causes skin cancer and eye damage.
Precautions	Not a problem, use sun tan cream.	Use total sunblock and cover up with long sleeved clothes.	This radiation does not reach ground level.

Table 2 Types of ultraviolet radiation.

Streetcar poisoning: Ozone at ground level

Figure 3 Bright sun and traffic add up to poison.

Questions

1 What chemical destroys ozone?
2 What type of radiation does ozone absorb?
3 What does this radiation do to our skin?
4 How should you protect your skin from this sort of radiation?
5 What is the formula for an ozone molecule?
6 What does ozone do to blood?

Ozone and traffic

- Car engines burn fuel at high pressures.
- Because of this, the exhaust gases contain nitrogen oxides (NO_x).
- Oxygen (O_2) in the air gets changed into ozone (O_3) when it reacts with nitrogen oxides (NO_x) and there is strong sunlight.
- The ozone that is produced is breathed in. It reacts with the blood and prevents it from carrying oxygen.
- It makes people's brains get too little oxygen.
- It is also very bad for people with asthma and breathing problems.

Remember

Copy and complete the sentences. Use these words:

CFCs radiation layer cream ozone cancers breathing

The ozone **l**________ in the atmosphere is getting thinner because of **C**________ destroying the ozone layer. This lets in ultraviolet **r**________. This radiation can cause skin **c**________ if you do not use sun tan **c**________ on your skin. **O**________ gas can cause **b**________ problems.

Sustainable development

Key words

environment Where we live

species One type of animal or plant

sustainable development Human activity that does not damage the environment

Air that you can't breathe without getting ill, water that fish can't live in, land so poisoned that you can't safely build on it – it has to stop! We can't go on treating the **environment** as a dustbin, because the bin is nearly full.

Sustainable development means living life without spoiling the environment for the future. But it does NOT mean giving up our useful technology to go back to horses and carts. It means designing things with the future in mind.

Cars

What was a shiny, new machine at the start of its life, becomes a useless lump of mixed materials at the end.

Possible action to be taken

Every car should have two taxes added to its price. One would pay the cost of all the pollution and ill health it will cause in its lifetime. The second would pay for recycling all the parts of the car when its life is over. But this costs money.

Fuels: Carbon tax

All fuels contain carbon. This burns in air to make carbon dioxide which adds to the greenhouse gases in the atmosphere. It costs a lot of money to repair the damage done by global warming.

Possible action to be taken

There should be an extra tax on every tonne of coal, every litre of motor fuel, every bag of charcoal and every unit of gas or electricity. This would pay for the damage that the extra carbon dioxide does to the environment. But this costs money.

Transport

Cars are very wasteful. Public transport, like buses and trains, makes much better use of fuel and space. Public transport is much less polluting than lots of small cars running everywhere.

Possible action to be taken

We need to have cheap, quick public transport.

Some examples may be:

- Pollution free, electronic cars and trams in towns.
- High speed rail networks instead of motorways.
- Offshore airports to cut noise pollution.

But this costs money and time.

Forestry

Trees are essential raw materials for newsprint, furniture and building. They are a valuable money earner when cut down. Trees absorb carbon dioxide from the air to grow. They help balance the amount of oxygen and carbon dioxide in the air. Cutting down lots of trees effects this balance.

Possible action to be taken

For every tree cut down and sold, there must be a new one planted. But this costs money.

Biodiversity

We spend our time clearing forests, ripping up hedgerows and draining wetlands to make farmland. When we do this we destroy the plants and animals that live in these places.

Possible action to be taken

Make sure that there are enough places for all the **species**. Protect endangered places such as wetlands. But this costs money.

Energy sources

Coal and oil burnt to make electricity are the major causes of acid rain. Oil tankers often pollute the seas. Renewable methods of making electricity, like wind or solar power, could provide all our energy needs.

Possible action to be taken

Insist that more renewable energy power stations are built. Design schools and shops that use lots of natural light rather than using lots of electricity.

Design 'green buildings' that can produce their own renewable energy and have built-in recycling facilities. But this costs money.

Recycling

Figure 1 A paper recycling centre.

We throw away mountains of rubbish each year. Rubbish needs to be sorted into what can be recycled and what cannot be.

Possible action to be taken

When you buy a fridge you should also pay the cost of getting it recycled safely.

We should sort out waste *before* it is collected. We could send all the glass, paper and card, metal and rubber for recycling. The rest could be burnt to generate electricity. Waste plant and food material should be composted to produce fertiliser.

But this costs time and money.

Activity

Sustainable development costs money. But there will be less problems from pollution in the future, and not so much pollution for the people who live now.

Design an advertising campaign. Try to tell people why sustainable development is good.

Design either slogans, a leaflet, a poster, a script for a radio advert, or a storyboard for a TV advert.

Finishing off!

Remember

What is pollution?

All human beings make waste. Waste in the wrong place is called pollution.

Acid rain

Coal and oil are burnt in power stations to make electricity. Sulphur dioxide and nitrogen oxide are produced. These are the substances that make rain very acidic.

Greenhouse gases

Our atmosphere is slowly heating up. This is causing higher temperatures, stormy weather and a rise in sea level.

Holes in the ozone layer

The ozone layer absorbs harmful ultraviolet rays from the Sun, before they reach us. These rays cause skin cancers.

Traffic smog, ozone and tiny soot particles

Petrol and diesel engines are part of our lives. The exhaust fumes they produce contain tiny particles of soot. These can get deep into our lungs and eventually cause disease and breathing difficulties.

Questions

1. Take a new page in your exercise book. Make a list of all the Key Words from the boxes in this chapter down the side. Take two lines per word. Try to write the meaning of each word without looking. Then go back and fill in any you did not know or got wrong.

   Now learn to spell them by the Look – Say – Cover – Write method.
2. How could the effects of acid rain be reduced where it falls to the ground?
3. What are the rays that can cause skin cancers?
4. Flooding and storm damage are blamed on the greenhouse effect. Explain what this means.
5. In Tokyo, Japan, many people walk the city streets wearing masks all the time. Explain why.
6. Fill in the grid to find the missing word.

a) Tiny p_________ of soot from car engines.

b) The o_________ layer is damaged by CFCs.

c) Acidic gases cause a_________ r_________.

d) S_________ is produced when things burn.

e) The sea is polluted by o_________ spills.

f) S_________ cancer can be caused by strong ultraviolet rays.

a)				■							
b)				■							
c)				■							
d)				■							
e)				■							
f)				■							

Web sites to visit:

Greenpeace – an environmental action group
http://www.greenpeace.org/~climate/

Southampton University – environment information
http://www.soton.ac.uk/~engenvir/index/enviro_index.html

Science Across the World
http://www.scienceacross.org

Gravity and space

Starter Activity
Balancing gravity

Here are some ways to provide an upward force to balance gravity:

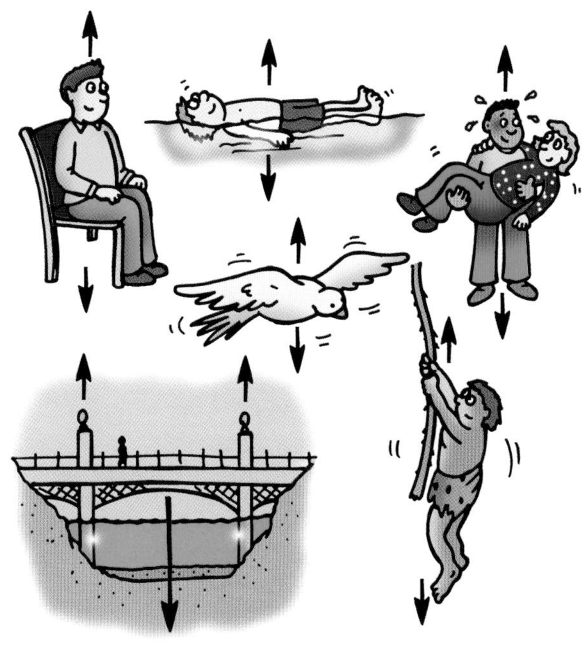

1 Sit (or stand) on a seat
2 Float on water
3 Get a friend to carry you
4 Be a bird and let the force of the wind on your wings support you
5 Be a bridge and let the pillars provide the upwards force
6 Be Tarzan and hang from trees by a vine

And here are some ways which will NOT balance gravity:

1 Cling on to a smooth wall by your fingernails
2 Flying, if you are not a bird and you are not in an aeroplane

We use springs to measure the weight of objects. The spring stretches until its upward force balances the force of gravity. We can see how much the spring stretches to measure the weight.

Questions

1 Describe what happens to the force you feel from a spring when you stretch it more and more.

2 A cyclist pedals along a road at a steady speed.
   a) Are the forces on him balanced or unbalanced?
   b) What will happen to his motion if he:
      i) increases his forward force?
      ii) decreases his forward force?

Parachuting on the Earth and Moon

Key words

terminal velocity Constant speed of a falling object

Figure 1 Air resistance on the sheet of paper makes it fall slower.

Take two pieces of paper, roll one up tightly, and drop them both at the same time. The flat sheet of paper takes much longer to reach the ground. Gravity pulls both down, but the air resistance force on the flat sheet of paper is greater. It does not accelerate as fast.

There is no air on the Moon. So there is no air resistance to exert an upwards force to slow down a falling body. The Moon's gravity is weaker than gravity on Earth. It only pulls down with 1/6 of the force of gravity on Earth. With no air on the Moon, parachuting there is deadly!

Parachuting on Earth

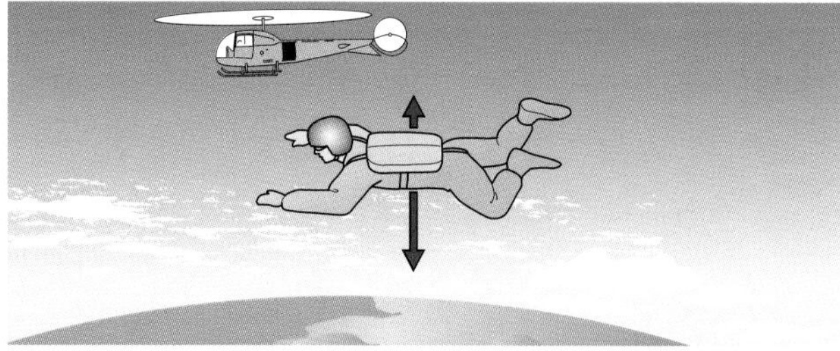

Figure 2 At the start of the jump, gravity pulls the person down. She is only moving slowly so the force of air resistance is small. The forces are unbalanced. Then motion changes and she accelerates towards the ground.

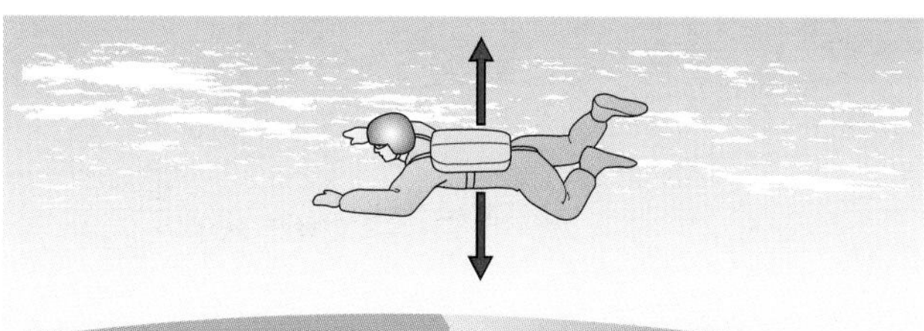

Figure 3 A bit later... She has accelerated and the air resistance force has increased. It is the same size as the gravity force. The forces are in balance. She falls at a steady speed, called **terminal velocity**.

Figure 4 The parachute opens. At first there is a large unbalanced upwards force of air resistance. This slows her down until the forces balance again and she reaches a slower terminal velocity. We see her as she drifts safely to Earth.

Figure 5 A comfortable landing. As she hits the ground it exerts a bearable upwards force on her. Her motion changes as her speed becomes zero.

Parachuting on the Moon

There is no air on the Moon so a parachute will not work. There can be no upwards air resistance force to slow down the parachutist to a terminal velocity.

Figure 6 Astronauts on the Moon dropped a hammer and a feather. With no air to slow them down they both landed at the same time.

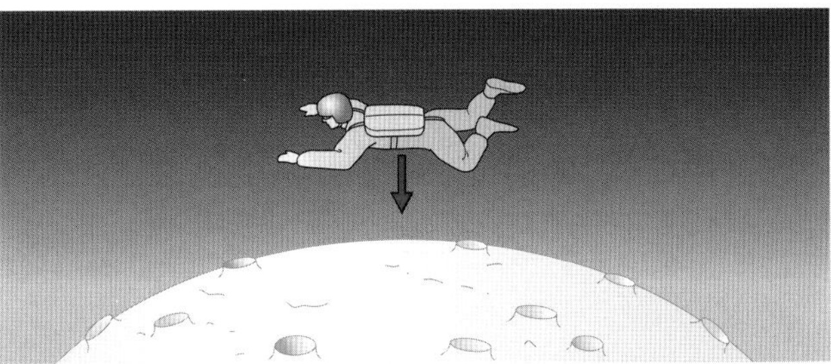

Figure 7 High above the Moon, near the start of the jump. ... The Moon's gravitational force pulls the parachutist down. There is no air resistance force acting in the opposite direction. The forces are unbalanced. There is nothing to slow him down. His motion changes and he accelerates towards the surface of the Moon.

Halfway down and nothing has changed. His parachute doesn't open. The forces are still unbalanced and he is going faster and faster towards the Moon's hard rocky surface.

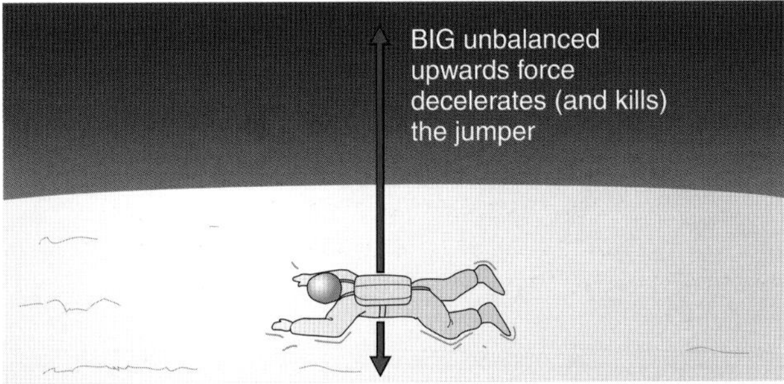

Figure 8 ... and a bit of a mess on the Moon ...

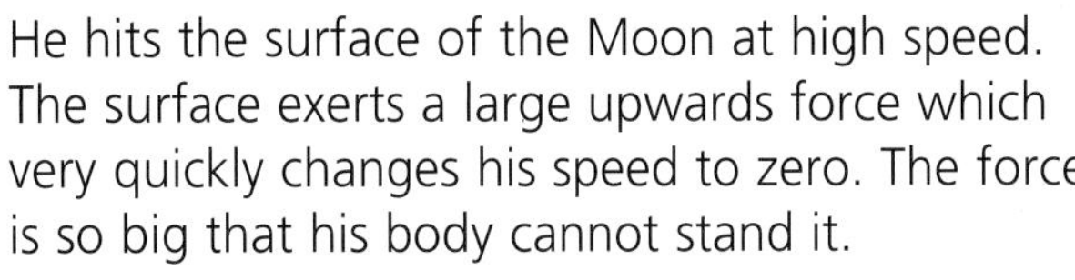

He hits the surface of the Moon at high speed. The surface exerts a large upwards force which very quickly changes his speed to zero. The force is so big that his body cannot stand it.

Worked example

A parachutist falls 60 metres in 10 seconds. What is his average speed?

average speed = distance ÷ time
= 60 metres ÷ 10 seconds
= 6 metres per second

Questions

1 Why can the forces on the Moon parachutist never become balanced during a fall?

2 When do both parachutists experience an unbalanced upwards force?

3 A parachutist falls 360 metres in one minute (60 seconds). What is his average speed in metres per second?

Remember

Copy and complete the sentences. Use these words:

opposite balanced air resistance friction unbalanced

The motion of a body always stays the same if the forces on it are **b**________. The motion always changes if the forces are **u**________.

Air resistance and **f**________ provide forces that act in the **o**________ direction to the motion. For a falling object, the force of **a**________ **r**________ acts upwards.

Houston, we have a problem

Key words

mass How much of an object there is.

weight The force of gravity acting on the mass of an object.

Figure 1 Film actor Tom Hanks plays Jim Lovell in the movie of the real Apollo 13 space mission.

The astronauts of the Apollo 13 space mission very nearly didn't make it back safely to Earth. Getting humans from space and back down to Earth's surface is not easy. People have bodies, and bodies have **mass**. We can measure the mass of a human body, or any kind of body in kilograms.

An astronaut has exactly the same body if he is on the Earth, the Moon or walking in space. There is no more or less of it. It isn't any bigger or smaller in one place than the other. It has the same mass wherever it goes. But the force of gravity on a body is NOT the same wherever it goes. An astronaut on the Moon experiences a smaller force of gravity than on Earth. When floating freely in space he experiences no force at all. The force of gravity acting on a body is also called its **weight**. Since weight is a force it is measured in newtons.

Kilograms or newtons?

In everyday life most people talk about weight and measure it in kilograms. But we need to be more careful with what we say when we talk about space. Then we MUST measure weight in newtons and mass in kilograms.

Weightless in deep space

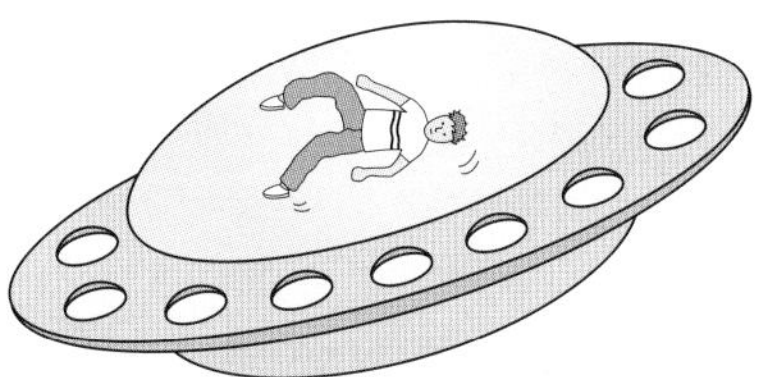

Figure 2 In a spacecraft a LONG way from Earth or other planets. There is no force of gravity. Objects are weightless.

As you travel further and further away from the Earth its gravitational pull gets smaller and smaller. When you are far away from any big body like the Earth, Moon, planets or stars, there is no force of gravity acting on you. Your mass is still the same. Your body isn't bigger or smaller. but you don't have any weight. You are weightless in deep space.

Weightless in orbit

The further away you go from the surface of the Earth or Moon the weaker the force of gravity on you.

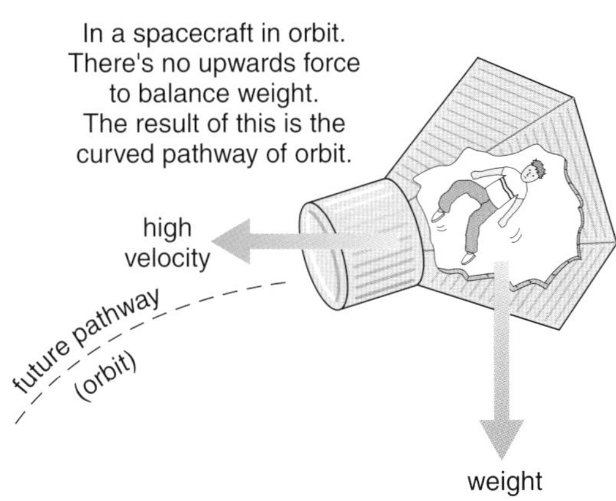

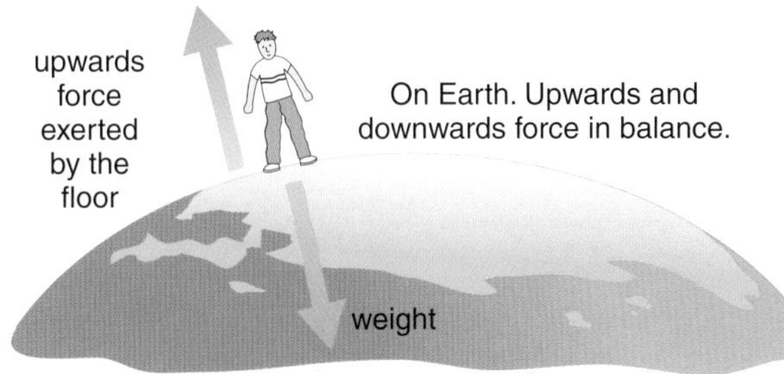

Figure 3 On the surface of the Earth, the floor exerts a strong force to balance the force of gravity. A spacecraft travels at high speed in a circle (orbit) round the Earth. The spacecraft floor exerts no force on you. You are weightless.

Astronauts in a space station orbiting the Earth are far enough away for the force of gravity to be a bit less than on the ground. But only a little bit. The Earth is still pulling on their bodies. This force changes their motion, so they keep turning. If they have the right speed at the right height, they keep turning in a circle. This matches the shape of the Earth. They are always 'falling' to the ground, but they never get closer to it. The walls and floor of the spacecraft don't exert any force on the astronauts (unless they bump into them). They feel exactly as they would in deep space, a long, long way from the Earth. They feel weightless.

A weight problem?

The size of a planet's gravity depends on its mass. The greater the mass, the stronger its gravity and the greater the weight of an astronaut on its surface.

Earth

Mercury

Jupiter

Figure 4

The gravitational force on the planet's surface is different for each planet. On Earth an astronaut and his suit might weigh 1000 newtons. On tiny Mercury the same astronaut would weigh only 400 N, but on mighty Jupiter a hefty 26 000 N. On the Moon, he would be a lightweight at only 170 N, BUT his mass of 100 kilograms would not change.

Questions

1 In space science, what is the unit for measuring **a)** mass, **b)** weight?

2 Why is it important to think about the difference between mass and weight when thinking about objects in space?

Remember

Copy and complete the sentences. Use these words:

newtons weightless deep space kilograms.

Weight is a force, and in space science must be measured in **n**________. Mass is a measure of the amount of substance in a body, and is measured in units such as **k**________. Any person or object in **d**________ **s**________ is **w**________ because there is no large body (such as a star, planet or moon) to exert a force of gravity.

The Isaac Newton story

Figure 1 Galileo was an Italian who died in the year that Isaac Newton was born. One of Galileo's original ideas was that moving objects keep on moving when they are left to themselves.

Figure 2 Isaac Newton was born on a farm in Lincolnshire on Christmas Day, 1642. His father died, and Isaac's mother got married again. Unfortunately, Isaac's new stepfather didn't have much time for children. Poor Isaac was sent to live with his grandparents. He had a lonely childhood.

Figure 3 Isaac had a strong curiosity. As a young man he put his finger between his eyeball and the bone around it – just to try to find out what was there. He was ill for several days, and was lucky not to go blind.

Figure 4 Isaac Newton developed ideas about force. We often think that the natural thing for moving objects to do is to slow down and stop. But Newton worked on Galileo's idea that the natural thing for moving objects to do is to keep on moving at the same speed. It takes a force to change the motion.

Figure 5 Air resistance and friction provide forces, so sometimes we make the mistake of thinking that moving objects always slow down and stop. Now that we can picture spacecraft moving where there is no air to slow them down, it's easier for us to see that steady motion IS what happens naturally.

Figure 6 Unbalanced forces change the speed and/or the direction of moving objects. This is a version of Newton's First Law.

Figure 7 Newton's other great achievement was to say that the everyday force that makes apples fall off trees is the SAME kind of force as the force that keeps the Moon in orbit around the Earth and keeps the planets in orbit around the Sun. This is the force of gravity.

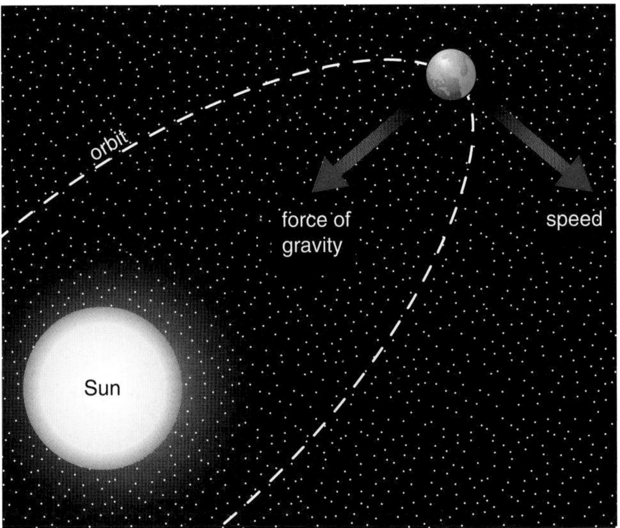

Figure 8 Isaac Newton said that the natural thing for planets and moons to do is to travel in straight lines at steady speed. He said that it was the continuous force of gravity acting on them that made their motion change, so they travel in curved paths and not straight lines. They stay in orbit because of the combination of their speed and the force of gravity.

Isaac Newton was a very clever man. He did a lot of work on forces and gravity. This is why the unit of force is named after him.

- He explained the refraction of light by lenses.
- He invented ways of making better lenses.
- He developed a better telescope.
- He investigated the dispersion of colours by a prism.
- He explained how rainbows are formed.
- He was a director of the Royal Mint and a Member of Parliament.

Questions

1 Think about these moving objects: A bag sliding across the floor, a rolling ball, a skater and a spacecraft.
  a) What does your 'common sense' tell you about what is more natural – steady motion or slowing down and stopping?
  b) Do you think that the ideas of Galileo and Newton agree or disagree with your 'common sense'?
  c) Is 'common sense' always a reliable way of understanding how the world behaves?

2 a) Why doesn't a satellite in orbit around Earth slow down?
  b) In what way is the satellite's motion changing?

3 What forces do the passengers feel in these situations:
  a) when a lift starts moving down?
  b) when the lift is falling steadily?
  c) when the lift stops at the bottom?

Remember

Copy and complete the sentences. Use these words:

resistance gravity directions motion planets orbit force same

Isaac Newton developed two very important new ideas – that **f**________ is what makes **m**________ change, and that the gravity we feel here on Earth is the **s**________ as the gravity that keeps the planets in **o**________ round the Sun. The planets' **d**________ change all the time as they follow their curved paths. It is the force of **g**________ that produces this change. In space there is no air **r**________ acting on a spacecraft. There is no resistance to the movement of **p**________.

6.4 Stories of the Solar System

If you watch the movement of the Sun or the Moon across the sky, it is easy to think that they travel around us. In the past, many people believed that the Earth was at the centre of everything – the centre of the Universe.

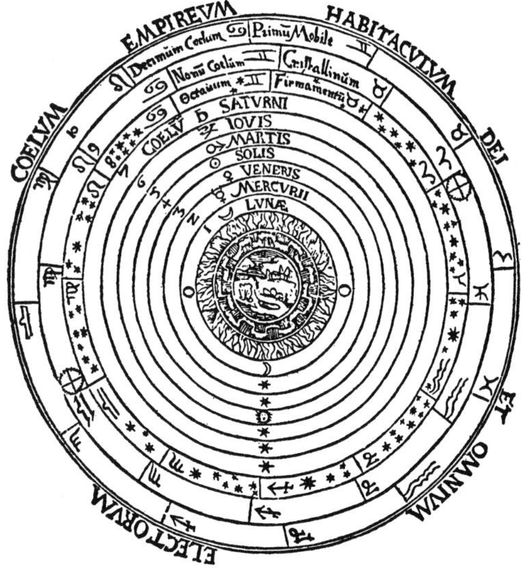

Figure 1 The Earth centred model of the Universe. In 1539 they thought that the Earth was at its centre.

If you follow the tracks of the planets, month by month, they move backwards and forwards. If everything goes round the Earth, then this is very hard to explain.

Copernicus was a monk who lived in Poland. He said that the Sun was at the centre of the Universe and that the Earth and other planets went round it. This provided a better explanation of the movement of the planets across the sky. It was a new idea but nobody liked it.

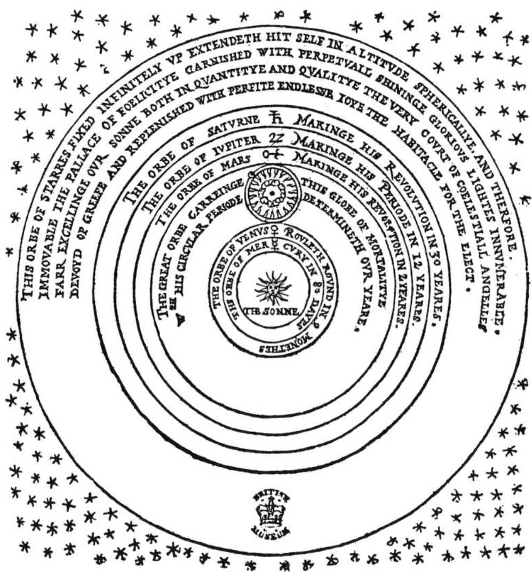

Figure 2 The model of the Universe with the Sun at its centre.

Figure 3 Johannes Kepler.

Later, Johannes Kepler worked with detailed measurements of the motions of the planets. He realised that the planets did not move in perfect circles. It was looking good for Copernicus's ideas.

Galileo arrested

Figure 4 Galileo Galilei.

Galileo used new technology – the telescope. He saw the shadows of mountains on the Moon, and moons in orbit around Jupiter. He saw with his own eyes that everything did NOT go around the Earth. This upset the people in authority who still believed that the Earth was at the centre of the Universe. Galileo was put under house arrest until he died.

The Universe

In Galileo's time, 400 years ago, people only knew of the Earth, and five other planets – Mercury, Venus, Mars, Jupiter and Saturn. Later people discovered Uranus, Neptune, and Pluto. Now, thanks to scientists like Isaac Newton, we know that it is the strong gravity of the huge Sun that holds the planets in their orbits.

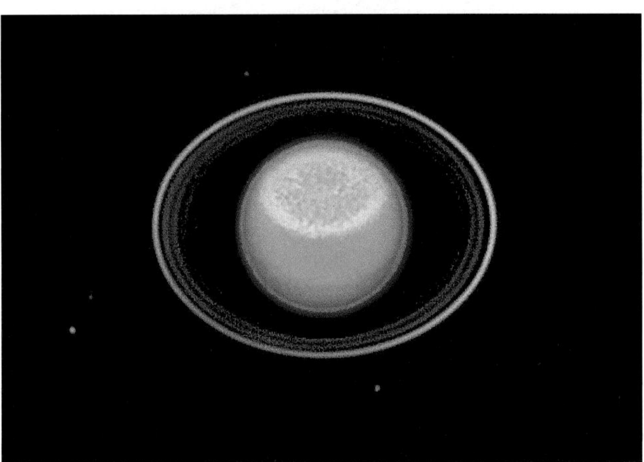

Figure 5 This picture of Uranus was taken by the Hubble Space Telescope.

Space is amazing. It's big and dark. At night we see tiny specks of distant light from stars like our Sun. We are surrounded by empty space, but protected from it by our atmosphere. We could not live outside our sea of air. Most of all, space is very, very scary.

Figure 6 Our galaxy looks like this one. Our Sun is a minor star on one of the spiral arms.

We now know that our Sun is just one star in a galaxy of billions of stars. There are billions of galaxies in the Universe. Some people say that there are more stars in the Universe than there are grains of sand on every beach in the world.

Questions

1 What new technology did Galileo use to observe objects in space?

2 What evidence did Galileo have that not everything in the Universe goes around the Earth?

3 Why is space scary?

Remember

Copy and complete the sentences. Use these words:

Galileo planets orbit telescopes Sun gravity Newton Copernicus

There are different ways to try to explain how we see the Sun, Moon, the **p**________ and stars moving across the sky. Some people said that the Earth was at the centre of the Universe. A Polish monk called **C**________ suggested a new idea with the **S**________ at the centre. **G**________ said his observations with **t**________ proved that the Sun was at the centre. **N**________ put forward the idea that the force of **g**________ acted across space. This provides the force that holds the Earth and other planets in **o**________ round the Sun.

Energy searches by satellite

Key words

geostationary A satellite orbit that takes 24 hours, so that the satellite stays above the same point on the Earth's surface.

satellites An object that orbits a planet.

Figure 1 A satellite in orbit above the Earth's atmosphere.

The Moon orbits the Earth. It is our natural **satellite**. The Earth has many artificial satellites. They are launched into space by rockets. They orbit the Earth well above the atmosphere so that there is no air resistance to slow them down. Once a satellite is in orbit, its speed and the Earth's gravity keep it there. If it stopped moving it would crash into the Earth. But it orbits the Earth at high speed, so it falls in a curve. It falls, but keeps missing the Earth.

Satellites at work

Satellites are extremely useful. Some have cameras on board which can check for diseases in crops as they orbit the Earth. They send information back to the ground so that the farmer can treat the crops. Others can search for different rock features. This helps people find out where fossil fuels, like coal, might be found underground.

Figure 2 A satellite picture of a weather system over the Atlantic Ocean.

The atmosphere is a layer of air around the earth. Energy from the Sun heats the atmosphere. Some places heat up more than others and this creates the wind and our weather. Satellites can take pictures of the clouds. We use the pictures to see where the wind is blowing and to make weather forecasts.

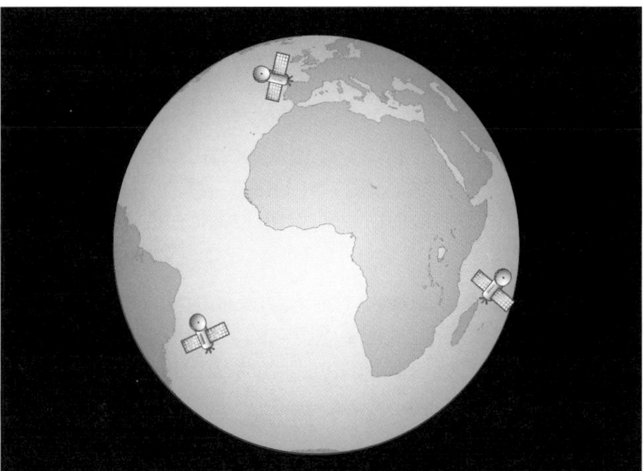

Figure 3 These satellites orbit the earth once every 24 hours. They appear to be stationary above the Earth. They can be used for communications and for transmitting TV programmes all over the world.

Some satellites are used to send TV pictures and telephone signals around the world. These satellites must orbit the Earth every 24 hours. They appear to be in a fixed position. They are called **geostationary** satellites. You may have a satellite TV receiver at home. The satellite dish always points in the same direction. If the satellite was not in geostationary orbit you could only watch TV when the satellite was overhead.

Figure 5 A sensitive camera on a satellite took this picture. It shows a huge patch of sea that's full of tiny living things called plankton. They get their energy from the Sun. Fish and whales eat plankton. Satellite pictures like these can help fishing boats to find the best places to search for fish.

Figure 6 This GPS hand held navigation aid helps walkers find their way.

Finding your way on open moorland can be difficult, but a group of satellites can pinpoint your position with great accuracy. They are called a Global Positioning System or simply GPS. Hand-held sets are available for walkers. Some cars are fitted with satellite navigation systems which tell the driver exactly where to turn.

There are several satellites, such as the Hubble Space Telescope, which are used by astronomers. Scientists from America and Russia are cooperating to build a big international space station.

Questions

1 Explain why satellite pictures are useful to:
 a) fishing boat crews
 b) the organiser of your school summer fair.

2 There could be a satellite above you now taking pictures. Do you think that is always a good thing?

Remember

These sentences are all cut into halves. Copy them into your book, matching up the halves.

a) Satellites travel . . .
b) Cameras on satellites . . .
c) The layer of air . . .

i) . . . around the Earth in orbit.
ii) . . . above the Earth is called its atmosphere.
iii) . . . can help us to find new underground energy resources like oil and gas.

Finishing off!

Remember

- ★ Mass is a measurement of the amount of material in an object. We measure mass in grams, kilograms or tonnes.
- ★ The weight of an object is a measurement of the force of gravity acting on it. In science we measure weight in newtons.
- ★ On Earth a mass of 1 kilogram weighs about 10 newtons. A 10 newton force is needed to lift a 1 kilogram bag of sugar.
- ★ On the Moon there is still 1 kilogram of sugar in the bag. The Moon is smaller than the Earth and so it has a weaker force of gravity. The weight of the bag of sugar will be just over 1.5 newtons.
- ★ The force of gravity exerted by a large object like the Sun, Earth, or Moon gets weaker as you move away from it. If you were a very long way from it you would be weightless.
- ★ People in orbit in a spacecraft are not a long way from the Earth, but they feel weightless. They float freely in the cabin.
- ★ People have watched the Moon, Sun, stars and planets for thousands of years. At different times there have been different ideas about the structure of the Solar System.
- ★ Now we know that the Earth is one of nine planets that orbit the Sun. We have been able to send spacecraft to visit distant planets.
- ★ The Moon is a satellite in orbit around the Earth.
- ★ We can send artificial satellites into orbit around the Earth.
- ★ Geostationary satellites orbit in time with the Earth's spin. They stay above the same place on the Earth.
- ★ Satellites are very useful for communication (radio and TV), navigation and surveying for resources, like fossil fuels.

Questions

1 Take a new page in your exercise book. Make a list of all the Key Words from the boxes in this chapter down the side. Take two lines per word. Try to write the meaning of each word without looking. Then go back and fill in any you did not know or got wrong.

Now learn to spell them by the Look – Say – Cover – Write method.

2 Write about an imaginary journey to Uranus. It will take many years. Think about:

- How you will get there.
- How much fuel you will use and how to overcome the gravitational pull of the Sun.
- Everyday activities, water for washing and drinking, and how much food you will take.
- If you will need to recycle the water from drinking and washing.
- If you will need to grow food on the journey or take it all with you.

Web sites to visit:

Space Telescope Science Institute – Hubble pictures
http://oposite.stsci.edu/pubinfo/

Plants, photosynthesis and food

Starter Activity
Flower Parts

Humans have complicated organ systems. Plants also have organ systems. They are not quite as complicated as human systems, but they are vital to the plant.

Flower: The flower contains the reproductive organs of the plant. It is often brightly coloured to attract insects. The flowers produce seeds and fruit.

Leaves: The leaves produce nearly all of the food that the plant needs. They store the food that the plant doesn't use immediately. The food is stored as starch in the leaf cells.

Stem: The stem supports the plant. Leaves are attached to the stem. The stem can move to help the plant to face the light so that photosynthesis can take place. The stem transports water, food, and other nutrients to all parts of the plant.

Roots: The roots support the plant and stop it from falling down or being blown over in the wind. More importantly, they take in water from the soil and minerals and nutrients dissolved in the water.

Questions

Read this letter from a local newspaper. Write a reply using what you know about how plants grow and what they need to be healthy.

Dear Sir/Madam

I recently bought a packet of rare orchid seeds from a garden centre. I was upset when none of the seeds grew after much love and care from me. I followed the instructions and planted the seeds in the soil and watered them. I covered them with plastic to keep them warm, but I could not find any clear plastic so I thought that I would be clever and use a black plastic bag to cover the seedlings. The seedlings began to grow, but went yellow instead of a nice shade of green, then they died. Could I go back to the garden centre and get my money back? As you are a good scientist could you explain what happened to my rare orchids!

Yours Mr Angry
South Croydon

Living on fresh air

Key words

biomass The amount of plant or animal material there is

photosynthesis The process that plants use to produce food using energy from sunlight, water and carbon dioxide

stomata Small holes on the underside of a leaf. Gases move in and out of the plant through these holes.

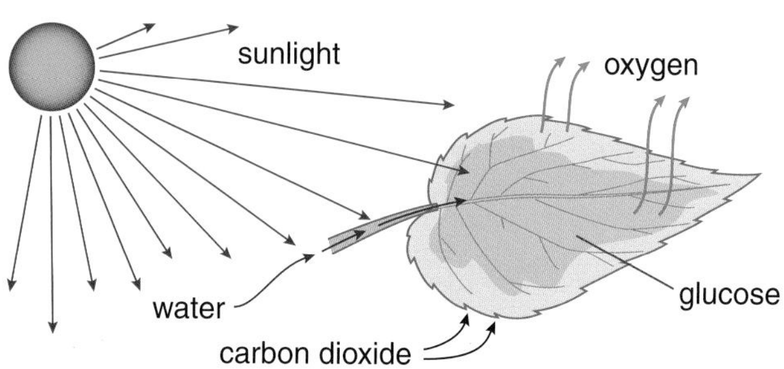

Figure 1 Photosynthesis in a leaf.

Plants make their own food. They use energy from sunlight to join together water from the soil and carbon dioxide from the air. The plant makes sugar and produces the oxygen as a waste product. This process is called **photosynthesis**. The word photosynthesis describes what the plant does, *photo* means light, and *synthesis* means making, so plants make food using light. We can use a word formula to show this chemical process. You will need to learn this equation.

$$\text{carbon dioxide} + \text{water} \xrightarrow[\textit{chlorophyll}]{\textit{sunlight}} \text{glucose} + \text{oxygen}$$

The carbon dioxide enters the leaf through tiny holes called **stomata**. The oxygen that is produced goes back into the air through the same holes. Any part of a plant that is green can photosynthesise, but it mainly happens in the leaves. Most of the stomata are on the underside of the leaf, but there are some on the top of the leaf and on the stem.

Plants cannot use all of the sugar that they make, so they have to store some. To do this they have to join units of sugar together to make starch. They store the starch in their leaves, so that they can use it when they cannot make food, for example in the dark.

Questions

1 As well as making sugar, plants also store food as starch. Where do they normally store the starch?

2 What two gases pass through the stomata of a plant?

3 Where are most stomata found on plants?

When plants photosynthesise they get bigger and heavier. This is called **biomass**. Amazingly the wood that makes up a tree has come mainly from the gases in the air and the water from the soil.

If a plant is going to photosynthesise it must have four things:

1 Sunlight
2 Water
3 Carbon dioxide
4 Chlorophyll

Figure 2 This plant has everything it needs to photosynthesise.

Three of these things, sunlight, water and carbon dioxide, affect how much food a plant can make and how fast the plant can make it. Temperature also affects how quickly and how much a plant will photosynthesise. Just like animals, plants work best when the surrounding temperature is not too hot and not too cold.

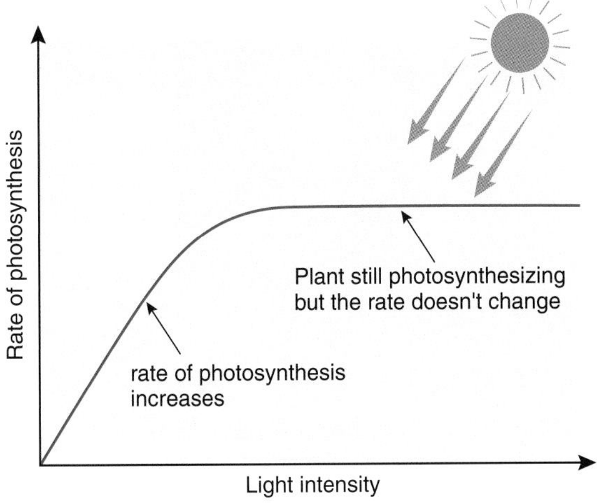

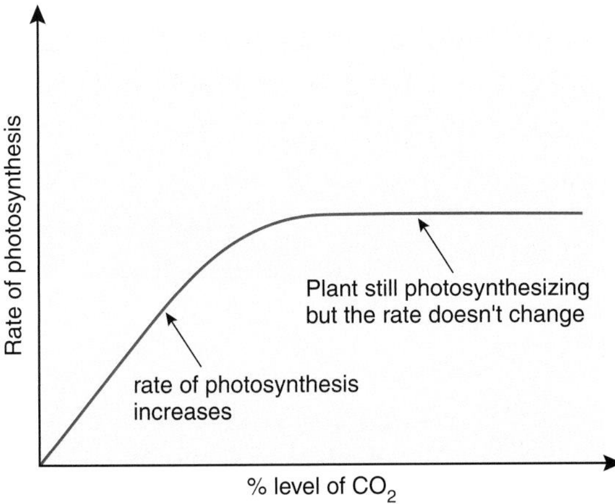

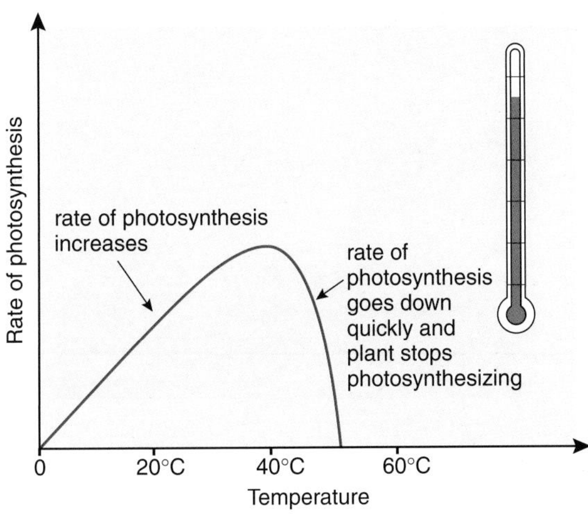

Figure 3 Factors affecting the rate of photosynthesis.

Look at the graphs in Figure 3. They show what happens when the factors that affect photosynthesis are changed.

Questions

4 Look at Figure 3. What is the best temperature to keep plants at if you want them to photosynthesise?

5 Look at Figure 3. What happens to the rate of photosynthesis if you increase the level of carbon dioxide?

Remember

Choose the correct word from each pair. Discuss your choice of word in small groups and check that you have the right answers with your teacher. Copy the completed paragraph into your exercise book.

Plants make their own **food/waste** by a process called **photosynthesis/respiration.** In this process **pollution/carbon dioxide** from the air is joined with **sugar/water** taken from the soil, to make the sugar **caffeine/glucose**. To do this the plant uses energy from the **wind/sunlight**. The gas **oxygen/hydrogen** is produced and is put back into the atmosphere.

Plants increase their biomass when they photosynthesise. Plants need the right amount of water, carbon dioxide and the right **temperature/vitamins** to photosynthesise well.

Discovering Photosynthesis

1 Van Helmont's Experiment

Figure 1 Joannes Baptista van Helmont

As long ago as the 1640s people were thinking about how plants lived and grew. Nearly everybody thought that the soil provided plants with everything they needed to grow, including their food. A Belgium scientist called Joannes Baptista van Helmont (1579–1644) did an experiment to prove that the soil didn't give plants very many nutrients and didn't give the plant any food to grow.

Van Helmont's experiment was very simple, but it took him 5 years to complete. He took 90kg of dried soil and planted a small willow tree weighing 2.5kg in the soil. He watered it carefully, making sure he knew exactly how much water he used. He let the tree grow for 5 years. Then he dried the soil and re-weighed it. He also re-weighed the tree. Van Helmont knew that no more soil had been added and that he only gave the tree water. He found that after starting with 90kg of soil he still had 89.5kg after 5 years, he had only lost 0.5kg. The tree weighed 77kg. This extra weight couldn't have come from the soil so Van Helmont decided that it must come from the water. It was a good idea but not quite right. He didn't know about the gas carbon dioxide.

2 Stephen Hales' Experiment

Figure 2 Rev. Stephen Hales

The English vicar Stephen Hales (1677–1761) found out how water was taken in by the roots of a plant and carried to the leaves. One of his best known experiments measured the water vapour given off by plants. He proved that water went into the roots, moved up the plant and left the leaves as water vapour. He also grew a plant in a container. He found that the amount of air in the container went down. Hales thought that this was because the plant was using up the air. He also showed that sap flowed upwards in plants.

3 Joseph Priestley discovers that plants make oxygen

Figure 3 Joseph Priestley

In 1772 Joseph Priestley suggested that plants must produce oxygen. He put a shoot from a plant into water and covered it with a jar to stop air getting to the plant. He then burned a candle in the jar until it went out. Later he was able to re-burn the candle in the same jar. He decided that the candle went out because there was no oxygen left in the jar. As no more air was let into the jar then it must be the plant producing more oxygen that allowed the candle to be re-lit and burn.

4 Jan Ingenhousz discovers that light is needed for photosynthesis

Figure 4 Jan Ingenhousz

The Dutch scientist Jan Ingenhausz (1730–1799) found out that the green parts of plants are where things happen. He discovered that the green parts of plants produce oxygen in light and that they don't produce oxygen in the dark. In fact we now know that plants give out carbon dioxide in the dark.

It has taken us over 350 years to really understand how plants make their own food and to find out that most of a plant, is actually made up from the gasses in the air that we breathe. Without photosynthesis there wouldn't be any life on Earth, and certainly no animals on the land. Photosynthesis means that plants can produce their own food, glucose. Food is stored as starch. The products of photosynthesis are useful to us as well as to the plant, giving us wood, oils, vegetable proteins and perfumes.

Questions

1 What does the word photosynthesis actually mean?

2 In Val Helmont's experiment how did he make it a fair test?

3 Which things couldn't Van Helmont control in his experiment?

4 Why did Stephen Hales do his experiment in a closed container?

5 Why do think the candle went out in Priestley's experiment?

6 Design an experiment that Ingenhousz could do to show that green plants produce oxygen in the light but not in the dark.

7.3 Roots

Key words

fibrous Root Lots of thin branching roots that spread out wide

tap root A long thick root that can grow deep in the soil

transpiration The process where plants lose water from their leaves

Roots are as important to a plant as its leaves. They take water and nutrients in from the soil. They help to stop the plant from being blown over.

Roots remain hidden underground. If you've ever dug up a plant or watched someone re-pot a houseplant, you might have seen what gardeners call the root ball. Some plants, even fairly small ones, can have a large network of roots that spread out in the soil.

Figure 1 The roots of this plant have nearly filled the flower pot. It's time to re-pot the plant to give the roots more room.

Roots are very simple, but very important. A root also helps to break up the soil. The root's main job is to absorb water from the soil that the plant then uses in photosynthesis. Figure 2 shows how the structure of the root helps the plant take up water.

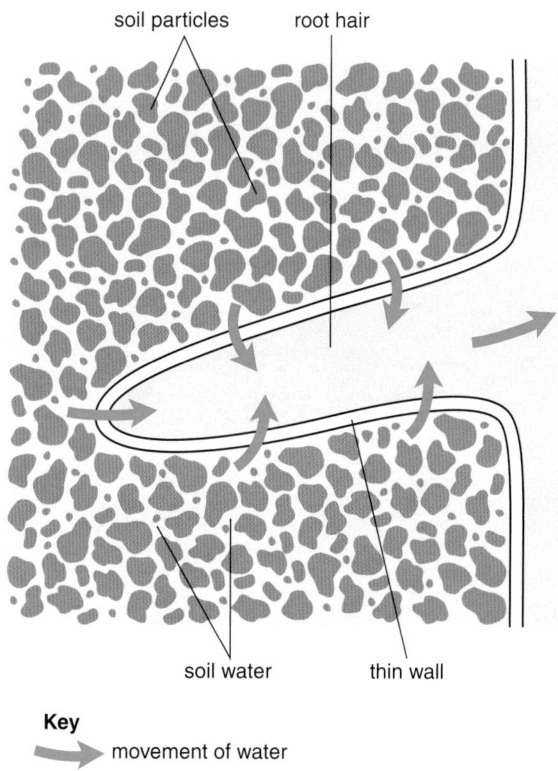

Figure 2 The root helps the plant to take up water.

Roots come in two main types, **tap roots** and **fibrous roots**.

A tap root is a thick root that is quite long. This sort of root is useful if the soil dries out and the plant has to go deeper to find water. Trees have tap roots and these stop them from being blown down easily.

Fibrous roots are the ones that you see on lots of garden plants. They are thin and there are lots of them that spread out from the plant, but they do not go down very deep into the soil. These roots are good at stopping plants from being uprooted by animals, but they cannot grow deep into the soil to search for water.

Questions

1 What are the two main types of roots that plants have?

2 If a large, heavy tree had only fibrous roots what might happen in the following circumstances?
   a) a long dry summer
   b) a gale in winter
   c) a very rainy month

Figure 3 The tap root on the left is long and thick. The fibrous roots are thin and widespread.

Plants need lots of water. Plants lose water from their leaves and this process is called **transpiration**. The roots need to take in water to replace what they lose.

Plants also need minerals to grow. It's a bit like us having a balanced diet. The minerals are dissolved in the water in the soil and taken in through the roots. Plants need a balanced diet of minerals and other chemical salts for healthy growth.

Questions

3 Apart from water what do plants get from the soil?

4 What do we call the process where plants lose water through their leaves?

Remember

Copy the following paragraph into your exercise book.

Plants need water to photosynthesise. Roots take in water from the soil. They also take in minerals dissolved in the water.

There are two main types of roots, tap roots and fibrous roots. Tap roots grow down deep into the soil to find water. Fibrous roots help stop small plants being uprooted.

7.4 Plants for food and plant nutrients

Key words

fertiliser Chemicals added to the soil so that more plants can grow in the soil

harvest A crop, like sweetcorn or potatoes, that is gathered or ripens during a particular season

nutrient A substance that provides nourishment, for example the minerals that a plant takes from the soil

Which parts of a plant do you normally eat? Different plants provide different parts that we can eat. In some plants it's the fruit. In others it is the seeds, or the shoots, roots or leaves. To grow healthy plants that we can **harvest** and eat we must also provide plants with the right **nutrients**.

Figure 1 We can eat all the plants in this photo. They can form part of a food chain for humans, though the food web that we are part of can be very complex.

We can eat all of the plants in Figure 1. You can probably think of lots of other plants that we eat for food. Make a table in your exercise book like Table 1. Use the plants in the photograph and ones that you think about in class to fill in the first column. Tick which parts of the plant we commonly eat.

Very often, the part of the plant that we eat is the part that contains starch. This is made from the glucose that the plant can't use immediately.

Questions

1 Looking at your table of plants that we eat, what is the most commonly eaten part of the plant?

2 Why do the seeds from a plant, like broad beans, need to have a store of starch?

Nutrients for plants

Gardeners and farmers know that if they are going to grow plants well, they need to add fertiliser to the soil. This provides the plants with all the nutrients they need for healthy growth. The three most important nutrients are nitrogen, phosphorus and potassium (known as N, P, K). Fertilisers often have the percentages of these three minerals on the front label of the bag, like the one shown in Figure 2.

	Parts of the plant that we eat				
Name of plant	**Leaves**	**Stem**	**Roots/bulbs**	**Fruits**	**Seeds**
Carrot	✗	✗	✓	✗	✗

Table 1

Figure 2 The percentages of N, P and K in this bag of fertiliser are shown on the bag, N = 20%, P = 8% and K = 14%.

Plants need small amounts of nutrients for healthy growth. Table 2 shows you the most common nutrients.

Nutrient	Why it is needed
Nitrogen (N)	The main nutrient needed by plants for new, green plant growth.
Phosphorus (P)	Helps the plant grow roots. It also increases the numbers of flowers on flowering plants.
Potassium (K)	Good for the overall health of plants. It helps them cope with very hot or cold weather and protects against diseases.
Calcium (Ca)	Needed to improve the growth of young roots and shoots.
Magnesium (Mg)	Needed to help seeds grow and to make chlorophyll.

Table 2 Plant nutrients.

Question

3 Why are the letters N, P, K used for fertilisers?

Remember

Copy and complete the sentences. Use these words:

tap roots leaves bulbs berries fertilisers onions

Many different plants provide us with food. Sometimes we will eat the **l**________, for example a lettuce, or we may eat the **t**________ **r**________ such as carrots, and **b**________ such as **o**________. Not all parts of the plant can be eaten. Some may produce **b**________ that are harmless to birds, but poisonous to humans. For plants to grow well we often need to provide them with **f**________.

Killing weeds

Key words

compete Fighting with other plants for space, light, water or nutrients

weedkiller A chemical that poisons unwanted plants

If you've ever been on a crowded train or bus you will know how difficult it is to move. We all need room to live. Just because plants don't move around doesn't mean they don't need room as well. Plants have to **compete** for space, nutrients, water and the sunlight.

If you look at a packet of seeds you buy in a shop, the instructions normally tell you how far apart the seeds should be planted. Farmers have to plant their crops very carefully to make sure that the plants have enough room and don't compete too much. This helps the farmer grow bigger plants and have a bigger harvest.

Figure 1 Plants competing with each other.

Weeds

Weeds are a big problem for farmers and gardeners. A weed is any plant that grows where we don't want it. Weeds are a serious threat to our food crops.

Weedkillers can be used to control weeds. Weedkillers can affect plants in two main ways. Some kill parts of the plant that they come into contact with. Others are absorbed (taken in) by either the roots or leaves of the plant. The chemical then moves through the plant, slowly killing it.

Questions

1 Weeds are plants and may be part of a food web. What could happen if a farmer decided to kill all the flowering plants in a field to plant a crop of lettuces?

There are three main ways to spray weekillers onto plants.

1 Crop Spraying

Figure 2 Crop sprayers are often seen in the countryside.

A farmer will spray the whole field, or an area of it.

2 Spot application

Figure 3 Council workers often use the spot method to kill weeds at the side of roads.

This method uses a small spray carried on a person's back, with a hand pump. Individual weeds or patches of weeds, such as thistles or docks, can be sprayed by this method.

3 The weed wiper

Figure 4 The wiper method can be used to kill weeds at different neights.

This method uses a wick soaked in weedkiller on a boom that sticks out from a tractor. The height of the wick is controlled so that only taller plants come into contact with the weedkiller.

Questions

2 One method of getting rid of weeds used to be ploughing all of the plants into a field and leaving it as bare earth. Why do the weeds grow back in the field after some time?

3 When council workers are spraying weedkillers along the roadside what safety precautions should they take to prevent the chemicals from harming them?

Remember

In small groups, discuss the following sentences and put them into a sensible order. Copy them into your exercise book. The first one has been done for you.

1 Just like animals, plants have to compete for light, water, nutrients and space.

- Killing the weeds can also affect other plants and animals in the food web.
- These chemicals are called weedkillers.
- Weeds, like all other plants are often part of a food web.
- Farmers need to control weeds to make sure that the crops they grow are not competing for resources with the weeds.
- Farmers and gardeners often use chemicals to control the growth of weeds.
- Plants that grow where they are not wanted are called weeds.

7.6 Pests

Key words

decline To go down or reduce in numbers
organic Crops grown without using chemicals
pest A living organism that can destroy crops
pesticide A chemical that kills pests

The word **pest** is used quite a lot. You could be a pest, or pehaps you've pestered your parents to buy you something. In biology a pest is any animal that destroys crops. Anything from field mice and cabbage white butterflies, to aphids, slugs and snails are pests. Farmers and gardeners need to control them in much the same way as they need to control weeds. To control the weeds they use weedkillers. To control the pests they use **pesticides**.

Farmers have been using more and more pesticides. But these pesticides cause problems for the bird population who need these same pests for food. The article below gives information on how the bird population in the United Kingdom has gone down in the last 25 years. Read it carefully and in small groups think about the answers to the questions at the bottom of the page. Write down your answers in your exercise book.

a) snail

b) cabbage white butterfly

c) aphids

d) slug

Figure 1 Common pests

Sharp decline in UK bird populations

Bird populations in many areas of the UK have **declined** dramatically in the last 25 years, according to a report by the Royal Society for the Protection of Birds (RSPB). The report links pesticide use with declining populations in a number of bird species. It says that the problem is not poisoning from the pesticides, it is the destruction of the birds' food sources. According to the report, pesticides can reduce birds' food sources in three ways:

- Insects are killed off. The insects are an important food source during the birds' breeding season.
- Weedkillers kill off plants, reducing the numbers of insects that live and feed off them.
- Weedkillers may also reduce the number of weeds and seeds that provide food for birds in winter and for some species during breeding.

The RSPB report showed that butterflies, moths, beetles and grasshoppers were important food sources in the diets of bird species that were declining.
The report makes several recommendations for change. It says that farmers should be encouraged to grow more **organic** food. They also should not use as much pesticides. Organic foods are grown without the use of chemicals to kill off pests

(a) starling

(b) lapwing

(c) finch

(d) grey partridge.

Figure 2 Some of the British bird species whose numbers are declining.

Questions

1 What is the main reason for the decline in bird populations in Britain?

2 How do weedkillers affect the bird populations?

3 How do pesticides affect the bird populations?

4 What could be done to protect the populations of birds?

Remember

For your school noticeboard, write 5 bullet points explaining why the RSPB report on the decline of bird populations is so worrying. Start with the heading '*Where Are all the Birds?*'

Finishing off!

Remember

In small groups produce a poster or flow chart that shows how photosynthesis takes place in plants. Use the words in the boxes below. You could draw a tree at the centre of your poster as a background, with a close up of the leaf structure and root structure. Make links between your words and diagrams.

fibrous root

biomass

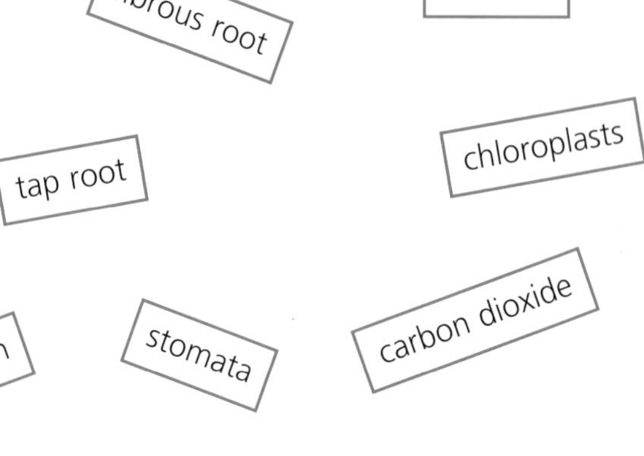

photosynthesis

starch

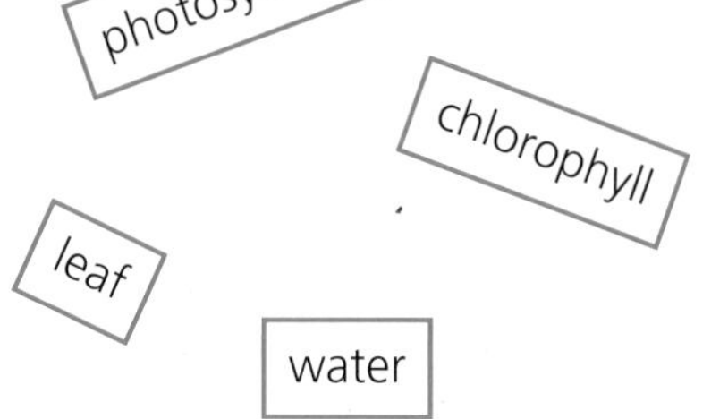

Questions

1. Take a new page in your exercise book. Make a list of all the Key Words from the boxes in this chapter down the side. Take two lines per word. Try to write the meaning of each word without looking. Then go back and fill in any you did not know or got wrong.

   Now learn to spell them by the Look – Say – Cover – Write method.
2. What does the term 'weed' mean?
3. How might weeds affect the amount of crops grown?
4. Name three common pests that attack plants either in fields or gardens.
5. Light and water are two of the five things needed by plants for healthy growth, what are the other three?

Web sites to visit:

Information about different types of fertilisers
http://www.fertilizer.com

Biological Control Virtual Information Centre
http://ipmwww.ncsu.edu/biocontrol/biocontrol.html

Royal Society for the Protection of Birds (RSPB)
http://www.rspb.org.uk

Using chemistry

Starter Activity
Get some energy

Energy is transferred as electricity and then as light.

Growing in sunlight. Photosynthesis enables plants to take energy in from the sun and store it.

Energy chemicals being transferred as movement.

The energy in the electricity is stored by the car battery.

Questions

1 What is a fuel? Make a list of as many fuels as you can.

2 What energy is transferred when a fuel burns?

3 What other substance is needed for a fuel to burn? (*Hint*: it's in the air)

4 When plants capture the energy in sunlight, what is that called? (*Hint*: Ph________syn________)

5 What gases are produced when methane burns?

6 What is the difference between heat and temperature? (*Hint*: movement of particles)

7 Which of the food groups provides the fuel to make our bodies go? (*Hint*: Ca________hyd________)

8 What is the name of the process that releases energy in our cells? (*Hint*: R________pir________n)

The rules of the game

Key words

electrons Tiny particles that orbit round the outside of atoms.

ion A particle with a positive or negative charge.

molecule A little group of atoms joined together.

state of matter Solid, liquid or gas.

temperature A hot temperature is to do with faster moving particles.

Particles react with each other to make new substances. The rules of chemistry explain how this happens.

1 Energy and Temperature

Particles of matter are moving all the time. Their **temperature** measures the speed of this movement. If the particles get more energy, they move faster and faster. They will have a hotter temperature.

Figure 1 Francis often had smelly cheese for lunch. The movement of particles makes smells spread.

2 States of matter

In solids, particles are neatly arranged.

In liquids, the particles are like a packed crowd.

In gases, the particles are flying about and are easy to get at.

Figure 2 Do you remember the carnival model of states of matter?

Questions

1 Write a few sentences to explain the idea of 'heat and temperature' to a junior school pupil. Use simple words a nine year old would understand. Here are some sentence starters to help you:

When a thing gets hotter, the particles . . .

The speed of the particles . . .

To make the particles move faster you need . . . . . .

Heat is the name we give to . . .

2 Draw a particle picture to show how the particles in two hot liquids mix together.

3 Energy transfers

When chemicals are broken up into atoms, energy is taken in.

When new chemicals are made, energy is released.

When fuels burn, more energy is released than is taken in. The extra energy heats up the surroundings.

4 How chemical reactions work

Nearly all atoms will make compounds. When they form compounds, it's all to do with **electrons**. They try to make a full shell of electrons on the outside of the atom. There are two ways that atoms can do this easily.

Figure 3

- **Metal with Non Metal** – The metal atoms get rid of electrons and gives them to non-metal atoms. This makes **ions**.

Figure 4 The hydrogen atom shares everything with chorine.

- **Non Metal with Non Metal** – Non metal atoms share electrons with each other. The electrons have to orbit both atoms, so this holds the atoms together in a little group. This makes **molecules**.

Figure 5 Chemistry is about arranging atoms into useful materials. Charcoal burns away on a barbecue. The atoms of carbon that make up the charcoal are now in carbon dioxide in the air.

5 You can't make atoms vanish

Figure 6 The tree next to the barbecue grows bigger. It's not creating atoms out of nothing. The tree uses the carbon from the carbon dioxide in the air. Of course this takes years, not minutes . . .

Remember

Copy and complete the simple rules. Use these words:

liquid energy electrons destroy hotter

1 **H**_________ particles are moving faster than cold ones.

2 Solid, **l**_________ and gas are the states of matter.

3 Breaking up chemicals needs **e**_________.

4 Compounds are made because atoms share **e**_________, or take other atoms electrons.

5 You can not **d**_________ atoms in reactions.

Question

3 When copper is heated in air, black copper oxide forms on the surface. Explain why the solid also gets heavier. You could use another particle picture.

Poison gas, combustion and explosions

Key words

carbon monoxide A poisonous gas.

combustion Another word for the burning reaction.

methane Natural gas.

soot Tiny particles of carbon.

Combustion

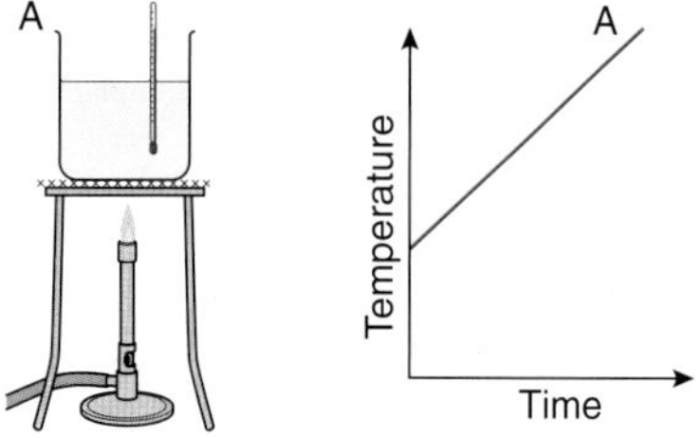

Figure 1 Burner A has a clean blue flame.

Burner A is producing lots of energy. The energy is transferred to the water. The water heats up quickly.

Burner A has the correct air/**methane** mixture. Burner A produces no soot, just carbon dioxide and water vapour.

Equation for burner A

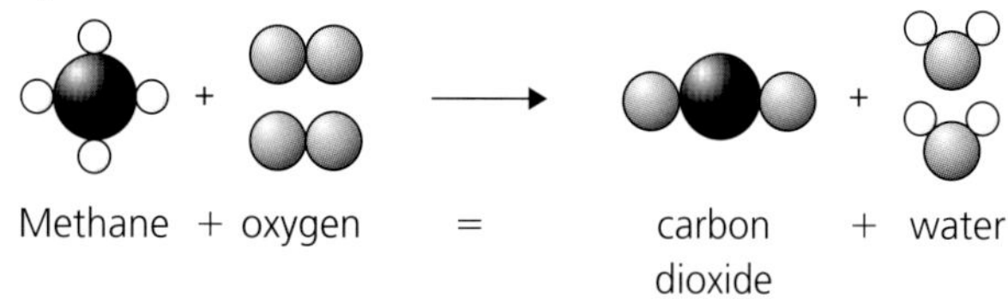

Methane + oxygen = carbon dioxide + water

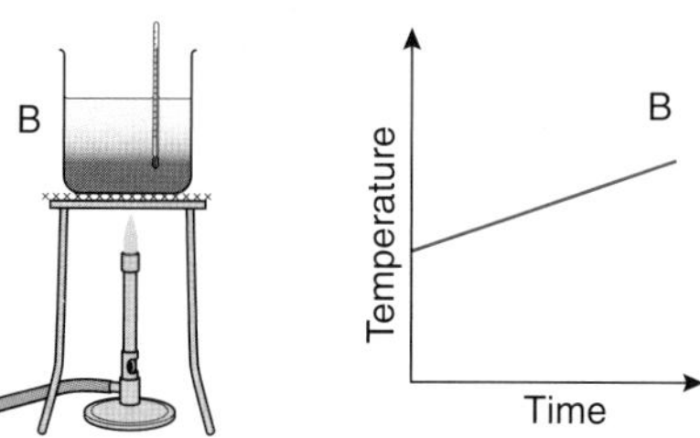

Figure 2 Burner B has a yellow flame.

The yellow flame is made by glowing **soot** particles in the flame. You can see the beaker has become all sooty.

Burner B has too little air to completely burn the methane gas, so less energy is made. The water heats up less quickly. Some energy is left in the unburned soot particles.

Equation for burner B

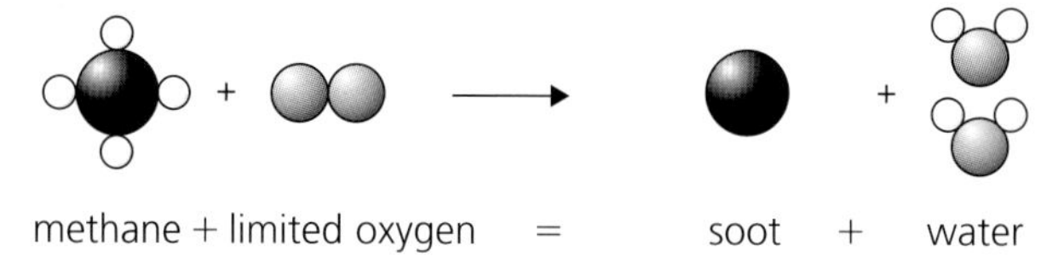

methane + limited oxygen = soot + water

Questions

1 Write a word equation for methane burning in a good supply of air.

2 What makes the yellow colour in a yellow bunsen flame?

Danger – poisonous gas

If there is too little air, **carbon monoxide** (CO) is produced when there is a burning reaction, or **combustion**. Carbon monoxide kills people. People die in accidents using gas heaters in closed rooms, or running a car engine in a closed garage.

Fireworks

Figure 3 Explosives in action.

Burning needs oxygen. Often the oxygen is taken from the air. In matches and explosives the oxygen atoms are in the chemicals themselves. When they burn, lots of heat is released very quickly. The gases expand quickly. This makes the explosion.

The chemicals in gunpowder are:

- Charcoal – this burns to give lots of heat.
- Sulphur – this also burns to give lots of heat.
- Saltpetre (potassium nitrate) – this substance contains lots of oxygen atoms.

Matches

A match is like a mini firework. Its head contains:

- Carbon to burn rapidly.
- Sulphur to burn rapidly.
- Potassium chlorate to provide the oxygen.

Questions

3 What is the poisonous gas that can be formed when fuels burn where there is too little air?

4 What is gunpowder made from?

5 Why can a match 'flare up' even if there is very little oxygen in the air?

Remember

Copy this into your books:

Combustion means burning a fuel. Combustion needs oxygen.

Not enough oxygen means the fuel is not completely burnt.

Explosives have oxygen atoms in their fuel. They burn fast and release all their energy at once. A match head is a tiny piece of explosive.

Hot food and cold relief

Key words

chemical change A permanent change in substances.

endothermic A chemical change that takes in energy.

exothermic A chemical change that gives out energy.

Figure 1 Self-heating coffee.

Push the button on the can. This breaks a water sachet and it heats itself up. Ideal for making a hot drink on a picnic. The chemical in the outer part of the can reacts with water to give out heat. This is called an **exothermic** reaction.

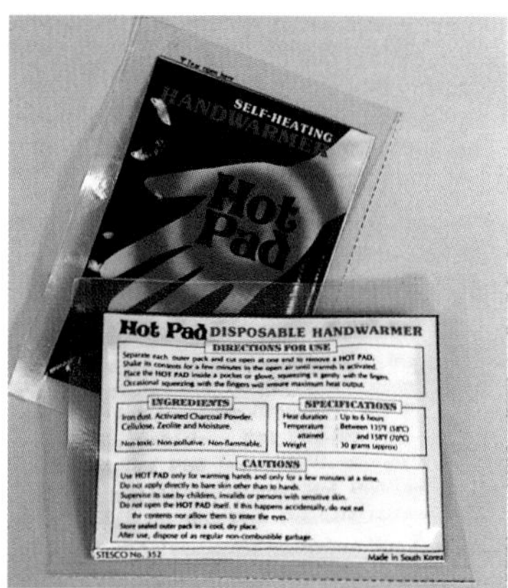

Figure 2 A cold pack for treating sprains.

Twist the pack and it gets cold enough to take away the pain of an injury. Cold helps to reduce pain and swelling. The chemicals combine to take in energy, so the pack gets cold. This is called an **endothermic** reaction.

Making cold

Chemical changes can produce cold. Dissolving separates particles, so it takes energy in.

100 g of water + 10 g sodium thiosulphate crystals	
Before mixing	After dissolving
20 °C	6 °C

Making heat

Acid particles join together with alkali particles to make water molecules. This is putting particles together, so it gives out energy as heat.

25 cm^3 of acid solution 25 cm^3 of alkali solution	
Before mixing	After dissolving
20 °C	29 °C

Questions

To make pottery a lot of heat energy needs to be put in the kiln.

Cooking food is a chemical change that needs energy put in.

Electrical energy is put in to change the aluminium ore into aluminium metal.

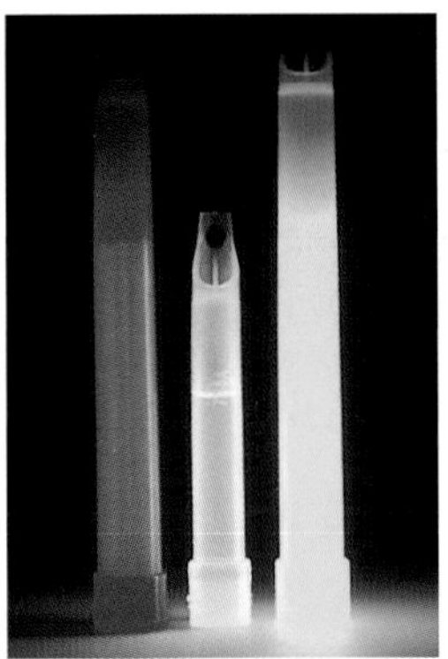

Light stick chemicals give out light energy

1 Copy and complete this table:

Chemical change	Endothermic or exothermic?
Sodium thiosulphate dissolving	
Acid – alkali reaction	
Firing clay pots	
Cooking vegetables	
Making aluminium metal	
Light stick chemicals reacting	

Electricity from metals

Metals contain energy. They often release this energy in reactions. Metals burn in oxygen to cause heating. Metals dissolve in acids and cause heating.

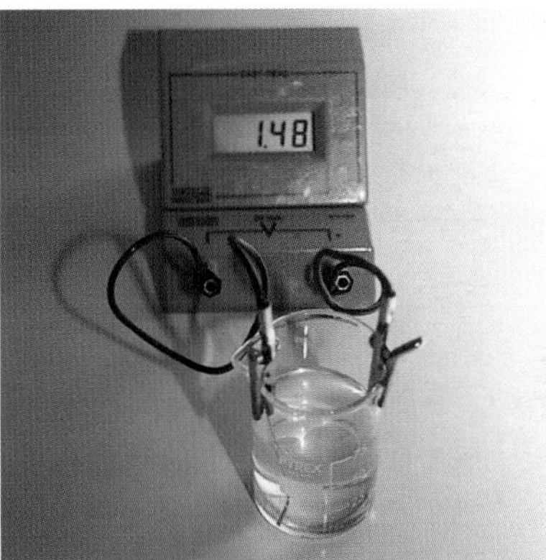

Figure 3 Metals releasing electrical energy.

Put the metal in an electric cell. Put the cell in a circuit. The chemical energy stored in the metal is released as electricity. You can get a voltage reading on the meter. More reactive metals such as lithium make more voltage than less reactive metals.

Remember

Copy and complete the sentences. Use these words:

in electricity energy give exothermic

Changes need **e**_________ to make them happen.

Endothermic changes take **i**_________ energy.

Ex_________ changes **g**_________ out energy.

Metals can release energy as **e**_________.

8.4 Bad air day

Key words

antioxidant A substance put in food to stop it reacting with oxygen. (The substance reacts with oxygen itself.)

corrode To rust and become useless.

galvanising Protecting steel metal with a thin layer of zinc metal.

oxidation Reacting with oxygen.

sour Nasty tasting, like bad milk.

Air is a dangerous chemical. Metals and foods react with oxygen in the air to make new substances. These new substances spoil the metal and food. The metals are **corroded** and food will taste **sour** and nasty.

Pie problems

Figure 1

Lis was annoyed. She had cut up the apple slices for a pie. She then made the pastry. But the apple had gone brown. What could she do?

Charlotte came to the rescue. She explained:

'Cut apple slices react with oxygen. The substances go brown.

This is an **oxidation** reaction.

You can put the apple in water. But there is oxygen dissolved in water and so the apple still goes brown, just slowly.

My advice is to use lemon juice on your apples. It contains sour tasting citric acid and vitamin C. These are **antioxidants**. They gobble up the oxygen on the apples. Then the apples stay a nice colour.'

That is exactly what Lis did. And her apple pies were perfect.

Questions

1. Why had the apple started to go brown?
2. Apple goes brown more slowly in water. Explain why.
3. What does citric acid do to stop the apple going brown?

Getting rusty

Charlotte knew her car was getting old and rusty. Lis was helping her sort out the problem. She said

'To stop rust:

- Clean off all the flaky rust.
- Cover the metal with a layer of paint or grease. Then the water and oxygen cannot get to it.'

Lis continued to explain. 'An object like a bucket or metal dustbin, is going to get banged about. First it gets dipped in molten zinc metal to protect it. This is called **galvanising**, The zinc isn't like paint. It reacts with any water and air, leaving the iron strong and not rusted.'

Figure 2 When water and oxygen get through a small hole in the paint, they react with the steel underneath to make flaky rust.

Questions

4 What would happen to Charlotte's car if she didn't stop the rusting?

5 What two substances together cause rust?

6 Why is galvanising not like painting?

Making Acids and Alkalis

Figure 3 Colours of some common oxides in universal indicator.

Look at Figure 3. The six gas jars have water in them. A different element is burnt in each one. The oxides produced dissolve in the water and Universal Indicator is added. Reactive metals combine with oxygen in the air to make alkaline oxides. Non-metals make acidic oxides.

Remember

corrode alkalis solutions food flavour

Oxygen can react with **f**________ to spoil the **f**________. Oxygen reacts with metals to **c**________ them. Acids and **a**________ are **s**________ of different oxides.

In control

Key words

cracking Breaking up big molecules into smaller ones

fractional distillation Process of separating liquids by boiling

monomer One unit of a polymer

polymer A long molecule made from many units

We control chemical reactions to make less useful substances into more useful ones.

We control chemical reactions to get energy from chemical changes.

We control chemical reactions to clean up dirt and pollution.

Polymers

Figure 1 Mrisi: 'Metals, glass and wood come from natural resources, but where do plastics come from?'

Will: 'They are made from oil products'.

Plastics are all man-made materials called **polymers**. Many natural materials are polymers. Proteins, starch, cellulose and DNA are all polymers.

A polymer is made from lots of smaller molecules joined together. The small molecules that get joined together are called **monomers**. Each different type of plastic (or polymer) is made from different monomers.

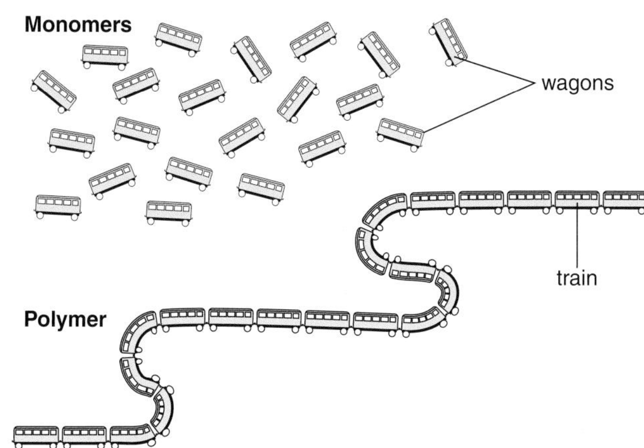

Figure 2 A good 'model' for the polymer reaction is putting wagons together to make a train. But thousands of monomer molecules get joined together to make a polymer molecule. This would be several kilometres long if it were a train.

Questions

1 Give three reasons for making chemical reactions happen.

2 What are polymers?

3 Draw an example of a model to show what a polymer molecule looks like.

4 Name as many different types of plastic as you can. How many of the names begin with 'poly'?

Better fuels

Crude oil (petroleum) is a mixture of lots of different fuels. Because they have different boiling points, the fuels can be separated using **fractional distillation**.

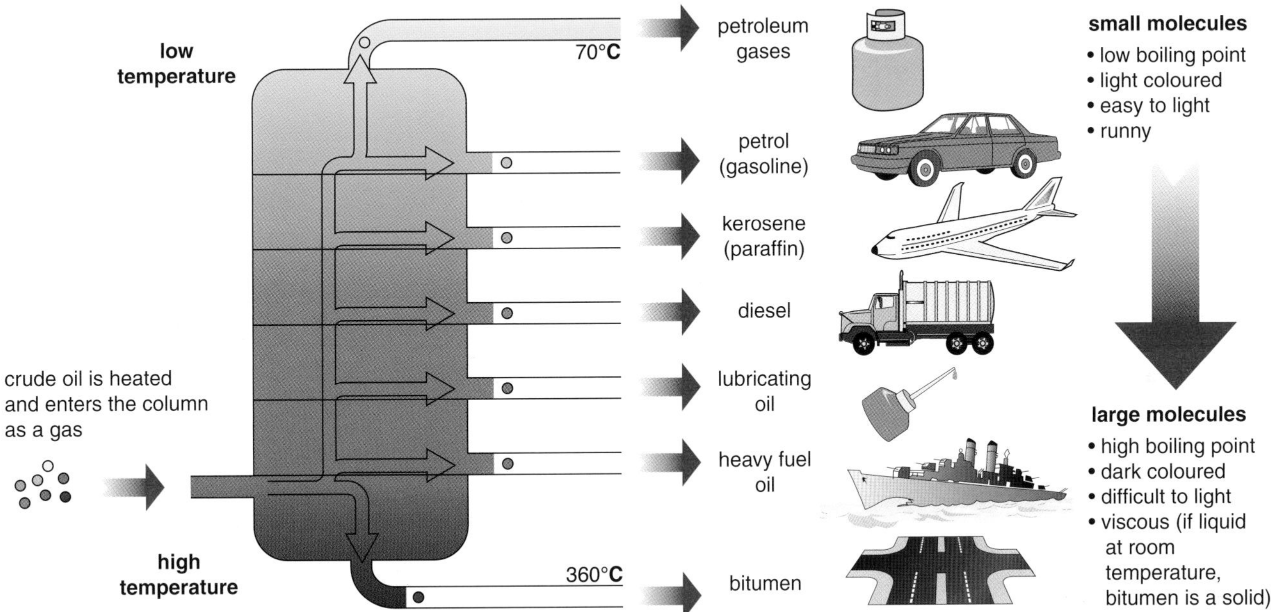

Figure 3 Fractional distillation.

Big long molecules can be broken up and made into smaller petrol sized molecules. This is called '**cracking**'.

Questions

5 Petroleum is another name for what substance?

6 How is the crude oil mixture split up to make it into more useful substances?

Summary

Complete the sentences. Use these words:

oil smaller plastics fuels distillation

P_________ are man-made materials called polymers. Polymers are made from lots of **s**_________ molecules joined together.

Crude **o**_________ is a mixture containing many **f**_________. Fractional **d**_________ is the process that turns crude oil into petrol.

8.6 Ideal partners

Key words

alkali metals A family of similar elements – very reactive metals

halogens A family of similar elements – very reactive non-metals

ions A particle in a salt, ions can be positively or negatively charged

Alkali metals and the **halogens** form very stable compounds together. The best known is common salt – sodium chloride.

Common salt (sodium chloride) has many uses as well as going on chips. It's a very useful material.

Figure 1 Common salt brings out the flavour in food, and it's used to preserve food as well. The microbes that make the food go bad are killed by table salt.

Figure 2 When it's icy the council puts salt on roads to keep them free of ice. Salt makes ice melt into water at a lower temperature.

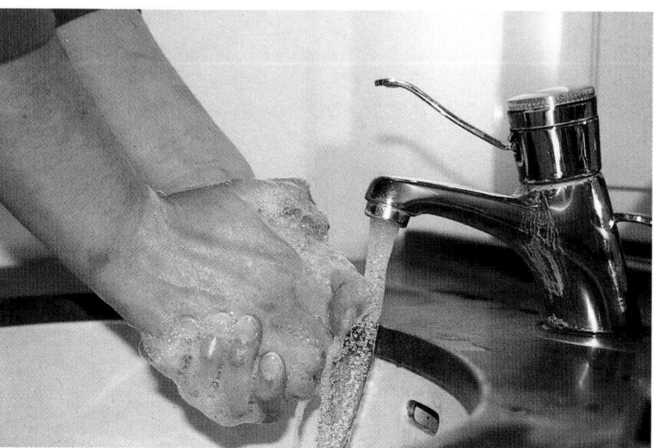

Figure 3 Salt is essential for making soap.

Figure 4 Salt is used to make washing soda, which is added to washing powder.

Questions

1. How does salt preserve food?
2. Why does salt make roads safer?
3. Name three materials that use salt in their manufacture.

Figure 5 Table salt is the starting material to make the bleach that keeps swimming pools free from germs.

The alkali metals start every new row of the Periodic Table. They are the most reactive of the metals. To react each alkali metal atom needs to lose one electron.

The halogens are at the other end of the row. They are the most reactive non-metals. To react each halogen atom needs to gain one electron.

One alkali metal atom reacts with one halogen atom. An electron passes from the alkali metal atom to the halogen atom. Now they both have a full outer shell of electrons and become very stable particles. These particles are called **ions**. The alkali metal atom becomes a positive ion, and the halogen atom becomes a negtive ion.

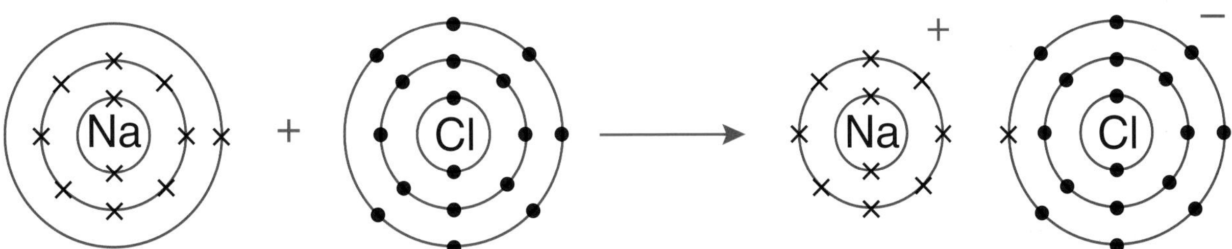

Figure 6 Sodium atom + chlorine atom = sodium ion + chloride ion.

Question

4 Copy figure 6 carefully. Write a sentence to say what has changed in the two halves of the diagram.

Remember

Spot the pattern in the names of the elements and compounds in the table below. Copy and complete the table.

The alkali metal	The halogen	The salt made by putting them together
Lithium	F____ine	Lithium fluoride
S_____	Chlorine	Sodium ________
Potass___	Bro____	___assium bromide
___idium	iodine	Rubid___ iod___

Two men of Science

Alfred Nobel, inventor of dynamite

Key words

detonator Device that starts an explosion
nitroglycerine Explosive in dynamite

Alfred Nobel was Swedish. His father was an engineer and inventor who moved to Russia to design torpedoes for the Russian government. Alfred worked for his father and found out about **nitroglycerine** for the first time.

Nitroglycerine is a very explosive liquid, but it's very hard to handle. If it gets bumped, knocked or dropped it tends to explode. In those days (1852) gunpowder was used by the army. Alfred could see that if you could make nitroglycerine easier to handle, it would be better than gunpowder.

Alfred, his father and Alfred's younger brother Emil tested nitroglycerine in their laboratory.

Sadly they had several explosions in their laboratory. A big one in 1864 killed Emil and several other people. This did not stop Alfred. He moved his laboratory to a barge on a big lake.

Finally, he came up with a solution. He mixed nitroglycerine with dry clay. This turned the liquid into a paste. The paste could be shaped and was safe to transport. It could even be burned if it was in small flakes.

To make it explode he invented a blasting cap (**detonator**). This contained mercury fulminate and could be set off by lighting a fuse. The product was patented with the name 'dynamite'.

The market for dynamite and detonators grew very rapidly. Soon Alfred was a very rich man. Alfred was always saddened by the military use of dynamite.

Alfred Nobel was interested in science, medicine, literature and peace. When he died in 1896 he used his fortune to establish a foundation that awarded Nobel Prizes each year. The Nobel Prizes are awarded for chemistry, physics, physiology, medicine, literature and peace.

Questions

1. Make a list of the seven underlined words and explain what they mean in this passage.
2. How do you make dynamite explode?
3. Why is dynamite safer than nitroglycerine?
4. Why do you think Alfred Nobel founded the Nobel Prizes?

To research

- What happens when someone is awarded a Nobel Prize?
- What does the prize consist of?
- Who won them last year?

Nylon and a troubled inventor

Key words

adipic acid Chemical used to make nylon
hexamethylene diamine Chemical used to make nylon
substitute To take the place of
synthetic (rubber) Man-made, not a natural product
textiles Cloth

Wallace Carothers was born in 1896 in Iowa in the USA, but he did not live to be old. He was the man who started man-made plastics, and the inventor of nylon. He was a brilliant chemist and inventor, but also a troubled soul.

Polymers are any natural or man-made substance made of very large molecules. These large molecules are made up of lots of smaller chemical units called monomers. Polymers make up many of the materials in living things, including proteins, cellulose, DNA, natural rubber and real silk.

Polymers made in laboratories are products such as plastics, resins, man-made **textiles** and **synthetic** rubber.

Carothers worked for the DuPont company. In 1931 he invented synthetic rubber (neoprene).

Most of all Carothers wanted to invent a **substitute** for silk. Silk came from Japan. Japan and the USA were about to go to war. Carothers made his new material by combining the chemicals **hexamethylene diamine** and **adipic acid** to create a very long, very smooth molecule.

The DuPont company decided to call the new material Nylon, because the work on its development had been done in New York and London. Nylon was a huge step forward in man-made textiles.

Carothers was never a happy man. He suffered from a condition called manic depression. He carried the poison cyanide with him all the time. In April 1937 he committed suicide by taking the cyanide. He had been severely affected by the death of his favourite sister.

Questions

1 What is neoprene?
2 What is nylon used for?
3 What natural material was nylon supposed to be like?
4 What is a polymer?
5 What two chemicals are used to make nylon?
6 Why was the new material called nylon?

To research

- How is nylon made now?
- What other synthetic fibres are there?
- Why was nylon used for parachutes?

Finishing off!

Remember

Equations and Formulae

Every particle of a compound has the same number of atoms in it. There is a quick way to show the number of atoms in each particle.

$$CuCO_3$$

This means one atom of copper, one atom of carbon, and three oxygen atoms joined to them. If there is no number after the atom symbol, there is only one atom of that type in the compound particle.

$$Ca(OH)_2$$

If there are brackets, it's the same rule as in Maths. Everything inside the brackets is multiplied by the same number. So this means one calcium atom joined to two oxygen and two hydrogen atoms.

Questions

1 Take a new page in your exercise book. Make a list of all the Key Words from the boxes in this chapter down the side. Take two lines per word. Try to write the meaning of each word without looking. Then go back and fill in any you did not know or got wrong.

Now learn to spell them by the Look – Say – Cover – Write method.

2 Copper carbonate dissolves in sulphuric acis, producing lots of froth and fizz.

$$CuCO_3 + H_2SO_4 = CuSO_4 + H_2O + CO_2$$

Write the word equation.

3 Lead is put out of solution by magnesium in the following reaction:

$$Mg + Pb(NO_3)_2 = Mg(NO_3)_2 + Pb$$

Write the word equation.

4 Ethanol burns to release heat energy.

$$C_2H_5OH + 3O_2 = 2CO_2 + 3H_2O$$

Write the word equation.

5 Magnesium burns in air in the following reaction:

$$Mg + O_2 = MgO$$

Write the word equation.

6 Match these types of reaction to questions 2–5:

combustion   oxidation   acid + base   displacement

Web sites to visit:

Wallace Carothers and the Nylon legacy
http://www.chemheritage.org/EducationalServices/nylon/nylon.html

NASA Spacelink
http://spacelink.nasa.gov/index.html

Royal Society of Chemistry
http://www.rsc.org

Chemistry Societies Network
http://chemsoc.org

Speeding up

Starter Activity
Swimming trunks

Elephants are good swimmers. They are not fast swimmers, but they have strong legs and big flat feet that make good paddles. These push them through the water in different directions so that they can turn.

They float in the water. There is an upthrust from the water which just balances their weight. They use their long trunks like snorkels to help them breathe. You could call them swimming trunks!

Questions

1 a) Name the force acting down on a swimming elephant.
b) Name the upwards force on the elephant.
c) Draw a simple sketch with arrows to show these forces.

2 Here are the names of some units:

metres seconds hours
kilometres per hour centimetres
metres per second kilometres miles
milliseconds miles per hour.

Sort them out into three groups – one for units of distance, one for units of time and one for units of speed.

Space speed

Key words

acceleration Changing motion, to move faster.

drag Friction when moving through a fluid such as air or water.

thrust A forwards force.

Figure 1 Space is empty. There is no air. So there is no air resistance or **drag** force to slow down spacecraft. They travel at high speeds and use rockets to change their motion.

Figure 2 Look at the rocket motors on top of the spacecraft. They can send jets out in four different directions. In the top of the picture the jet produces a forwards **thrust** and gives it forwards **acceleration**. In the lower part of the picture, the sideways thrust gives sideways acceleration, allowing the fighter to turn.

Speeding to the rescue

Figure 3 Jake must protect his planet from the Evil Empire.

The Evil Empire is about to launch an attack on the peaceful planet Gaia. The countdown has started. Jake has 500 seconds to destroy the dreaded Garth Radar. He is 10 000 kilometres away. His speed control must be set now. What speed must it be set to?

Figure 4 Will he make it in time?

The answer to Jake's problem:

$$\text{speed} = \frac{\text{distance}}{\text{time}}$$

$$\text{speed} = \frac{10\,000\ \text{(kilometres)}}{500\ \text{(seconds)}}$$

speed = 20 kilometres per second

Remember

Copy and complete the sentences. Use these words:

drag speed resistance thrust hour

In space there is no air **r**________ and so there is no force of **d**________. We can work out speed from the formula:

$$\text{average } \mathbf{s}\_\_\_\_\_\_ = \frac{\text{distance}}{\text{time.}}$$

The units of speed include kilometres per **h**________ and metres per second. In space a **t**________ force is not needed to balance drag.

Questions

1 Imagine that you are the pilot of a spacecraft. You have rocket motors at the front, rear and both sides of the spacecraft.

a) Which way will you move the lever to:
   i) accelerate forwards?
   ii) slow down (or accelerate backwards)?
   iii) turn left?

b) Which rocket motor will fire to make it:
   i) accelerate forwards?
   ii) slow down or accelerate backwards?
   iii) turn left?

2 A space station is 80 000 kilometres away. You must get there in 1000 seconds. How fast must you go. Write down your calculation like the one on the left.

9.2 Every 0.01 second counts

Key words

instantaneous speed Speed at any one instant in time. The speedo on a car measures instantaneous speed.

precision Accuracy. In sporting events we measure to one hundredth of a second. If we want a higher precision we measure to a thousandth of a second.

We can compare how fast athletes run by measuring their time. The timing is measured with high **precision**. It is measured to the nearest hundredth of a second. We write this as 0.01 seconds or just as 0.01 s.

0.01 s might not sound very long, but a sprinter can travel 10 centimetres in that time. So 10 cm and 0.01 s, can mean the difference between winning and losing.

Average speed

Even long distance events like the 10 000 metres are timed to the same precision of 0.01 s. The women's world record in the year 2000 was 29 minutes and 31.78 seconds, set by Wang Junxia.

Let's work out her average speed for the 10 000 metre race. The time of 29 minutes and 31.78 s is 1771.78 seconds.

So now we can use this formula:

$$\text{average speed} = \frac{\text{total distance}}{\text{total time}}$$

$$\text{average speed} = \frac{10\,000 \text{ (metres)}}{1771.78 \text{ (seconds)}}$$

$$\text{average speed} = 5.64 \text{ metres per second}$$

Figure 1 This race was timed to one hundredth of a second.

Instantaneous speed

The athlete does not run at exactly 5.64 metres per second for the whole race. Her speed changes, slowing down and speeding up. At the start she is not moving. It takes a second or two to accelerate. Perhaps she will slow down a little in the middle of the race. Then near the end she makes a quick sprint for the finish line. The speed she has at any one particular instant is called her **instantaneous speed**.

a) Starting off – her speed increases instant by instant.

b) Speed changes as the athletes jostle for position during the race.

c) Speed increases during the final sprint.

Figure 2 An athlete has only one average speed for the race. She has lots of different instantaneous speeds.

Questions

1 Write these times in decimal form:
   a) one hundredth of a second
   b) two hundredths of a second
   c) a tenth of a second.

2 A sprinter runs 10 cm in 0.01 s, what is their speed in:
   a) centimetres per second?
   b) metres per second?

3 What is an athlete's speed at the instant that the gun goes off?

Remember

Copy and complete the sentences. Use these words:

average speed metres per second instantaneous speeds total distance precision total time

Athletics events are timed to high **p**_________, usually to the nearest 0.01 s.

For a complete race, an athlete has an average speed which can be worked out by dividing **t**_________ **d**_________ by **t**_________ **t**_________.

At different instants of time, the athlete might have different **i**_________ **s**_________. Sometimes these are bigger than the **a**_________ **s**_________ and sometimes they are smaller.

All speeds, average speed and instantaneous speed, can be measured in **m**_________ **p**_________ **s**_________.

High Street travellers

Key words

gradient Slope or steepness.

We can use graphs to show the stories of different journeys.

The High Street is 500 m long. It has shops, banks and cafés. There are two busy junctions with traffic lights and pedestrian crossings, just like any other shopping sreet.

Matt, Vicky, Ellie and Ali travel along the street at about the same time. Matt is walking, Vicky is on a bike, Ellie is riding in a bus, Ali is in a car.

They take different times to travel along the street. They have different average speeds for their journeys. They stop and start in different ways. They have different instantaneous speeds.

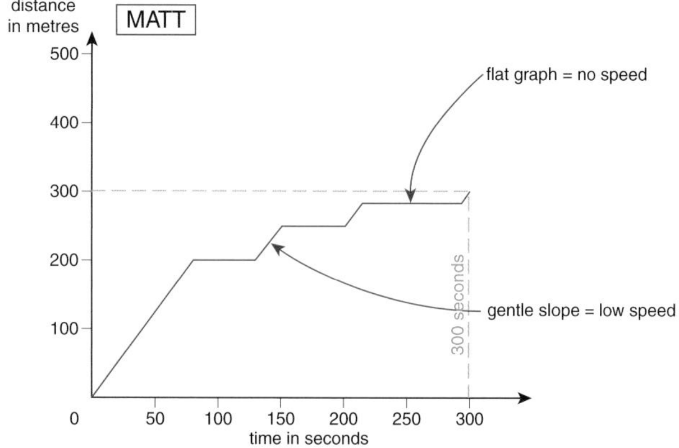

Figure 1 The distance-time graph for Matt as he stops to cross roads and look in shop windows.

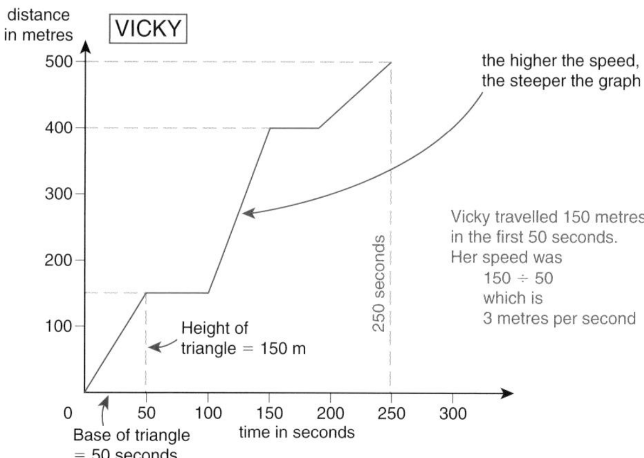

Figure 2 The distance-time graph for Vicky as she cycles down the High Street.

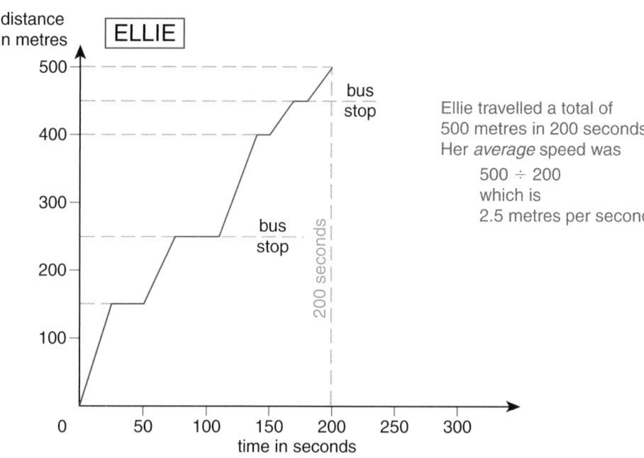

Figure 3 The graph for Ellie on her bus journey.

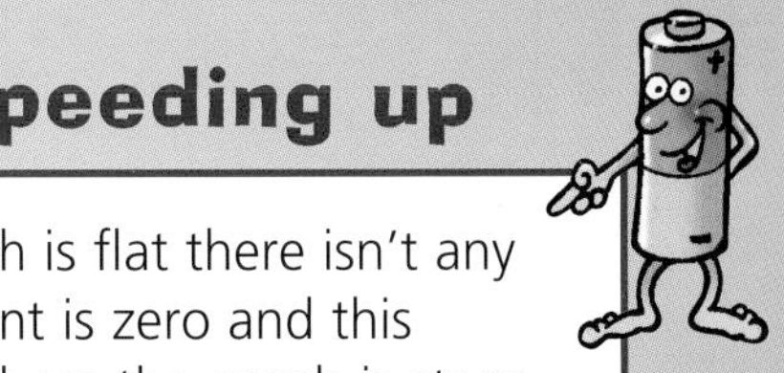

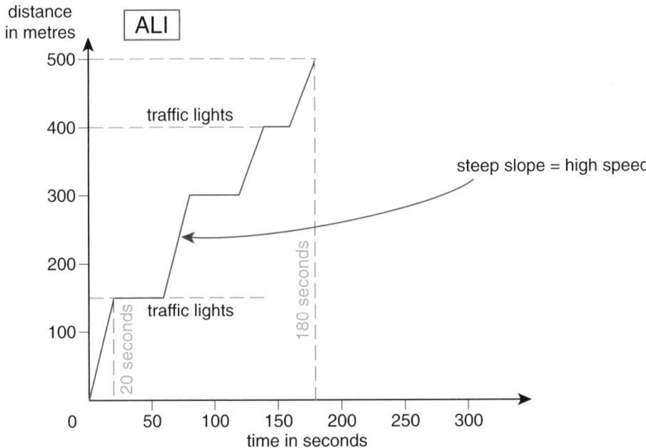

Figure 4 The graph for Ali as he travels down the High Street in his car.

Matt stops to cross roads and to look in shop windows. Vicky stops at the traffic lights when they turn red. Ellie stops at bus stops. Ali's car stops to let his brother get out.

We can use distance–time graphs to tell us how they travelled down the High Street.

Distance–time graphs

The graphs show:

- where they have stopped.
- when they stopped. The distances don't change, the graphs become level lines.
- when they set off again, the lines become slopes.
- the faster they go, the steeper the slopes.

We can use the graphs to:

- work out average speed, because the graphs tell us total distance and total time taken for the journey.

  $$\text{Average speed} = \frac{\text{total distance}}{\text{total time}}$$

- work out speed at any instant. For this we look at the steepness or **gradient** of the graph. When the graph is flat there isn't any steepness – the gradient is zero and this matches the speed. Where the graph is steep, the speed is large.

Let's work out Vicky's speed in the first 50 seconds.

We use the line of the graph as part of a triangle. We measure the height of the triangle to find the distance. We measure the base of the triangle to find the matching time.

Height of triangle = 150 m
Base of triangle = 50 s

$$\text{Speed} = \frac{\text{distance (m)}}{\text{time (s)}}$$

$$\text{Speed} = \frac{150\ \text{(m)}}{50\ \text{(s)}}$$

Speed = 3 metres per second

Questions

1 a) How big is the gradient of a distance-time graph for a traveller who is not moving?
b) What happens to the gradient of the graph as the traveller moves faster and faster?

2 Work out the average speeds for Matt and Vicky.

Remember

Copy and complete the sentences. Use these words:

speed distance-time average speed level total distance gradient

A **d**________ **t**________ graph tells us where the traveller stops and how long they stop for. The gradient of the line can tell us the **s**________ at that time. The steeper the graph, the higher the speed. We can work out the **g**________ from the height and base of the triangle.

When the speed is zero, the distance stays the same. Then the graph is a **l**________ line and the height of the triangle is zero. The gradient is zero and so the speed is zero.

The graph also tells us the **t**________ **d**________ of the journey and the total time it takes. We can work out the **a**________ **s**________ for the whole journey.

Air speed 1

Key words

acceleration Any object that's changing either its speed, or its direction, or both, is accelerating.

deceleration Slowing down of a moving object.

Vertical forces ...

Figure 1 This bird is being pulled down by the force of gravity. This force is also called its weight. There is not enough upwards force acting on the bird to balance its weight. The forces are unbalanced. The bird goes faster and faster – it **accelerates**.

Figure 2 The weight force on this bird is just balanced by the lift force from its wings. Lift is a force that acts upwards. When the weight force is balanced by the lift force, the up-down forces or vertical forces are in balance.

... and horizontal forces

The bird in Figure 2 also experiences forwards and backwards forces. These are called horizontal forces. One of these is the forward push from the wings, or thrust. The other is air resistance, or drag, which acts in the opposite direction. On its own, drag always causes slowing down or **deceleration**. When thrust and drag are in balance, the bird flies at a steady horizontal speed.

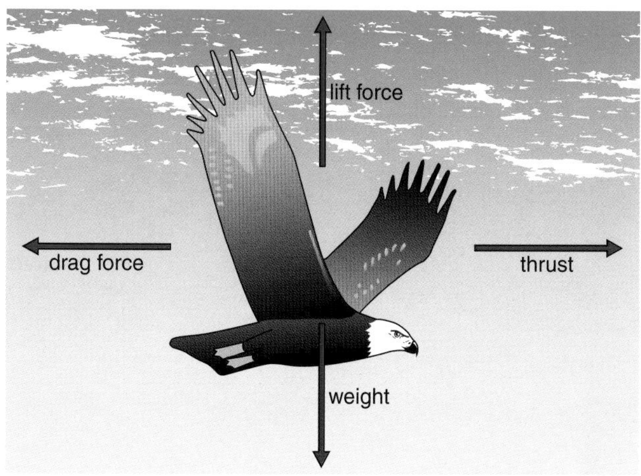

Figure 3 The vertical forces are balanced. The horizontal forces are balanced. The bird flies at a steady speed without acceleration or deceleration.

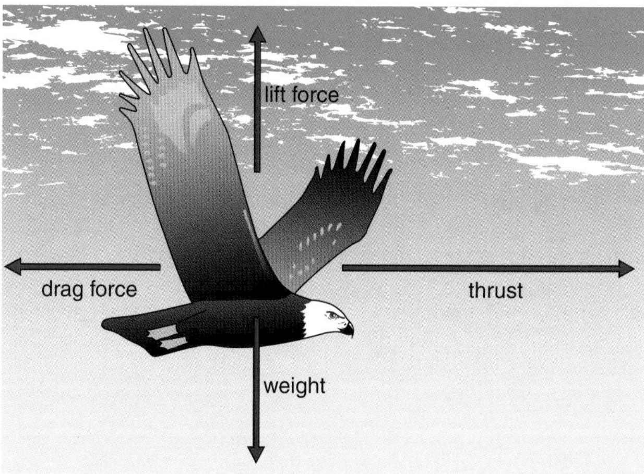

Figure 4 The vertical forces are in balance, but the horizontal forces are not. Thrust is greater than drag. The bird accelerates forwards.

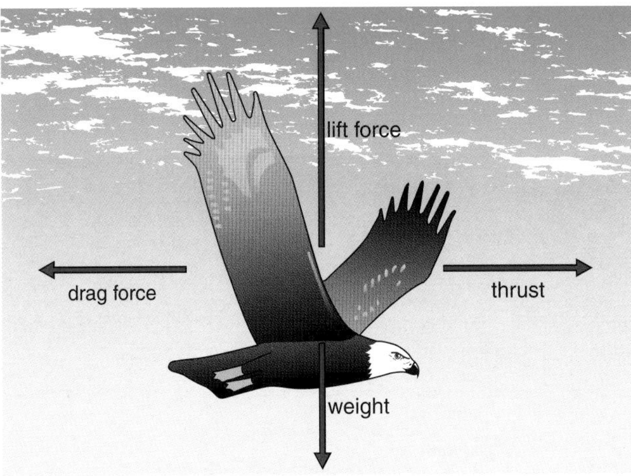

Figure 5 Now the vertical forces are *not* balanced. The lift force is greater than the weight force down. The bird accelerates upwards. The bird has to work hard to create such a strong force of lift.

Bird speed

Bird	Maximum speed in metres per second
Swift	45
Pigeon	28
Sparrow	8

Table 1 Bird speed.

A bird travels 100 metres in 5 seconds. Find its average speed.

Use this formula:

$$\text{average speed} = \frac{\text{distance}}{\text{total time}}$$

$$\text{average speed} = \frac{100 \text{ metres}}{5 \text{ seconds}}$$

So average speed = 20 metres per second

Questions

1 Which bird cannot fly at 20 metres per second?

2 What happens to a bird when:
a) drag is bigger than thrust?
b) thrust is bigger than drag?

3 Sketch a diagram to show the forces acting on a bird that is accelerating forwards.

Remember

Copy and complete the sentences. Use these words:

forces balanced distance metres horizontal acceleration drag lift

A flying bird experiences vertical forces of weight and **l**_________. When it flies without accelerating up or down, these forces are **b**_________.

The bird experiences **h**_________ forces of thrust and **d**_________. When it flies without experiencing backwards or forwards **a**_________, then these force are in balance.

Balanced **f**_________ always result in no acceleration.

Speed is measured in **m**_________ per second. You can work out the average speed by dividing **d**_________ by time.

Air speed 2

Key words

streamlined Shaped to have a smooth air flow over its surface.

turbulence The breaking up of streamlines; unsmooth air flow over a surface.

Reducing air resistance

The faster you travel through the air, the faster you have to push air out of the way. When you ride a bike you can feel the wind in your face. You are feeling a force of air resistance or drag.

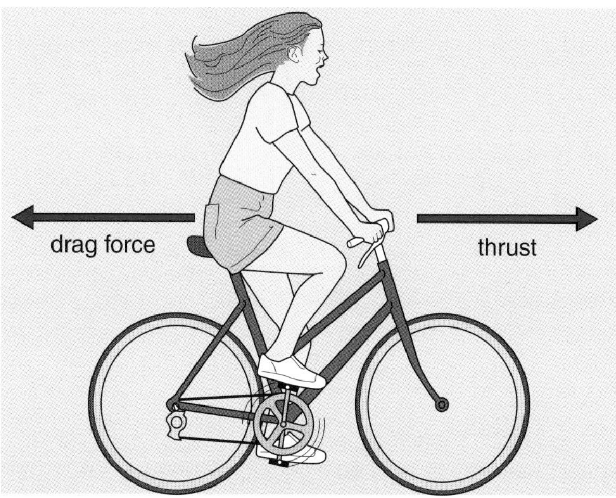

Figure 1 You have to pedal to provide a force of thrust to balance the drag force.

Figure 2 The difference between smooth and turbulent flow.

Figure 3 A good car design makes the air flow across the surface in smooth streamlines. This car has tapes fixed to it to show which way the air is moving at different places.

The faster you go, the bigger the drag force. It isn't a problem on a bike, but cars go much faster and they are much bigger. The more air resistance there is, the more work the engine has to do to overcome it. The car uses more fuel and causes more pollution.

Car makers want to design cars which have a low drag. They put their designs in wind tunnels. They blow air and smoke over the car in the tunnel. The lines of smoke show the air's streamlines. If the streamlines are smooth, then drag forces are not too big. We say the car is **streamlined**. If the streamlines break up into swirls, the drag forces become much bigger. This breaking up of streamlines is called **turbulence**. Cars are designed to stop turbulence.

Questions

1 If a car is 'streamlined', what does it mean?

2 What is the cause of drag?

Air resistance and particles

An airliner flies from New York to London, a distance of 5580 km, in 6 hours 40 minutes. It goes very fast, so it has to push a lot of air out of the way very quickly. It collides with the particles in the air. These particles are not very big, but there are a lot of them. The plane hits them hard.

The result of all these particle crashes is that the particles in the plane's metal are made to vibrate more rapidly. The metal gets hotter.

Figure 4 Concorde flies faster than sound. Its outer surface gets very hot. Special metals have to be used to stop it melting.

Figure 5 The space shuttle enters the Earth's atmosphere at 24 000 kilometres per hour (15 000 mph). Its surface temperature reaches 1500 °C. No metal can stand this temperature without melting. So the shuttle is covered with a layer of heat proof tiles to protect it.

Questions

3 Why does a plane experience much more drag force than a person on a bike?

4 Is a plane's average speed always the same as its instantaneous speed? Explain your answer.

Remember

Copy and complete the sentences. Use these words:

drag thrust collide streamlines turbulence balanced

A cyclist, a car and a plane can only go at a steady speed if the forces on them are **b**________. They must exert a forwards **t**________. This is the force that balances the backwards force of **d**________. Drag is caused by air resistance.

Air resists the motion of cyclists, cars and planes because air must be pushed out of the way. This means the air particles **c**________ with the particles in the moving body.

S________ show the flow of air. Car makers use smoke to help them study streamlines. If the streamlines are smooth, then drag is quite low. If the streamlines show **t**________, then drag is high.

Finishing off!

Remember

- ★ We can work out average speeds using the formula:

$$\text{average speed} = \frac{\text{distance}}{\text{time}}$$

- ★ If we measure distance in metres and time in seconds, then average speed is in metres per second.
- ★ We can also work out distances when we know average speed:
  distance = average speed × time
- ★ Most moving objects change their speed. Their speed varies instant-by-instant. Their speed at just one instant is called their instantaneous speed.
- ★ When speed is changing, instantaneous speed and average speed are usually not the same.
- ★ We can use graphs to show how the distance travelled by an object increases and decreases on its journey. A distance-time graph tells the story of the journey.
- ★ Unbalanced force can change the speed of an object. Unbalanced force can also change the direction of a moving object. Unbalanced force always does at least one of these things.
- ★ When balanced forces act on an object it moves with a steady motion. It stays at the same speed and moves in a straight line.
- ★ Air resistance creates a drag force. Drag force can be balanced by thrust force. Air resistance also makes moving objects get hotter.
- ★ Fast vehicles and aeroplanes are 'streamlined' to reduce drag.

Questions

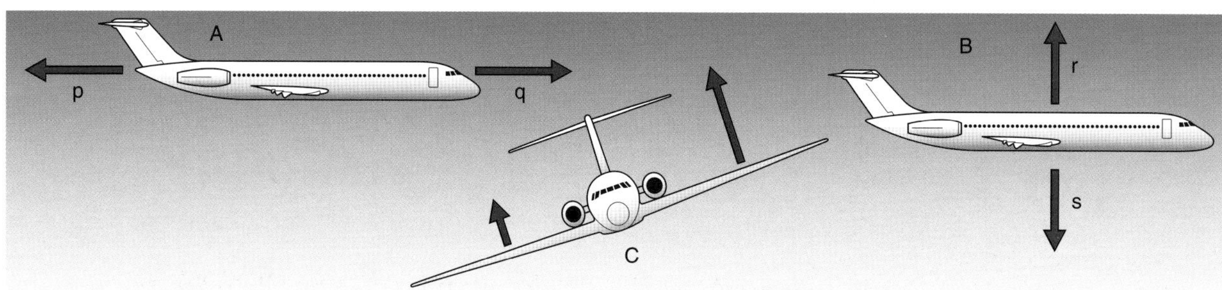

1 Take a new page in your exercise book. Make a list of all the Key Words from the boxes in this chapter down the side. Take two lines per word. Try to write the meaning of each word without looking. Then go back and fill in any you did not know or got wrong.

Now learn to spell them by the Look – Say – Cover – Write method.

2 Which diagram shows:

a) horizontal forces in balance?
b) vertical forces in balance?
c) forces having turning effects?

3 What are the names of the forces labelled p, q, r and s?

Web sites to visit:

International Amateur Athletics Federation – World records
http://www.iaaf.org/Results/index.asp

Forces in action

Starter Activity
Shoe technology

Every Akibide shoe has a gas-filled heel – the bubble that you squash at every step.

It is scientifically developed to protect your joints. The bubble contains particles of gas. They get closer together when your weight comes down on the bubble. And since there's plenty of space between the particles in the gas, there's plenty of room for them to get closer together. You get a nice soft landing, even on the hardest surface.

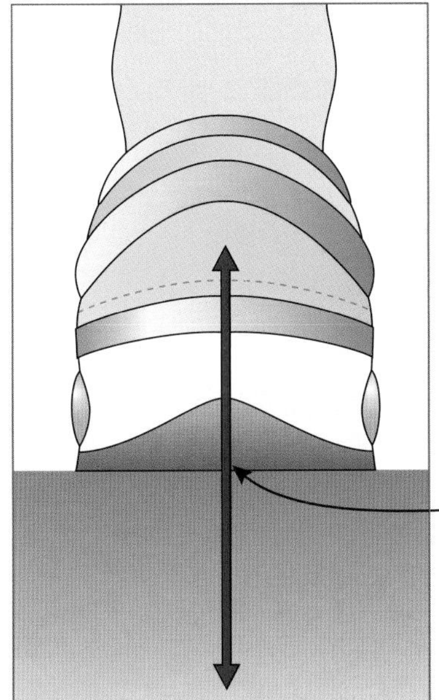

Every time your foot comes down, the ground pushes upwards. If it pushes in the wrong place, the upward force combines with your weight to twist your foot. But with Akibide shoes, there's no turning effect and you keep your balance

Questions

1. Particles in a gas are far apart. Particles in a liquid are very close together. How does this explain why the shoe designers don't use bubbles of liquid in the heels of their shoes?
2. Name some materials, used in the home, which contain lots of air bubbles.
3. Write down another example of the use of bubbles of gas (big or small) to provide cushioning. (*Hint*: think about safety devices in a modern car)

Elephant pressure

Key words

area The size of a surface.

inverse relationship A relationship where one variable gets larger as the other gets smaller.

pressure Force per unit area.

Figure 1 An elephant exerts a pressure on the ground. The pressure depends on the weight of the elephant. It also depends on the area of foot that is touching the ground.

Everyone knows that it is easier to push a sharp stick into the ground than a thick one. If you are an elephant you need big wide feet to stop you sinking into the ground.

The large feet of an elephant spread its weight over a large **area** so that its big weight doesn't have too much effect on the ground below. The larger its feet, the smaller the **pressure** is on the ground. For an elephant's feet in a muddy place, big area is good, small area is bad.

If you want to dig into the ground then you need a small area. If you use your pointed tusks then you can exert a large pressure and can dig deep in the ground. For digging, small area is good, big area is bad.

Pressure

There is an **inverse relationship** between pressure and area. The bigger the area, the smaller the pressure. When one gets bigger, the other gets smaller.

Figure 2 The cat ladder makes the area bigger and the pressure on the fragile roof smaller.

When you want to cut things then you need to have a high pressure.

Figure 3 The sharp edge of the knife has a small area. There is a big pressure under the blade.

How much pressure do you exert?

We can work out pressure like this:

$$\text{pressure} = \frac{\text{force}}{\text{area}}$$

The pressure depends on the force. The force you exert on the floor is your weight. We can measure it with a newton meter.

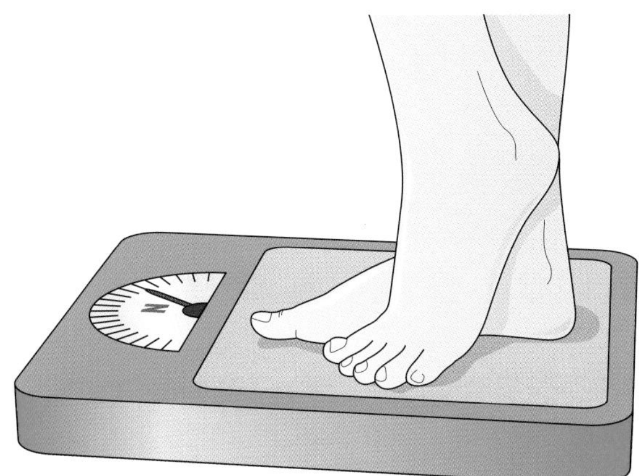

Figure 4 Your weight can be measured with a newton meter.

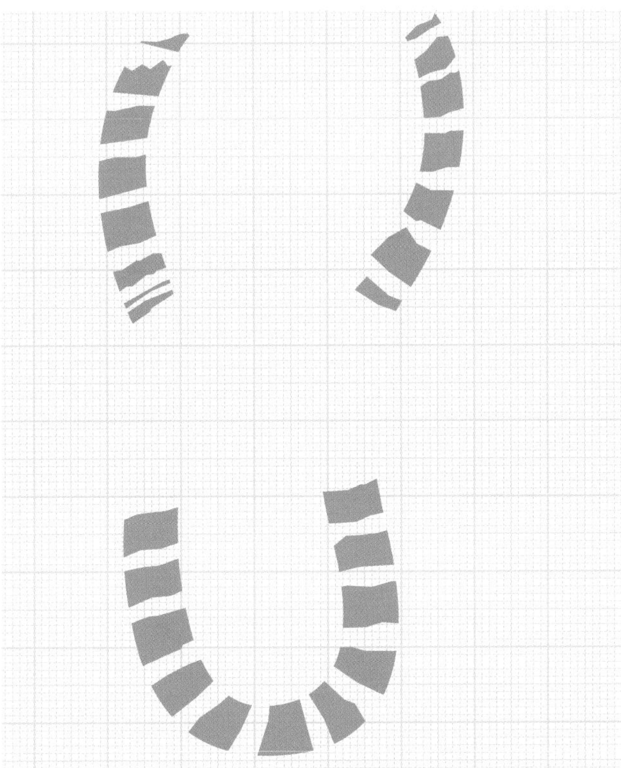

Figure 5 You can use squared paper and coloured chalk to measure the area of your foot which is in contact with the floor.

The pressure also depends on the area of your foot which is touching the ground. This can change. If you stand on your toes the area will be smaller and the pressure greater. Pointed high heels have a very small area and so people who wear them can exert a lot of pressure. The pressure can be so high that it can damage wooden floors. An ice-skater's blades have a small area. The high pressure makes the ice more slippery. Skis and snow boards have a large area so that people will not sink in the soft snow.

Questions

1 What does pressure depend on?

2 What happens to the pressure when the area is: **a)** increased, **b)** decreased?

3 Use the words area and pressure to explain how a knife can cut through cheese.

Remember

Copy and complete the sentences. Use these words:

smaller area surface Pressure inverse

The size of a surface is called its **a**_________. **P**_________ is a measure of the effect of a force acting on a **s**_________. If the force acting doesn't change, then as the area gets bigger, pressure gets **s**_________. There is an **i**_________ relationship between pressure and area.

10.2 Working under pressure

Key words

atmospheric pressure The pressure exerted on us by the air above us.

pascal Unit of pressure – 1 newton per square metre.

Figure 1 On Earth the air above us exerts a pressure on us. Our bodies on the insides of our skin push out to balance the pressure. In space there is no atmosphere, so there is no air pressure. Astronauts have to wear pressurised space suits. Their bodies would explode if they did not wear them.

We live at the bottom of a sea of air. It is called our atmosphere. It exerts a pressure on our bodies. It is called **atmospheric pressure**.

Atmospheric pressure is about 100 000 newtons per square metre. The area of a human body is about 1 square metre. This means there is a total force of 100 000 newtons acting on our body. That's nearly 10 tonnes!

$$\text{pressure} = \frac{\text{force (newtons)}}{\text{area (square metres)}}$$

One way to measure pressure is in units of newtons per square metre. This unit is called a **pascal**.

1 newton per square metre = 1 pascal or Pa for short

The pressure of air at, or close to sea level, is about 100 000 Pa.

Water pressure

Figure 2 As divers go deeper, the water pressure increases.

When we go below the surface of water, it exerts a pressure on our bodies. The deeper we go, the greater the pressure. At 11 metres under water, the pressure is double that at the surface. At 22 metres it's trebled.

Divers do not have to go very deep before the pressure becomes dangerous. Nitrogen gas starts to dissolve in their blood. If they come back up too quickly bubbles of nitrogen start to form in their veins. The bubbles are like those you get when you open a fizzy drink. The bubbles are painful and can kill. Divers call it *'the bends'*.

Question

1 Name the unit of each of these quantities:
  a) force,
  b) area,
  c) pressure.

Working out pressure

$$\text{pressure} = \frac{\text{force}}{\text{area}}$$

There is an inverse relationship between pressure and area. The bigger the area over which you spread the force, the smaller the pressure.

Figure 3 The wide crawler board has a large area. The pressure under it is low.

Let's work out:

1 The pressure under the firefighter's feet –

$$\text{Weight of firefighter} = 800\text{ N}$$

$$\text{Area of feet when standing on roof} = 0.01\text{ m}^2$$

$$\text{Pressure when standing} = \frac{\text{force}}{\text{area}}$$

$$\text{Pressure} = \frac{800}{0.01}$$

$$\text{Pressure when standing} = 80\,000\text{ Pa}$$

2 Pressure under the crawler board –

$$\text{Area of crawler board} = 1\text{ m}^2$$

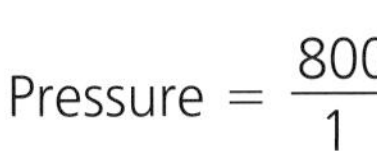

$$\text{Pressure} = \frac{800}{1}$$

Pressure when on crawler board = **800 Pa**

Figure 4 A small area has a bigger pressure. The point of the firefighter's axe has a big effect on any surface it hits.

Questions

2 What does it mean that there is an 'inverse' relationship between pressure and area?

3 What does it mean that there is a 'direct' relationship between pressure and force?

Remember

Copy and complete the sentences. Use these words:

inverse pascal atmosphere depth pressure increases square force newtons

P________ = force ÷ area. There is a direct relationship between pressure and force. Increasing the force **i**________ the pressure (provided that the area stays the same). There is an **i**________ relationship between force and area – increasing the area decreases the pressure (provided that the **f**________ stays the same). If force is measured in **n**________ (N) and area measured in **s**________ metres (m^2), then the unit of pressure is the **p**________. The **a**________ exerts a pressure. Water also exerts pressure. Water exerts more pressure at greater **d**________.

Robot Force

Key words

compressible Can be squeezed or squashed into a smaller size.
hydraulic Transferring force by liquid pressure.
incompressible Not able to be squeezed.
pneumatics Transferring force by air pressure.

Hydraulics

When you apply pressure to a gas, the gas is squashed. Its volume gets smaller. When you apply pressure to liquids, the volume does not get smaller. We can use this to transfer forces in machines.

small force in here
a large force is produced here
robot arm
piston
piston movement
piston
piston movement
liquid
Slave cylinder
Master cylinder

Figure 1 A small force on the piston in the master cylinder produces a large force on the robot arm.

A **hydraulic** system has two cylinders. One is called the master, the other the slave. The master cylinder has a piston with a small area. The slave cylinder has a piston with a large area.

If the piston in the master cylinder is pushed down it exerts a pressure on the liquid. The liquid volume can't change. So the liquid presses on the piston in the slave cylinder. The liquid 'transmits' the pressure from one cylinder to the other.

The pressure in each piston is the same, but the area of the slave piston is much bigger. The pressure acts on a bigger area and so exerts a bigger force on the slave piston. A small force on a master cylinder can exert a large force on the slave cylinder.

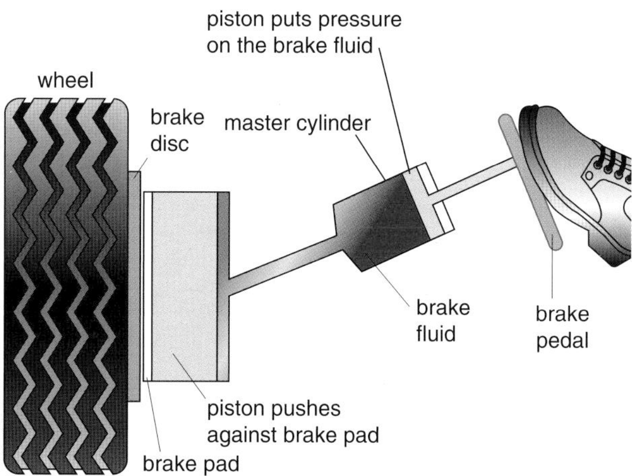

Figure 2 The brakes in a car use hydraulics. The brake pedal is connected to the master cylinder. A large force is exerted at the slave cylinders on the wheels.

A car's brakes use hydraulics. The liquid in the pipes connects the brake pedal master cylinder to the slave cylinders on each wheel.

It is dangerous to get air in the brake pipes. Air is not like a liquid and its volume does change when pressure is applied to it. If a car has air in its brake pipes, the air will squash when the driver puts the brakes on. So all the pressure is not transmitted to the wheels, and the car does not slow down.

Question

1 How do they design a hydraulic system so that the force exerted by the slave piston is bigger than the force exerted by the master piston?

Pneumatics

Gases like air can change their shape and volume under pressure. When something can be squashed we say it is **compressible**. Water and hydraulic fluid cannot be squashed. We say they are **incompressible**. Liquids are good for hydraulic systems, but gases are not.

Air can be used to transfer small forces in machines. They are called **pneumatic** systems. They work in the same way as hydraulic machines. There are times when the compressibility of a gas is useful, see Figure 3.

Figure 3 The compressibility (or sponginess) of air in the tyres gives a less bumpy ride.

Particles

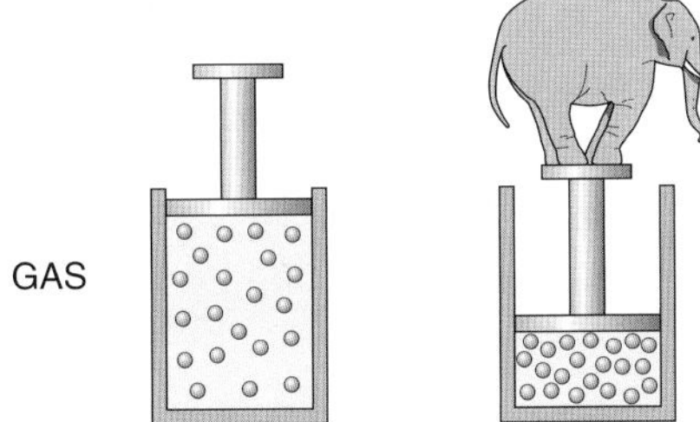

Figure 4 a) In a gas, the particles are a long way apart and it is easy to push them closer together.

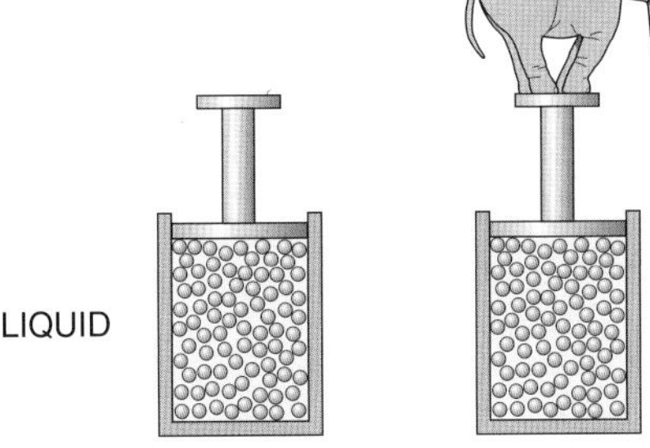

Figure 4 b) The particles in a liquid are very close together. It is very hard to push them even closer together.

Questions

2 Air can be compressed. Give an example of where this is: **a)** a good thing, **b)** a bad thing.

3 If you put your finger over the end of a bicycle pump and push the handle you can feel the sponginess of the air inside. What would happen if you filled the pump with water and tried to do the same thing?

Remember

Copy and complete the sentences. Use these words:

compressed incompressible particles liquid hydraulic force area pressure

A **h**________ system can change a small force into a bigger force. The system is filled with a liquid which is **i**________.

The force acting on the piston in the master cylinder acts over a small **a**________ The **p**________ is transmitted through the liquid, so the same pressure acts on the piston in the slave cylinder, but it acts over a bigger area. The same pressure acting over a bigger area produces a bigger **f**________.

A gas is no use in a hydraulic system because it can be **c**________ Pressure acting on a gas pushes the **p**________ closer together. In a **l**________ the particles are already close together and it's very hard to move them even closer.

Safe forces at play

Key words

moment Turning effect of a force.

newton metre Unit of turning effect or moment.

pivot The point around which a force turns

principle of moments Total clockwise moments = total anticlockwise moments.

Turning effects

Most of the time the forces on you are balanced. Sometimes the forces combine to put you in a spin. The diagrams below show you some examples.

Figure 1 These forces are not in balance. The arrows show the size and direction of the forces. They are the same size but they do not act at the same point on the gymnasts body. They make her turn.

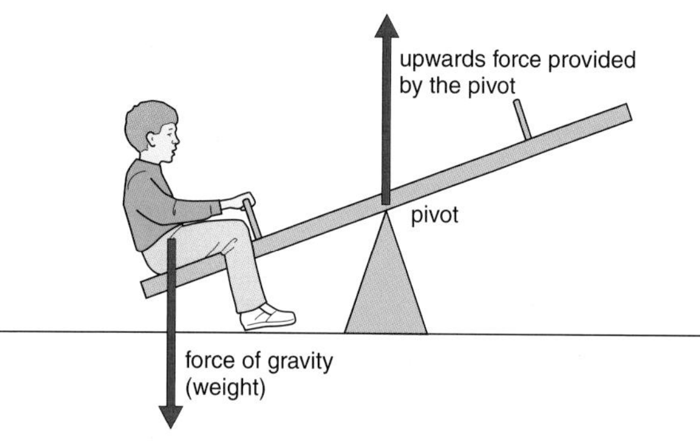

Figure 2 On a see-saw, the force of gravity can produce a turning effect.

Figure 3 The force of gravity acting on a second person can also produce a turning effect.

How big?

The variables that affect the size of the turning effect are:

- The size of the force – more weight means more turning force.
- The distance of the force from the **pivot** – the bigger the distance means more turning force.

Figure 4 A smaller person can have a bigger turning effect than a heavier one by sitting far away from the pivot.

The size of the turning effect on a see-saw is the force multiplied by the distance from the pivot.

For a see-saw:

turning effect = force × distance of force from the pivot

Question

1 What do we mean by the 'moment' of a force?

Another name for the turning effect of a force is the **moment** of the force. We measure force in newtons and distance in metres. So turning effects, or moments, are measured in **newton metres**.

The principle of moments

Jeff has built a see-saw for his children, Liam and Jodie. However they are not the same weight. To find out where they must sit we must use the **principle of moments**. A force that has a clockwise turning effect is called a clockwise moment. For the see-saw to balance, the total of the clockwise moments must equal the total of the anticlockwise moments.

total clockwise moments =

total anticlockwise moments.

Liam and Jodie sit on the see-saw and move about until it is balanced.

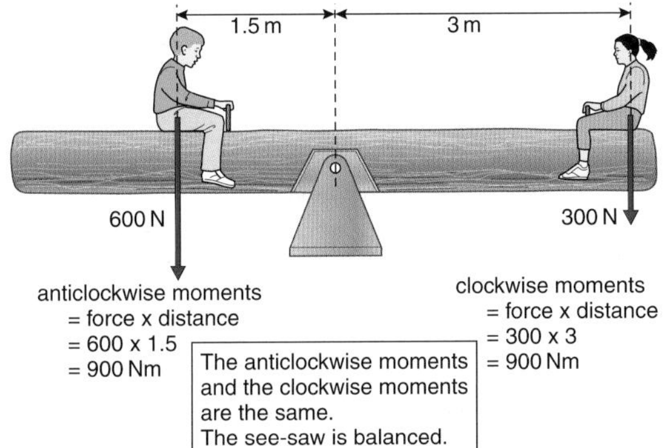

Figure 5 Liam and Jodie just balance the see-saw.

Jeff made the see-saw out of a log. A beam that swings up and down is a hazard. He needs to think about making it as safe as possible. He writes a list of the hazards and risks:

Falling off, with special risk to head.

Being hit by beam moving up and down, again with special risk to head.

Sudden movement, with special risk of neck damage if very sudden.

Jeff changes his see-saw to reduce these risks.

- He puts extra weights at the bottom of the beam to keep it balanced and prevent sudden movements.
- He covers the ground under and around the beam with log shavings.

Questions

2 What is the principle of moments?

3 a) Calculate the moment of a force of 100 N when it acts 1 m, 2 m, 3 m, 4 m from a pivot. Copy and complete the table below using your answers.

Distance from pivot	Moment
1 metre	
2 metres	
3 metres	
4 metres	

b) Add another column to your table to show the distances that a 50 N force must be from the pivot to *produce a balance* for each position of the 100 N force.

Remember

Match the half sentences together. Copy the complete sentence into your book.

a) We measure force in units . . .
b) The size of the turning effect of a force depends on . . .
c) The turning effect of a force about a pivot . . .
d) A moment is equal to the size of the force . . .
e) The unit of moment is the newton metre, and it can be clockwise . . .

i) . . . or anticlockwise.
ii) . . . called newtons.
iii) . . . is called its moment.
iv) . . . the size of the force and the distance of the force from the pivot.
v) . . . multiplied by its distance from the pivot.

Body balance

We can use the principle of moments to help us to understand a wide range of situations.

Figure 1 The gymnast is turning round and round. The unbalanced force of gravity gives her an anticlockwise moment. Her hands on the bar act as a pivot. The principle of moments is *not* being satisfied. The total clockwise moments do not equal the total anticlockwise moments. So the gymnast experiences a turning (rotational) acceleration.

Figure 2 They say that if you kiss the Blarney Stone at Blarney Castle in Ireland, then you'll be a good talker. The trouble is that the stone is high up on the Castle. You have to lean a long way out to kiss it. It could be dangerous. For the tourists, there are strong arms to reduce the risk of falling. It's really important to obey the principle of moments!

Figure 3 This tightrope walker is using a pole to make smooth and well-controlled adjustments to the moments. This avoids too much violent arm-waving. The weight of each half of the pole is a quite a long way from the pivot.

Questions

1 Draw a pin person sketch of the gymnast in Figure 1. Add an arrow to show the force of gravity. Explain why the force has a turning effect.

2 For the tightrope walker, where is the pivot?

Levers at work

We use the turning effect of forces every day. Here are some examples:

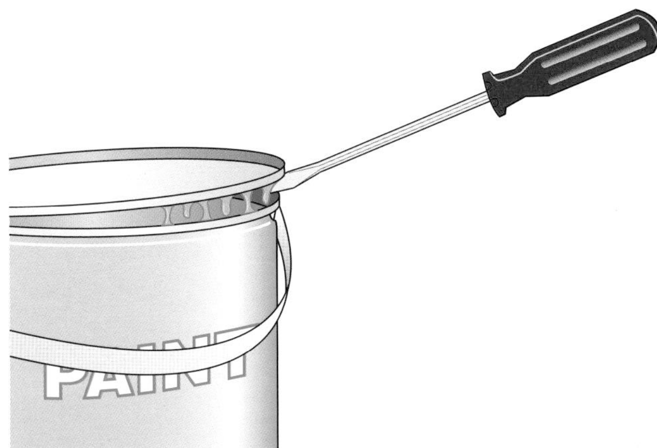

Figure 4 A small force on the end of a long screwdriver enables us to exert a large force to lever the lid off the can.

Figure 5 The scissors enable us to cut thick material easily. The joint in the middle is the pivot. The closer the material is to the pivot the easier it is to cut.

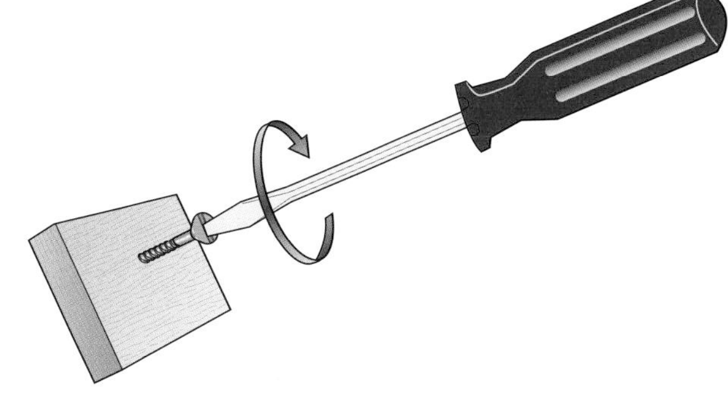

Figure 6 The screwdriver exerts a turning force on the screw. The wider the handle, the easier it is to turn.

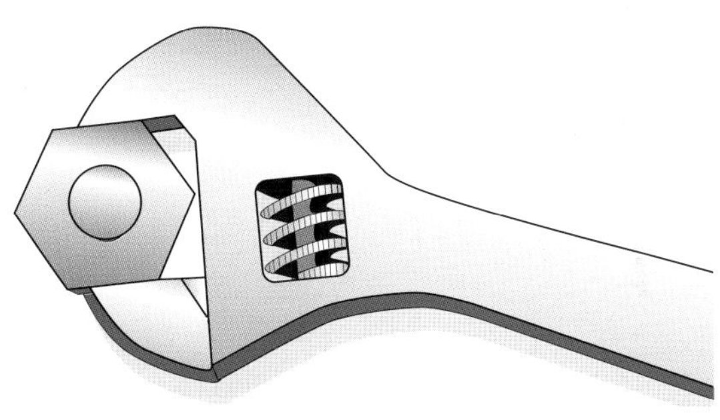

Figure 7 The spanner exerts a turning force on the nut. The longer the spanner, the easier it is to turn.

Question

3 For the lever on the paint can lid in Figure 4, where is the pivot?

Remember

Copy and complete the sentences. Use these words:

moment bigger total clockwise pivot

A **p**________ can be anywhere on a body. The further a force acts from the pivot, the **b**________ the moment of the force.

M________ = force × distance from the pivot.

To be in balance, the principle of moments must be satisfied:

total **c**________ moments = **t**________ anticlockwise moments.

Finishing off!

Remember

- ★ Pressure is force per unit area.
- ★ Pressure = force ÷ area, with pressure measured in pascals, force in newtons and area in square metres.
- ★ Pressure increases whenever force increases, provided that the area does not change.
- ★ Pressure decreases whenever area increases, provided that force doesn't change.
- ★ Snow shoes have a large area. They reduce pressure on the snow. A sharp blade has a small area. This increases the pressure, making it cut easily.
- ★ Hydraulic systems use liquids to transmit pressure. Liquids cannot be compressed.
- ★ Pneumatic systems use air. Gases can be compressed. They cannot transmit large forces.
- ★ The turning effect of a force is called its moment. The size of the turning effect depends on the force and the distance of the force from the pivot.
- ★ If force is measured in newtons and distance in metres, the moment of a force is measured in newton metres.
- ★ For a balanced beam, the total clockwise moments = the total anticlockwise moments. This is the principle of moments.

Questions

1 Take a new page in your exercise book. Make a list of all the Key Words from the boxes in this chapter down the side. Take two lines per word. Try to write the meaning of each word without looking. Then go back and fill in any you did not know or got wrong.

Now learn to spell them by the Look – Say – Cover – Write method.

2 The tightrope walker on page 132 is in a hazardous situation.

a) What is the main risk?

b) How does the tightrope walker reduce the risk?

c) Do you think that the tightrope walker is taking an 'acceptable' risk?

Web sites to visit:

Association of Women in Science and Engineering
http://www.awise.org

Institute of Physics
http://www.iop.org/Physics/Schools

Engineering Council
http://engc.org.uk

Revision hints and tips

This page will help you to find the revision method that suits you.

- Simply reading is not revising. Revision is about learning facts, but it is also about understanding the work that you have done.
- Having the TV on will distract you, but music can help you concentrate. The type of music that works best is soothing music. If you have music on with words, that could distract you.
- The best revision is done in the month before the exam.
- Leaving it until the last minute is not helpful. There will be too much to learn in one evening.
- Your exercise book is a guide to what to revise – but it can be full of mistakes.
- Bedtime is for sleeping. You don't revise well if you are sleepy.

How should I plan my revision?

- Draw up a timetable for revision.
- Plan your timetable so that you have regular breaks and don't exclude all the fun things.
- Plan to revise topics for no more than half an hour and have a 10-minute break between each half-hour session.
- Rather than missing your favourite TV programme, arrange it so that you do work before the programme, then go back to work after it has finished.

Where's the best place to revise?

Organise a space for your revision. Make sure you have everything before you start, like your textbook, revision guides, some paper or file cards and pens (at least two different colours, or perhaps a highlighter). Make sure the room is comfortable, but not too warm.

What's the best way to revise?

Method 1

Some people revise best by making concept maps. First read through your notes on a topic and any other information. Write the name of the topic in the middle of a clean page. Write down on the paper around the topic as many words as you can remember that are linked to that idea. Now join the words up, making connections between them.

Method 2

Use file cards to organise your revision. At the top of the file card write the name of the topic and an important word or phrase. Underneath write down the meaning of the word or phrase and how it links with other words or phrases in the topic. Soon you will have lots of file cards.

Different people learn in different ways:

- Some people like to record notes on a cassette and listen to them on the way to school or when they have a free moment.
- Some people like to see how things work, or like to learn using diagrams.
- Other people learn by doing things. Remember activities you did in class? When you revise, try and picture what happened in the class on that day.

Whichever method you use, **good luck** in all of your exams and tests!

Experimental skills – a checklist for experiments

Use these points to help you when you write up an account of your experiments

- Have a question that you want to answer.
- Make a list of the things you need to use.
- Write step by step instructions.
- What will you measure?
- Give an explanation of the science in your question using proper scientific language.
- Do trial runs of your experiments and get some readings.
- Find information from textbooks about your question.
- Say how you will work safely.
- Make sure your work is a fair test and explain why it is fair.
- Decide how many readings you need to take for accurate results.
- Explain why your experiment is accurate.

- Make tables of your results.
- Decide whether there are enough results for an accurate answer, and repeat your readings.
- Make charts or graphs to show your results.
- Draw lines of best fit on graphs, they could be curves.

- Explain what the graphs show.
- Present all your calculations.
- Explain how the answer given fits with the readings.

- Do you have any doubtful results i.e. results which don't seem to fit your pattern. Don't include them in, do more repeats.
- Explain how you could improve the methods or equipment used.
- Decide if you had enough results to be certain you were right.
- Were your repeats of results close in value?

Physics Post-test chapter

Scientific questions

How can we see more?

Figure 1 At a simple level we look and record what we see. We can use instruments to help us. Astronomers and astrophysicists like Dominique use telescopes and radio telescopes. She uses the radio telescope you can see behind her.

Figure 2 Photographs can help us to study things. You can't see the colour in stars, but a photograph shows that colour is there. Stars can be put into groups according to their size and colour. One type of star is a red giant. Another is called a white dwarf star.

Questions

1 Telescopes and photographs help us to see things. What can we do to help our ears to hear?

2 List any other ways in which we use photographs to help us to see things that our eyes can't see on their own.

How can we explore invisible worlds?

Using echoes

If we make a sound, we can hear its reflection or echo. Submarines and fishing boats do that. A geological surveyor uses explosives to make a large sound. The reflections tell the geologist about the layers of rock underground.

Using X-rays

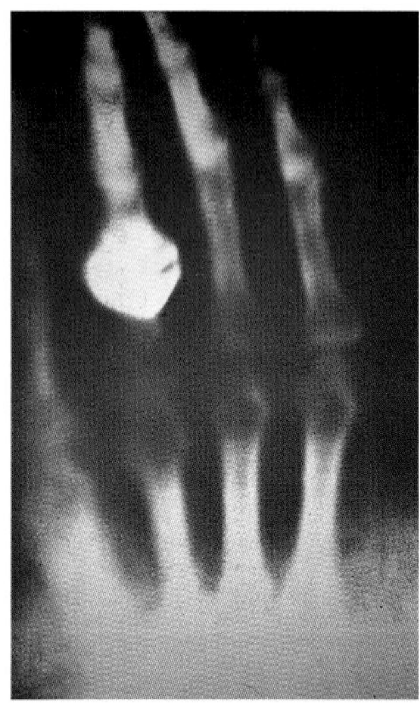

Figure 3 X-rays can be used to 'see' inside your body. X-rays travel easily through most parts of your body. They do not travel easily through bone. They make shadow pictures of your bones and other things they can't pass through. The bones and metal ring show up clearly on the photographic film.

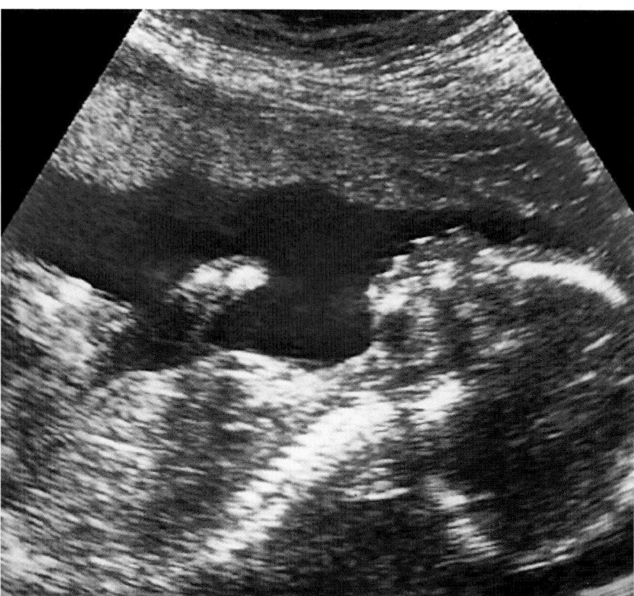

Figure 4 A radiographer in a hospital uses high frequency sound or ultrasound. The reflections provide information to make an image of the unborn baby.

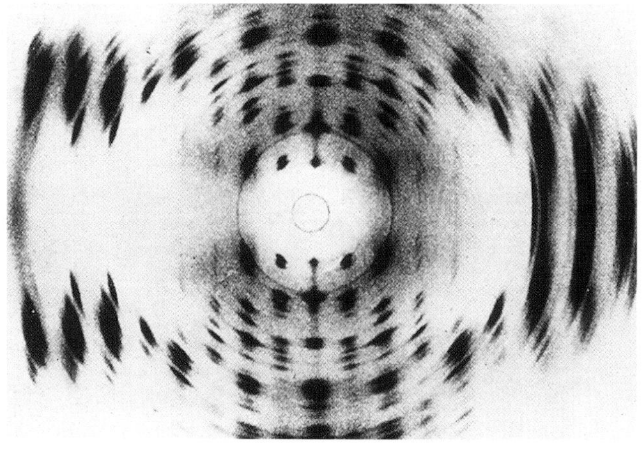

Figure 5 Atoms are much too small to see. If we shine X-ray beams onto a crystal we get a pattern like the one shown. The patterns tell us how the atoms are arranged in the crystal. This photo shows the arrangement of atoms in DNA.

Question

3 Read this page again. Then write down the ways in which ultrasound and X-rays are:

a) similar

b) different.

Why do we measure?

Key words

analogue Something which changes in the same way
variable Something which can change

As far as we know other animals don't count. Counting is a human thing. It is very useful.

But we don't just count, we measure. Measuring is a way of comparing. We can write measurements down so that we don't forget them.

With the right measurements we can make predictions. We can predict how many cakes we bake, how big a building or a bridge will be. We can find out about relationships between **variables**.

How do we measure?

When we make measurements we use units. Metres, seconds, kilograms and °C are all units. We have to use units sensibly.

2 metres + 2 metres = 4 metres
but
2 metres + 2 seconds doesn't equal anything at all.

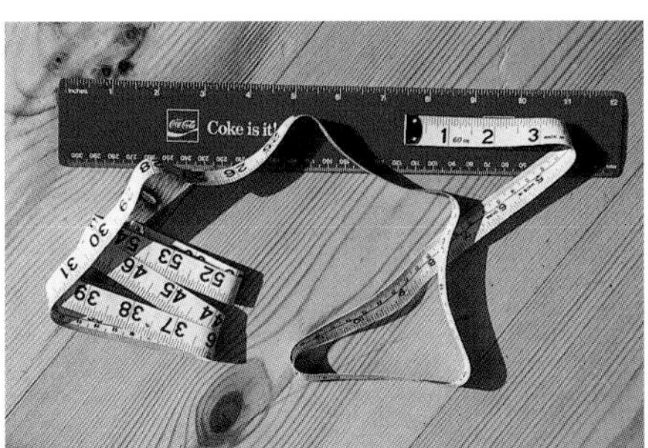

Figure 6 We measure length using numbered scales. Usually a scale is printed onto wood or plastic, and then we call it a ruler. Sometimes the scale is printed on a length of tape. The markings on the scale are evenly spaced. All rulers have the same spacing. We can all agree on the measurements whichever ruler we use.

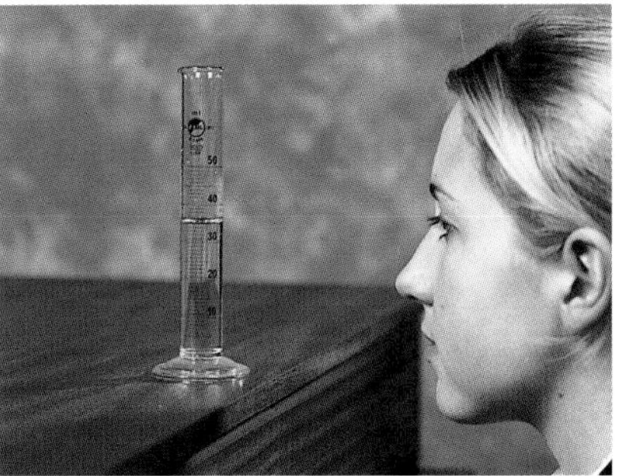

Figure 7 We use measuring cylinders to measure the volume of liquids. The measuring cylinder has a scale marked on it.

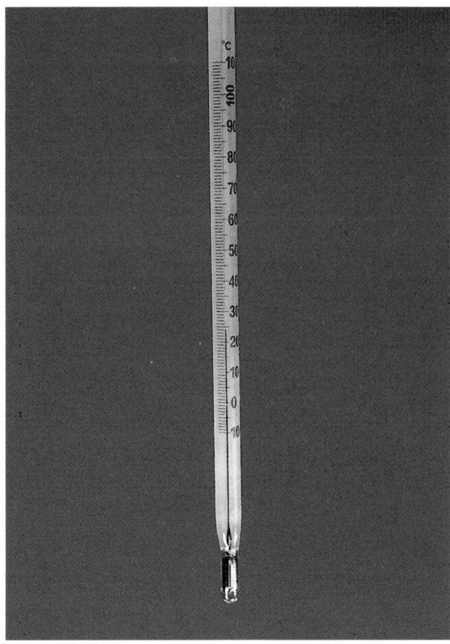

Figure 8 Measuring temperature is not quite so easy. We know that some materials expand when they are heated. So to measure temperature we use the expansion of a liquid in a tube.

The length of a thread of liquid in a tube is not temperature, but is related to temperature. We use the length of the thread as an **analogue** of temperature. The liquid-in-glass thermometer is an analogue measuring instrument.

Analogue and digital instruments

Key words

digital Scale made up of numbers that change

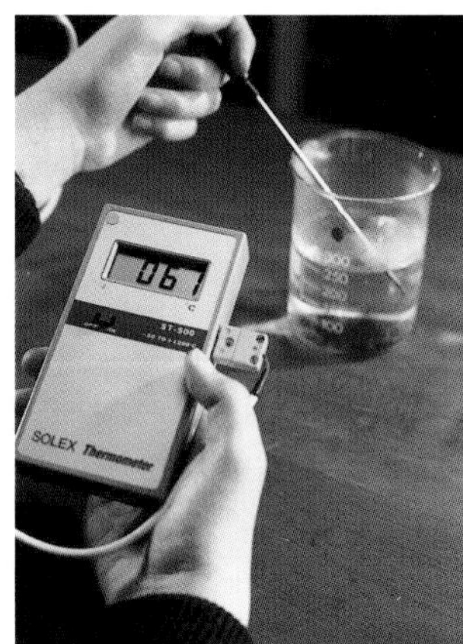

Figure 9 Some thermometers are not analogue. This is a **digital** thermometer. The temperature is shown as a number.

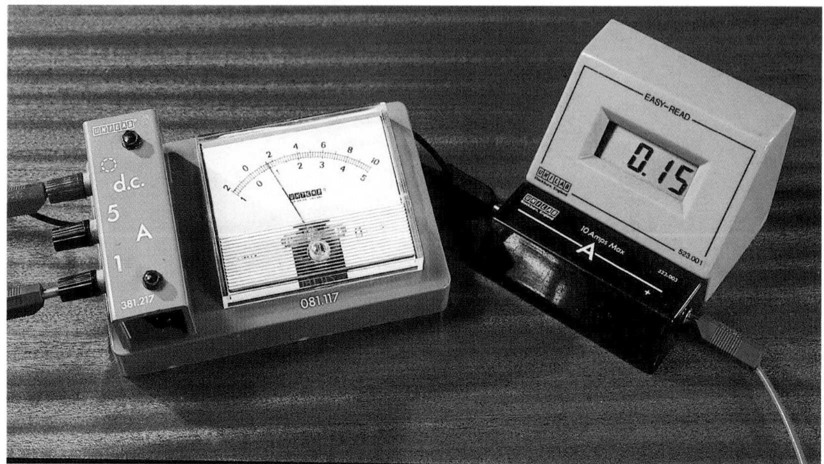

Figure 10 Ammeters and voltmeters can be analogue or digital. The analogue ammeter has a needle which moves across a scale. The digital ammeter is easier to read.

Figure 11 Most car 'speedometers' are analogue, Concorde is fitted with a digital 'speedometer'.

Questions

4 We know that 2 + 3 = 5, But can:
a) 2 dogs + 3 cats = 5 camels?
b) 2 cm + 3 mm = 5 mm?

5 What does 2 cm + 3 mm equal
a) in cm?
b) in mm?

6 What are the readings on these instruments?

How do we investigate variables?

Key words

input variable A variable that we can control

output variable This variable changes when we change the input variable. We have no direct control over it

You have grown since you were born. We say your height has varied. Soon you will stop growing. Then it won't vary any more. It won't be a variable, but will be constant. Your weight is likely to continue to change. It will be a variable for longer. Variables are quantities that we can measure. They are quantities that can change.

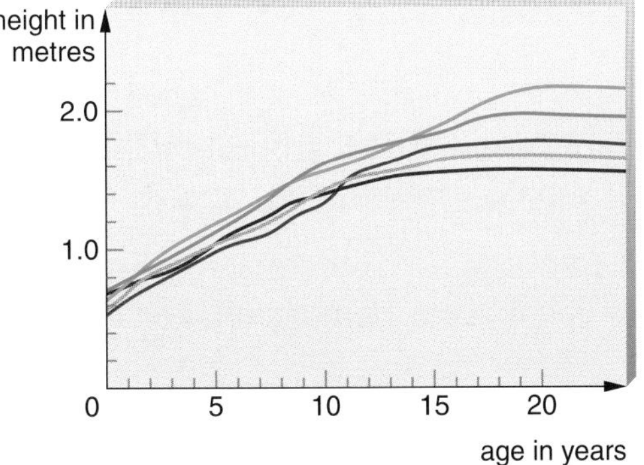

Figure 12 This graph shows how the heights of five people changed as they got older. You can 'see' a pattern. They grew taller as they got older and then stopped growing before they were twenty years old. Height and age are variables. The graph shows that height and age are related variables.

Science helps us to find simple patterns from what at first appear to be complicated things. As always, we have to do a fair test. If the test is to be fair we must investigate *two* variables. If the test has more than two variables it will be impossible to get a fair result.

Usually in an experiment we control one variable. We decide how to change it. This is called the **input variable**. You can also call it the *controlled* variable.

Then we watch what happens to the other variable. We have no direct control over it. We just wait to see what happens. This variable is called the **output variable** of the experiment.

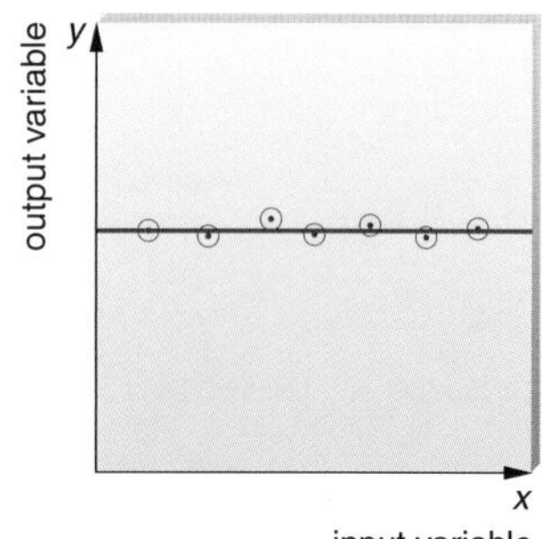

Figure 13 The graph is horizontal (level). This means that as x increases, y stays almost the same. We say that y is independent of x (it does not depend on x).

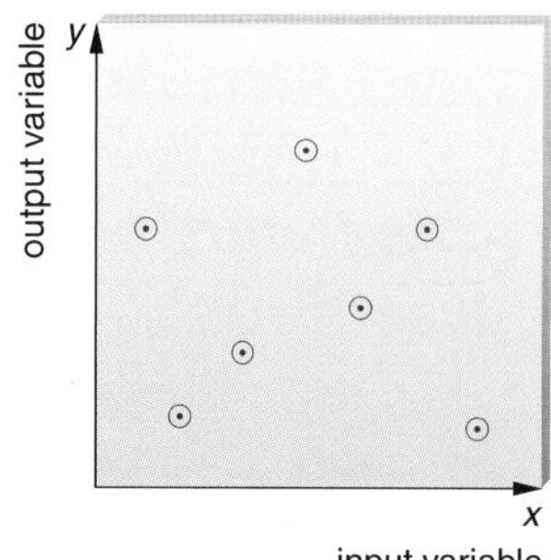

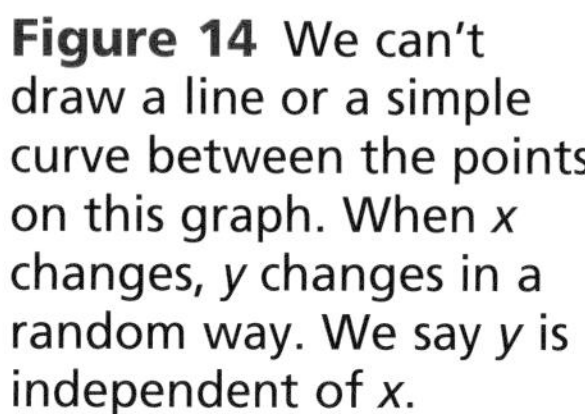

Figure 14 We can't draw a line or a simple curve between the points on this graph. When x changes, y changes in a random way. We say y is independent of x.

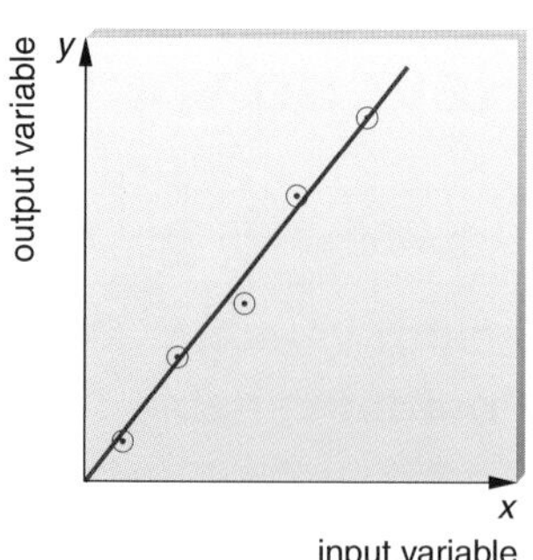

Figure 15 This graph is a straight line. We find that when x changes, y changes by the same proportion. We say that y is dependent on x.

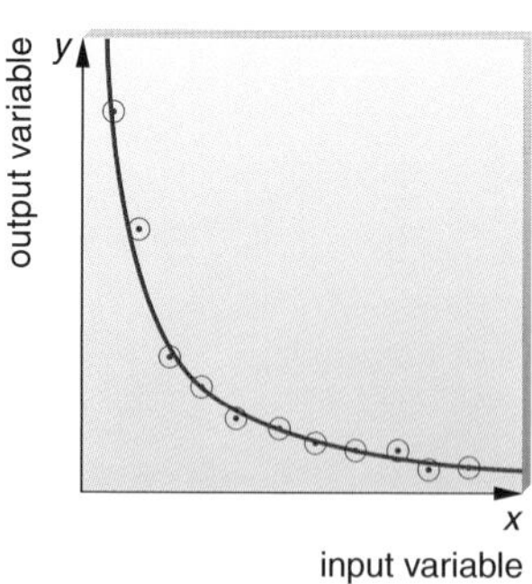

Figure 16 This graph is a curve. When x gets bigger y gets smaller. We say that y is dependent on x.

These graphs show that the output variable doesn't change when we change the input variable. We say the variables are independent of each other.

We plot graphs to see if there are any relationships between variables. We plot the input variable on the bottom axis (x-axis). We plot the output variable on the side axis (y-axis).

The graphs in Figures 15 and 16 show that both variables change in a clear way. The output variable is dependent on the input variable.

Questions

7 a) For each of the graphs below:
- i) name the input variable
- ii) name the output variable.

b) Which of the variables do you control when you do an experiment?

c) Say whether the output variable is *dependent on* or *independent of* the input variable.

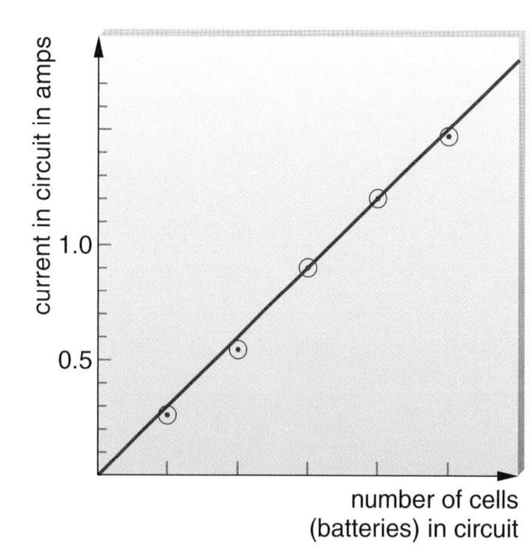

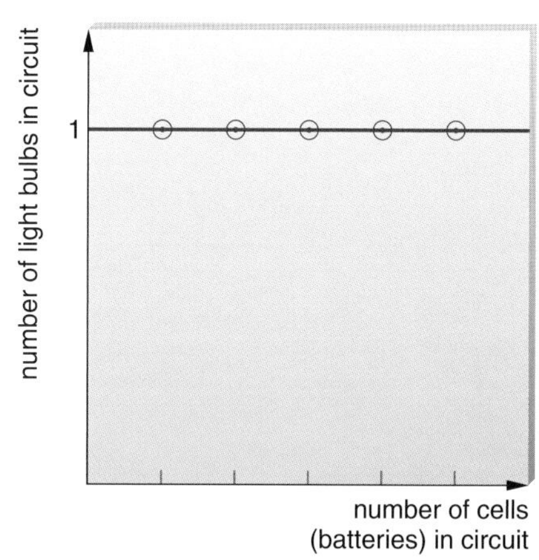

What is a scientific question?

A scientific question is one that we can investigate by doing an experiment.

These are scientific questions:

- Does a wet surface cool down more quickly than a dry one?
- How can we make water evaporate more quickly?
- What is the relationship between the saltiness of water and how high ships float?
- How do fish control upthrust?

These are some questions that are not scientific. They are still important questions, but we can't find the answers from scientific experiments:

- Who is the world's best singer?
- Are elephants beautiful?
- Who is the world's best football player?

How do we test ideas and answer scientific questions?

First we must do an experiment. The purpose of the experiment will be to answer a question. These are the different stages in an experiment:

Step 1: I have an idea that's based on what I know so far. I'm not sure if it's a good idea. I can write my idea as a question.

Step 2: Depending on the answer to my question, if I do **X** . . .

Step 3: . . . then I'd expect **Y** to happen. Now I have a prediction that I can test.

Step 4: If **Y** does happen then my idea is probably a good one.

(This is usually good because it says you might be on the right lines with your idea.)

Step 5: If **Y** doesn't happen then my idea must be wrong. I need a new idea. (This is almost always good, because it makes you have to think about new ideas. Being wrong is the start of new ideas. It can be very useful to be wrong!)

This way of working is called the scientific method.

Here is an example:

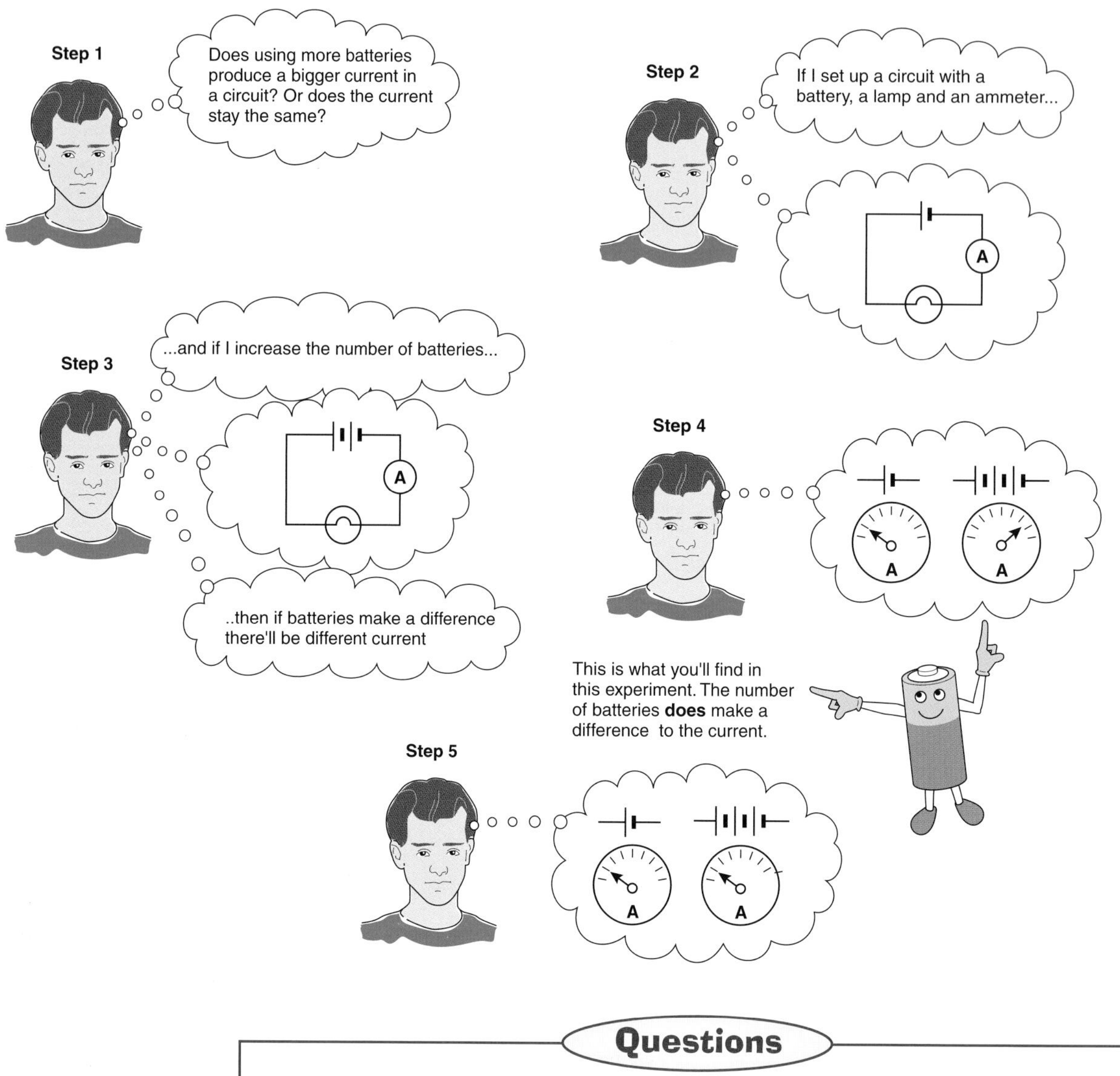

Questions	
9	What is a scientific question?
10	How do you find the answer to a scientific question?
11	Give an example of a scientific question.

How do we know that the conclusion is good?

Scientists might not believe that your answer is right. They must check your experiment for themselves. If everyone gets the same answer then they believe you. They must be able to replicate your results (repeat your experiment and get the same results).

If they get different results it could be because:

- their measurements are unreliable
- they don't have enough measurements so that their conclusions are not valid.

Some BIG questions for elephants

Elephants are warm-blooded animals. The temperature of an elephant's body has to stay the same or it will die. We humans are warm blooded too.

On most days the temperature of the elephant's body is higher than the air around it. Energy transfers out from the elephant to its surroundings. To keep its temperature the same it eats food. Its food reacts with the oxygen it breathes. This provides the energy the elephant needs to keep warm.

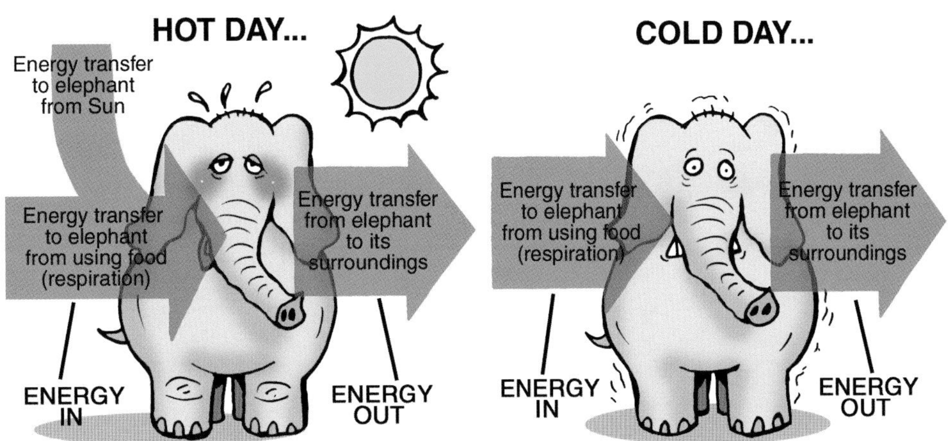

Figure 17 On a cold day energy transfers out from the elephant to its surroundings. The elephant eats food and can keep at the right temperature. On hot days, there can be a problem. Getting too hot is as dangerous as getting too cold.

Figure 18 This elephant is squirting water over itself to cool down.

On a hot day animals have to make energy transfer outwards much quicker. People cool down by sweating. Salty water comes out of their skin and evaporates at the skin surface. It cools them down. Dogs can't sweat from their skin, so they pant. They breathe hard over their wet tongues. The water evaporates and cools them down.

Elephants can use their trunks to squirt water over themselves. The water evaporates, and carries energy away from their skin.

Investigating the cooling effect

We can investigate questions that are important to elephants (and people) trying to keep cool. For each question we start by making a prediction. It might be a good one or it might not, but we can test our prediction.

Question A:

How do we know when evaporation is taking place?

A prediction we can test: If evaporation is taking place, then the mass of liquid should decrease.

Question B:

How do we know that evaporation causes cooling?

A prediction we can test: If evaporation causes cooling, then we should be able to measure a bigger temperature drop when a wet object cools than when an identical dry object cools.

Question C:

Does evaporation cause cooling only of hot objects?

A prediction we can test: If evaporation only causes cooling of hot objects, then the fall in temperature of cooler objects will be the same whether they are wet or dry.

Question D:

Does surface area make a difference? If so, how much?

A prediction we can test: If the surface area makes a difference, then the bigger the surface area that is wet, the bigger the fall in temperature. We could control the size of the wet surface (the input variable) and then measure what happens to the size of the temperature fall. (the output variable). To do a fair test we must make sure that the other variables do *not* change.

Question E:

How can we make evaporation go faster?

A prediction we can test: We can measure how quickly evaporation takes place by measuring the change in mass of the water.

Here are some variables which might affect evaporation:

- starting temperature of warm object
- rate of flow of air across the wet surface.

Questions

10 Choose one of these questions and write down a plan for an experiment. Your plan should include:

a) what variables you will measure
b) which is the input variable and which is the output variable
c) make a guess at the highest and lowest values for each variable
d) which measuring instruments you will use
e) how you will record your results
f) what you will do with the results to look for a pattern
g) what pattern you think you are likely to find. (It doesn't matter if your experiment shows you are wrong on this.)

Some questions for sailors and salmon

A liquid provides a force of upthrust. If this force balances the weight of an object, it will float.

The upthrust in salty water is different from the upthrust in fresh water. Some fish like salmon spend part of their lives in salty sea water, and part in rivers which are fresh water. They have to be able to vary the size of the upthrust.

Some ships also move between rivers and the sea. They have to be loaded so that they can float in sea water and in fresh water.

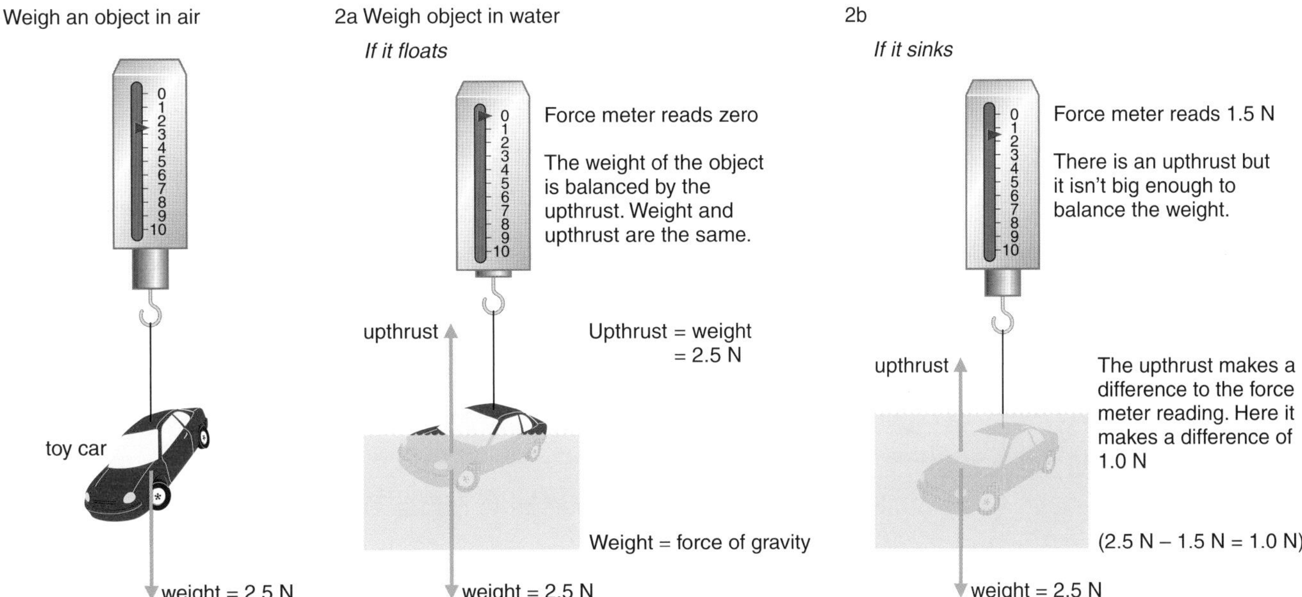

Figure 19 Upthrust and how to measure it.

Variables that *might* affect upthrust include:

- the saltiness of the water
- the weight of the object
- the volume of the object

Questions

These are some important questions for these ships and for salmon.

A Does salty water provide more or less upthrust on a body than fresh water?

B What happens to the upthrust as we vary the saltiness of water?

11 For each of these questions, suggest some predictions you can test. Your teacher might ask you to do some investigations of your predictions and write a report on them. At each stage check your ideas with your teacher.

Chemistry Post-test chapter

Key words

data Measurements, readings and things you see that you write down.

models A way of thinking about how a scientific idea works. It is a similar thing that you can see in your imagination – like particles and Carnival People.

Science and experimenting

Science is about explaining how things happen.

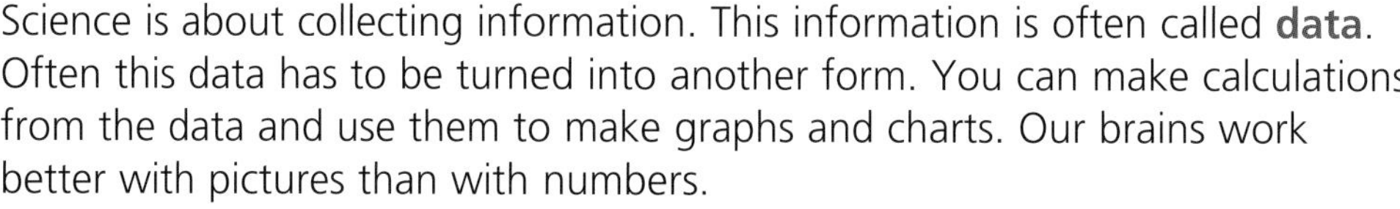

Science is about collecting information. This information is often called **data**. Often this data has to be turned into another form. You can make calculations from the data and use them to make graphs and charts. Our brains work better with pictures than with numbers.

Figure 1 Is this a scientist?

This information is used to find patterns in the way natural things work. If they can find a pattern, people working scientifically can use that pattern to make predictions about the way things will happen in the future.

Not all scientists look like the person in Figure 1.

A nurse is a scientist. Nurses have to use data to try to make patients better.

A gardener is a scientist. Gardeners use data to find out how much fertiliser to add to the soil to produce the best crop.

A chef is a scientist. Chefs must choose the right mixture of ingredients to make the perfect meal.

A builder is a scientist. Builders have to make the correct concrete mix to build safe buildings.

Stuff is made of particles because ...

Science is about using models.

Models are a way of thinking about how things work. In science the small particles like atoms and molecules are far too small for us to see. Particle models can be used to help us explain the behaviour of most materials.

Chemistry is about understanding how substances behave. To do that we have to see patterns in how substances change, and explain them using the 'because' word.

Figure 2 People do chemistry to make better materials – materials for better clothes, for cosmetics, for people's health, for improving crops, for counteracting pollution – the list is endless.

'Because' Questions

Complete the explanation for each of these observations. If possible, try to use a 'model' to explain your idea.

1. Candle wax melts at 58 °C because ...
2. A bike tyre feels hard even though it is full of air because ...
3. A peeled orange smell spreads across a room because ...
4. Copper conducts heat and electricity because ...
5. Black ink can be separated into many colours because ...
6. Nail varnish is cleaned off by nail varnish remover, but not by water because ...
7. When water evaporates from your skin you feel colder because ...
8. Rocks get broken up by water freezing because ...
9. Iron rusts and cream goes sour because ...
10. When heated, magnesium flares up and becomes a white powder because ...
11. Litmus paper turns blue in soapy water because ...
12. Magnesium reacts with acids because ...
13. Tartaric acid and sodium bicarbonate (baking powder) makes scones spongy because ...
14. Vinegar will cure wasp stings because ...
15. Powdered lime is put into lakes affected by acid rain because ...

Key words

displace A more reactive element that will kick a less reactive one out of a compound and take its place.

reactive Combines easily with other elements to make compounds.

subliming Turning from solid to gas with no liquid state, melting and boiling at the same temperature.

unreactive A very stable element that needs lots of energy put in before it will form compounds.

A family of non-metals

Science is about finding patterns.

The halogens are a family of **reactive** non-metals. They all occur in the same column or period of the Periodic Table, just before the noble gases. They have very similar chemical reactions. This is one of many 'patterns' that can be found in the Periodic Table.

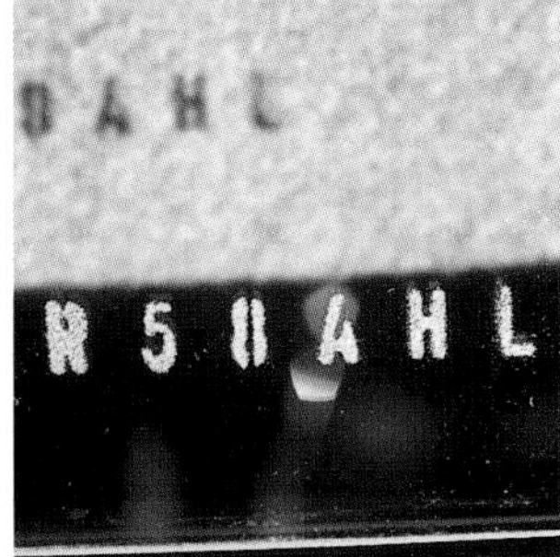

Figure 3 Security marking car windows with the registration number.

Eating into glass

Glass is a very hard material. Glass is almost totally chemically **unreactive**. That's why we use it so much as containers for food and chemicals. Glass is much less reactive than metals or plastics. Both of these give nasty tastes to food, but glass does not. To attack glass you need a really reactive chemical. That chemical is hydrofluoric acid

When car windows are marked with their registration number, a mask is used to protect the surrounding glass. The chemical is put on as a jelly so it stays in one place. It eats into the glass, dissolving the surface and leaving a rough patch that is a contrast to the smooth surface.

The halogens

Figure 4 Some of the halogens: chlorine, bromine and iodine.

The halogens are a group. They are Group 7 of the Periodic Table. They are typical non-metals:

- low melting points,
- do not conduct electricity or heat,
- react strongly with metals.

They have similar chemical reactions but they are not the same. They react differently with living things. They range from very dangerous to a strong antiseptic. There is a reactivity series for halogens. They will **displace** each other from solution.

Fluorine

This is the most reactive and the most dangerous. It will make wood and rubber burst into flame. The molecules are so small that they diffuse through flesh and attack your bones directly! This is one chemical you never want to see in the laboratory. It is far too dangerous.

Chlorine

Chlorine is dangerous. If you get it into your lungs it attacks them, causing septic pneumonia. If you have asthma, take care! But when it is diluted it is used in swimming pools and as a disinfectant because it kills bacteria easily. Domestic bleach also contains chlorine.

Bromine

Bromine is a liquid element at room temperature. It gives off a choking brown gas as it vaporises very easily. The gas is harmful. Bromine dissolves in water. It is a dilute solution called 'bromine water' that we usually use in science labs.

Iodine

Iodine is the pretty one in the family. At room temperature it is shiny grey crystals. But when you heat it, it turns into a beautiful purple coloured vapour. It goes directly from solid to vapour with no liquid state. This is called **subliming**.

For many years a solution of iodine was used to clean cuts and wounds. It is antiseptic, but it stings really badly!

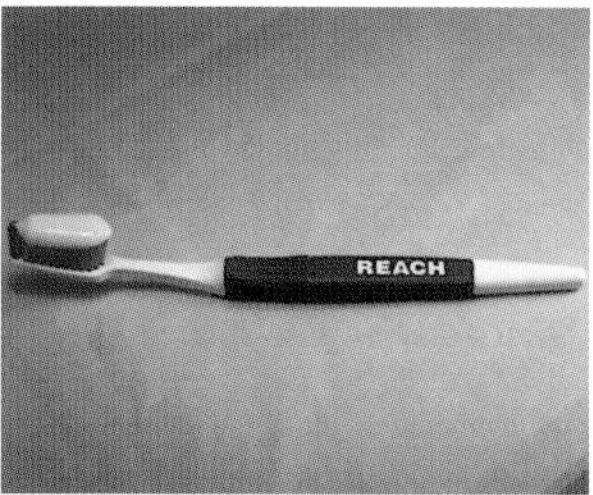

a) small quantities of fluoride make your teeth much stronger and resist attack by tooth decay.

b) silver bromide is used in photographic film and paper. Silver bromide becomes silver and bromine when light falls on it.

c) People need some iodide ions in their diet. It is one of the minerals we need for health. Iodine is needed for the thyroid gland to work properly.

Figure 5

Questions

16 Why is the glass etching chemical in the form of a jelly?

17 The people who do the security marking wear rubber gloves and eye protection. Explain why.

18 All the halogens can be used to kill germs. Find the reasons from the text.

19 Why can silver be extracted from used photographs?

20 What halogen is needed to make the thyroid gland work properly?

Key words

collisions Two particles actually have to bang into each other hard for them to react.

collision theory This is how we explain the rate at which chemicals react. Some reactions are very fast (explosions) and some are very slow (rusting).

How Fast?

Science is about applying theories.

For chemical reactions to happen, particles have to hit against each other with enough energy.

If there are more **collisions** between particles, reactions work faster.

The harder the collision the more likely it is that a reaction will happen.

This is called the **collision theory** of chemical reactions.

Cooking spuds

Figure 6 Spuds with everything.

Cooking potatoes is a chemical change that sometimes takes ages and sometimes only a minute or two. Cooking potatoes follows the same rules as speeding up any chemical reaction. If you make the potatoes hotter, they cook faster.

Chips are deep-fried in oil. They cook in 2–3 minutes, but it takes about 20 minutes to boil potatoes. That's because deep fat fryers work at a much higher temperature than boiling water.

If you cut the potatoes up smaller, they cook faster. Crisps only take 20–30 seconds to deep fry. The thin slices cook through much faster. Crinkle cut chips cook faster than straight chips. The crinkle cut exposes much more of the surface to the cooking oil, so the chips cook quicker.

This all fits with the collision theory for reactions.

- **Higher temperature** means the particles are moving faster. This causes more collisions AND collisions with more energy.
- Smaller pieces or crinkle cut pieces mean **more surface area** is exposed. This means there are more potato cells exposed, so the cooking reaction happens faster.

Get your concentration right

Use of chlorine	Concentration in parts per million (ppm)
To clean drinking water	0.001 ppm
In swimming pools	1 ppm minimum level
Minimum level to detect smell	3.5 ppm
As a restaurant surface cleaner	50–200 ppm
As a poison gas	Over 1000 ppm. Fatal after a few deep breaths.

Chlorine is a greenish yellow gas, but it dissolves in water. A dilute chlorine solution is used to clean surfaces in restaurants, to purify tap water, and to kill germs in swimming pools.

But chlorine is also very bad for the lungs. It is so dangerous that it was used as a war gas in 1915. More concentrated chlorine solutions react much faster, and can be very dangerous. When there are more particles, there are more collisions, so the reaction is faster.

Figure 7 Chlorine is used in solution to kill germs in swimming pools.

Questions

Explain these different observations using ideas about collision theory.

21 Food goes off slowly in the fridge.

22 Wood shavings catch fire easily.

23 Exhaust pipes on cars rust quickly.

24 Powdered limestone, rather than lumps, is used to treat lakes affected by acid rain.

25 You should use a hot wash for very dirty clothes.

26 Draw a diagram to show the increased surface of a crinkle cut chip.

Figure 8 Chemical reactions can be good or bad, but they follow the same rules.

Summary of the collision theory

- Particles can only react if they collide with each other.
- Some of the particles have to be a liquid or a gas, as their particles move about.
- Not all collisions result in a reaction. There has to be enough energy transferred as the particles smack together to make the reaction happen.
- To make reactions happen faster you can do three things:
  - increase the number of collisions OR
  - make the collisions have more energy OR
  - reduce the energy needed to react.

Biology Post-test chapter

What is biology?

Biology is a science that looks at how living things work. Living things are divided into five main groups: plants, animals (including humans), bacteria, single-celled organisms and fungi. Biology uses knowledge from other sciences as well: we need chemistry to explain how chemical reactions take place in living things, and physics to explain how living things move. These are just two examples. Knowledge and understanding of biology is also used to explain how living and fossilised organisms are related to each other.

Figure 1 Representatives from some of the five groups of living things.

Science is all about asking questions and finding the answers if possible. It is also about solving problems. In biology there are a lot of questions that scientists can ask about how living things work, how they live and where they live. Scientists test their ideas by carrying out experiments. Experiments are done to try and answer questions. Not all questions can be answered by doing an experiment. For example the question 'Which make of trainer looks best on me?' is not a scientific question.

Look at the list of questions below. Which ones do you think are scientific questions, that we could find the answers to by doing an experiment. Which ones are questions that cannot be answered by doing experiments?

Where do living things come from?

Figure 2 The recipe for mice?

For thousands of years people believed that many living things just 'appeared'. This sounds silly today. In the 17th century, people believed that they could make mice appear from some sweaty underwear and the husks of wheat. These were placed in an open jar and, after about three weeks the theory was that the sweat from the underwear would soak into the husks of wheat and they would change into living mice!

Question

1 Do you think that mice appeared in the jars and why?

Maggots and Meat

Figure 3 Francesco Redi was a physician and poet.

If you leave meat lying around in the warm it will rot and maggots will appear. The maggots don't come from thin air. In 1668, a scientist called Francesco Redi was the first person to prove that maggots came from flies. He had a theory that flies laid eggs on the meat and that the maggots came from the eggs. He put meat into a number of glass bottles or flasks. Some of the flasks were open to the air, some were sealed from the air and others were covered with cloth that prevented the flies landing.

Questions

2 Do you think maggots appeared on the meat in the open flasks? Why?

3 Do you think maggots appeared on the meat in the sealed flasks? Why?

4 Do you think maggots appeared on the meat in the flasks covered with gauze? Why?

Not everyone was convinced by Redi's experiment. Some scientists showed that even if a flask was sealed, fungus and other living organisms grew on the meat.

Louis Pasteur's experiment

Key words

microbes Living organisms too small to see with the naked eye.

pasteurised A process of heating foods to a high temperature for a short time to kill off any microbes.

Figure 4 Pasteur made special flasks with S-shaped necks.

Louis Pasteur was a French scientist who lived in the 19th century. He asked the question 'Why does food go off if left in the open air?' He came up with the theory that **microbes** were responsible. Pasteur planned an experiment. He put some meat broth into a glass flask and heated it to kill anything that might be living in the broth. He then heated the neck of the flask until the glass began to melt and curved the neck into an S shape. He sealed the flask by heating the end until the glass melted. Nothing grew in the sealed flasks.

Then he broke off the end of the flask to let the air in, but the curved neck trapped any microbes floating in the air. When Pasteur tilted the flask and let the broth come into contact with the neck area the broth very quickly went cloudy. Pasteur had proven that microbes do make food go off. They are everywhere, even in the air we breathe.

Pasteurised milk is milk that has been heated to a very high temperature for a very short time. This kills off the microbes and makes the milk safe to drink. Pasteur also found a cure for a deadly disease called rabies.

Maggots and murder

Figure 5 Maggots have helped the police to solve many murders.

Maggots can help the police solve serious crimes like murder. When a murder takes place, the murderer often tries to hide the body by dumping it or burying it. Insects are the first things to settle on the body and they do this very quickly.

Trained scientists, called forensic scientists, examine the scene of the crime looking for evidence to tell them how the person was murdered. They try to find out where the person was murdered and most importantly when. Flies are always looking for somewhere to lay their eggs and a dead body is perfect. Forensic scientists will look for evidence such as fly eggs, maggots, dead flies or other insects. By studying them carefully they can work out what species they are and how old they are. The scientists can work backwards and pinpoint when the first flies laid their eggs to help them find the time of death. The number of different insects can show if a person was killed in the spring or summer, autumn or winter. More than one murderer has been caught by a maggot on a dead body!

Humans as organisms

Nutrition

Fifty years ago science fiction films and stories would often have humans eating pills instead of real food. They showed people wearing silver suits, flying around in 'hover cars' and getting all their nutrients from a single pill, washed down with a glass of water. Would you like to live in a world like this?

Figure 6 Food is kept in packs like these, the astronauts need to add water before they eat it.

In real life, astronauts need to have a balanced diet, just like us. They cannot take lots of fresh food into space. Inside the space shuttle there is only a small space to prepare and cook the food. Much of the food astronauts eat is dried. It is pre-packed and in order to eat the food they simply add either hot or cold water through a special nozzle that makes sure the water doesn't escape into the cabin.

Questions

5 What are the basic food groups that an astronaut needs in order to have a balanced diet?

6 What problems might astronauts have eating and drinking in a weightless environment?

Movement

Many of our muscles work in pairs. Our arms are a good example. The muscles are attached to our skeleton by tendons. Figure 7 shows how these muscles work.

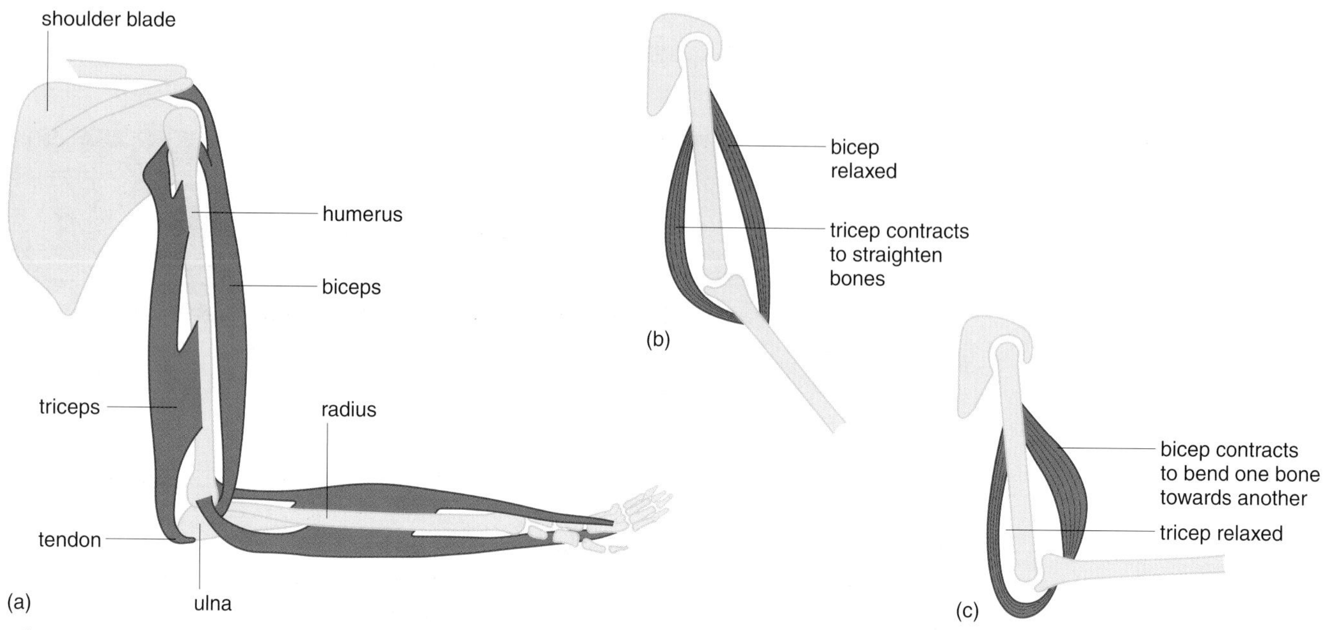

Figure 7 The biceps and triceps are the pair of muscles in the upper arm.

The skeleton and muscles work together to produce movement. If we damage a muscle or break a bone it can make even simple movements very difficult.

Questions

7 When the bicep contracts, what happens to the tricep?

8 Think of another pair of muscles that could work in the same way as the arm muscles. Write down where you would find them (you don't need to know the actual names of the muscles).

9 What sort of movements would be difficult if you broke a bone in your wrist? What help would you need to do everyday things?

Reproduction

Key words

dander The dead flakes of skin that normally make up most of the dust in a house.

donor A person that gives sperm, eggs or other organs for the benefit of others.

infertility The name given to a condition where a person cannot have a baby naturally.

in vitro fertilisation (IVF) When an egg is fertilised outside a woman's body, normally in a glass dish. The word vitro means glass.

Sadly some couples cannot have children. If a person cannot have a baby the condition is called **infertility**. Sometimes men can be infertile and don't produce sperm. Sometimes it is the woman who cannot produce eggs. Often, the couple will talk to their doctor about fertility treatment.

The newspapers used to refer to children born after fertility treatment as 'test tube babies'. This is actually not true. A test tube is not used. An egg is removed from the woman and put in a glass dish. Sperm, either from the father or from a **donor**, is then added to the dish. If the sperm joins with the egg and fertilises it, then the egg is placed back into the woman's womb. This type of treatment is known as **In Vitro Fertilisation** or **IVF** treatment.

Many cases of infertility can be treated with drugs. Hormones can be given to encourage the body to produce either sperm in men or eggs in women.

Breathing

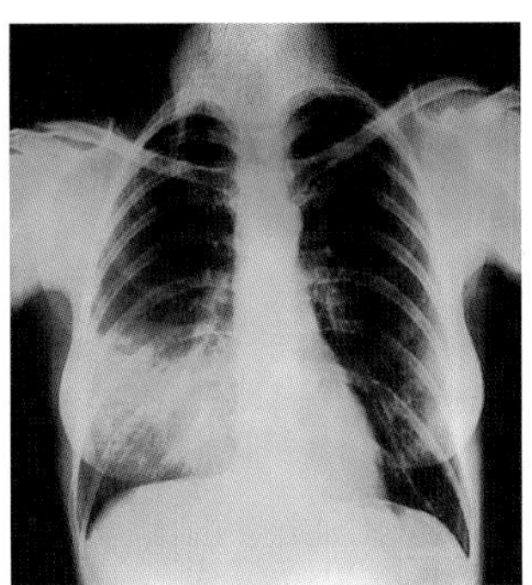

Figure 8 An X-ray of the lungs can be used to check for diseases like bronchiolitus.

There are lots of tiny particles in the air that we breathe in. These may be bacteria, viruses, spores, dust, or lots of different particles like pollen that we may be allergic to. Pollen is the commonest cause of hay fever.

The lungs work hard to provide us with oxygen and to get rid of the waste gas carbon dioxide. Any lung disease can be serious. If we get an infection, like a cold or 'flu it can irritate different parts of the lungs. Pneumonia (inflammation of the lung) is usually caused by bacteria or viruses and is more serious.

A common lung problem is asthma. People who suffer from asthma find it difficult to breathe. The tubes that supply air to the lungs contract, or get smaller, stopping air getting deep into the lungs. The cause of asthma can be pollen, house mites, fungal spores and **dander**. The dander from humans makes up most of the household dust we have in our homes.

Questions

10 What do we normally call the condition where people are allergic to pollen?

11 Explain why some asthma sufferers cannot have household pets such as cats or dogs.

Respiration

Respiration provides the body with all of the energy it needs. For a quick burst of energy we need to take in glucose – perhaps in an energy drink. For a slower burst of energy, we can take in starch that is broken down by digestion into glucose. Both starch and glucose are called carbohydrates, because they contain the elements carbon, hydrogen and oxygen. The energy is produced in our cells, where glucose is combined with oxygen. This produces water, the waste gas carbon dioxide, and releases energy. It can be summed up in the following equation:

glucose + oxygen → carbon dioxide + water + energy

$$C_6H_{12}O_6 + 6O_2 \rightarrow 6CO_2 + 6H_2O + \text{energy}$$

The energy is needed for many things – to maintain our breathing, heartbeat, body temperature and other functions. This is called our metabolism. People often talk about having a high or low metabolic rate. What they mean is how quickly we use up energy. When we take exercise or if we are under stress, our metabolic rate increases. When we are resting or sleeping our metabolic rate slows down.

Questions

12 What common name do we give chemicals such as glucose, sucrose and fructose?

13 What are the three basic elements needed to produce chemicals called carbohydrates?

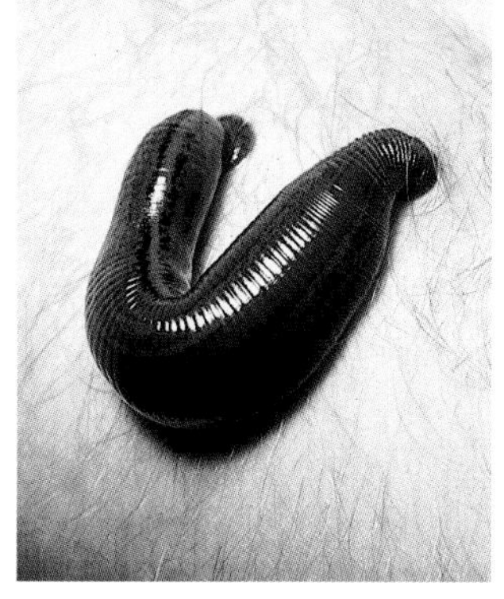

Figure 9 This medical leech will suck blood from a patient and drop off when it is full.

Health

We have come a long way from the days when doctors prescribed leeches for almost every disease. The leeches were placed on the sick person and allowed to suck the 'bad blood' out. They dropped off the patient's body when they had had their fill of blood. It often had little to no effect.

Modern medicine is now learning a thing or two from the past. Medical leeches are still used today, but only to drain bits of clotted blood from a wound. The leech has a painless bite and their saliva has a chemical that stops blood from clotting. This can cause a leech wound to bleed for several hours after the leech has filled with blood and dropped off. Leeches do not carry any infections and are not thought to transmit any diseases.

Doctors are also using maggots to clean infected wounds. Maggots only feed on dead rotting flesh. When someone has a bad wound that is infected, special sterile maggots are placed in the wound and they will literally eat the infected flesh, leaving behind the healthy flesh. This helps the wound to heal a lot faster and is more effective than treating the wound with antibiotics or other drugs.

Questions

14 What sort of medicine is used to treat someone who has a bacterial infection – an antibiotic or an antihistamine?

15 What are the different ways in which diseases can be spread among humans?

Plant Biology

Key words

autotrophs Living organisms that can produce their own food, like plants that make sugar during photosynthesis.

cellulose A type of sugar that makes up the cell walls of plants. It helps to give a shape to the cells.

Versatile cellulose

Cells are the building blocks of life. Groups of cells make tissues and tissues make up organs. Biologists use their knowledge and understanding of science to work out the functions or jobs that different cells have. But biologists can also use some of the properties of cells to make useful products that we use everyday. There are many similarities between plant and animal cells, but one big difference is that plant cells have a cell wall. This wall is made up of a type of sugar called **cellulose**. Cellulose is a very useful chemical and scientists have managed to use it and change it to make many useful things.

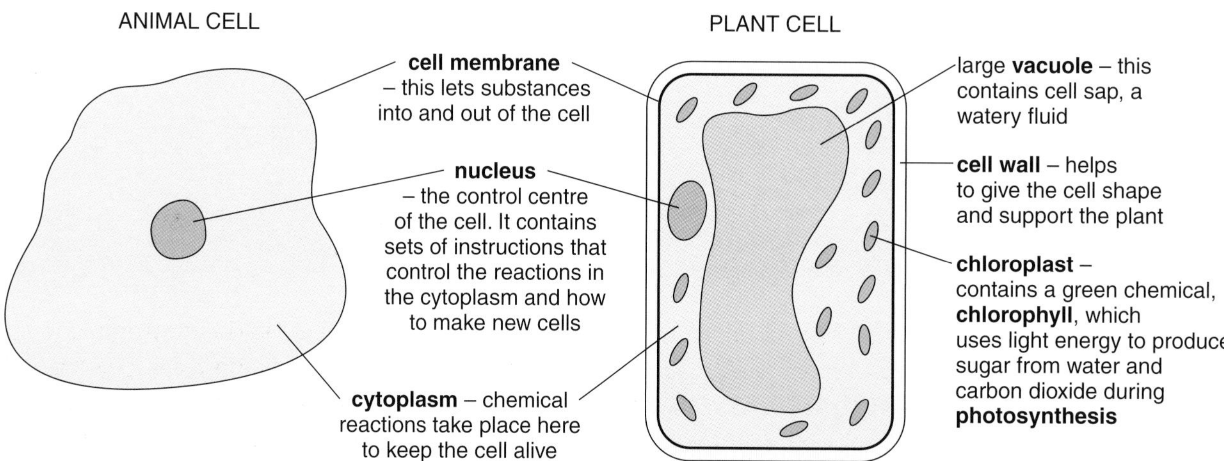

Figure 11 Plant and animal cells.

Plants in the cinema

Have you ever wondered why films are called films? A film in science is simply a thin layer. A film used in the cinema is a strip of clear plastic with a thin layer of chemicals on it that holds the image we see on the screen. Did you know that the thin layer of plastic actually comes from plants? It is a man-made chemical called cellulose acetate. The plastic is also used in car windscreens to stop the glass breaking into sharp pieces. This chemical can also be made into fibres that can be used to make clothes.

Figure 12 One of the uses of cellulose acetate.

Question

16 What other plant fibre is commonly used to make clothing?

Painting with plants

Cellulose lacquer is also a man-made chemical that can be used to put a clear plastic-like coat on top of paints. It is like a varnish. Paints that contain cellulose are often used to paint cars.

Wearing plants

You are probably wearing some clothes that contain viscose (check the label on your neighbour's blazer or jumper). Viscose is a man-made chemical that comes from cellulose. It is used in hundreds of garments and is often used with cotton, another fibre that comes from plants.

Figure 13 Sleeping bags are made from viscose

Photosynthesis

Plants make their own food by joining together water and carbon dioxide to make sugar, using the energy from sunlight. The green chemical, chlorophyll, is also needed as a place for this to happen. This process is called photosynthesis and because plants make their own food they are called **autotrophs** (*auto* means self and *troph* means feeding, so they are self-feeding).

We can write a word formula for photosynthesis like this:

$$\text{carbon dioxide} + \text{water} \xrightarrow[\text{chlorophyll}]{\text{sunlight}} \text{glucose} + \text{oxygen}$$

We can also write it using chemical symbols, like this:

$$6CO_2 + 6H_2O \xrightarrow[\text{chlorophyll}]{\text{sunlight}} C_6H_{12}O_6 + 6O_2$$

Scientists use chemical symbols as a sort of short hand way of writing down long, difficult chemical names. The symbols also tell us what atoms there are in the chemical and how many atoms each chemical has.

Carbon dioxide is made up of two types of atom, carbon (C) and oxygen (O). There is one atom of carbon and two atoms of oxygen. The number 6 in front of the chemical symbols means that there are 6 lots of carbon dioxide present.

Many people see plants as quite boring as they never move. This is not really true. Plants do move to face the light. If you leave a potted plant on a window sill facing in one direction, the plant will bend towards the light. If you then turn the plant around it will bend back towards the light (try it out over the summer holidays).

Questions

17 Apart from those things listed in the formula, what else do plants need in order to photosynthesise well?

18 What do farmers and gardeners often add to the soil to help plants grow, and what are the three elements they contain?

Genetically modified (GM) plants

Potatoes have had genes inserted into them that are normally found in rice. These genes produce extra vitamin A. By growing potatoes that have extra vitamin A, it can help to reduce the number of people suffering from a lack of this vitamin.

Plants are also being used to make plastics. Plastic is normally made from crude oil. Some bacteria naturally produce a type of plastic and genes from these bacteria have been inserted into rape seed plants that normally produce rape seed oil. These plants then make plastics that can be extracted from them. Whatever plants are, they most certainly are not boring!

Question

19 Where are the genes found in plant cells?

Ecology

Ecology is the study of plants and animals, the environment in which they live and how they interact with each other. Ecology is a very important branch of biology. Until scientists began to understand how living things affected each other, and how changing the environment affected them, man caused many problems. Our actions probably made many thousands of plants and animals extinct.

We now have many laws in this country and abroad, designed to protect and save plants and animals from extinction. The problem is that many of us are willing to save the cuddly animals like the panda from extinction, but we don't feel as strongly about an ugly reptile or a boring plant.

Zoos are places that now spend a lot of time and money protecting thousands of different species from extinction. The Millennium Seed Bank has been created at Kew's country estate in West Sussex. They are carefully storing seeds of species that are nearly extint.

Glossary

Acceleration Any object that's changing either its speed or its direction, or both, is accelerating 118, 119

Acid Substances that can have dangerous reactions. 18, 20, 21

Acid rain Pollution dissolved in the water in clouds that makes the rain more acid 58, 59

Addictive Something you cannot stop taking once you've started 50, 54, 55

Adipic acid Chemical used to make nylon 109

Alcohol A colourless chemical found in alcoholic drinks 52, 53

Alkali metals A family of similar metals, very reactive 28, 29, 106, 107

Alkali A different set of substances that can also have different dangerous reactions 18

Alloy A mixture of metals. 16

Alveoli Small damp air sacs at the end of each bronchiole, through which oxygen enters the body and carbon dioxide leaves 46

Analogue Something which changes in the same way 139, 140

Antarctic Continent round the South Pole – totally frozen 30

Antioxidant A substance put in food to stop it reacting with oxygen 102

Area The size of a surface 124

Arthritis A condition in which a person's joints become painful, swollen and stiff 48, 49

Artificial selection Selecting two plants or two animals with specific traits to breed together 4, 5

Atmospheric pressure The pressure exerted on us by the air above us 126

Autotrophs Living organisms that can produce their own food, like plants that make sugar during photosynthesis 165

Ball and socket joint The type of joint you have in your shoulder and hips 48, 49

Base In chemistry, this is a substance that neutralises an acid 20, 60, 61

Biomass The amount of plant or animal material there is 82

Breed A particular group of animals that have the same characteristics 6, 7

Brittle A brittle material does not bend, it snaps apart 16, 17

Bronchi Two pipes that branch off the trachea, one pipe (bronchus) for each lung. 46

Bronchioles Small tubes that take air deep into and out of the lungs. 46

Bronze A mixture of copper and tin metals 24

Carbon monoxide A poisonous gas 50, 98, 99

Caustic A substance that will damage flesh and skin 28

Cellulose A type of sugar that makes up the cell walls of plants. It helps to give a shape to the cells 164, 165

CFCs Ozone destroying chemicals. 64

Chemical change A permanent change in substances 32, 100

Chromosomes Threads of DNA, a human has 46 chromosomes in 23 pairs 2, 3

Collision theory This is how we explain the rate at which chemicals react. Some reactions are very fast (explosions) and some are very slow (rusting) 152, 154

Term	Definition	Pages
Collision	Two particles actually have to bang into each other hard for them to react	153
Combustion	Another word for the burning reaction	98, 99
Competition	Fighting with other plants for space, light, water or nutrients	90
Compressible	Can be squeezed or squashed into a smaller size	128, 129
Conduction	Lets energy pass through easily	16
Corrosion	Metal reacts with water and air to become a brittle material and flakes break off the surface	22, 26, 102
Cracking	Breaking big molecules into smaller ones	104, 105
Dander	The dead flakes of skin that normally make up most of the dust in a house	161
Data	Measurements, readings and things you see that you write down	148
Deceleration	Slowing down of a moving object	118
Decline	To go down or reduce in numbers	92
Detonator	Device that starts the explosion	108
Digital	Scale made up of numbers that change	140
Displace	When a more reactive metal takes the place of another one in a compound	20, 21, 26, 27, 31, 151
Dissipate	Spread out into the surroundings	34, 35
DNA	The chemical that makes up the nucleus of every cell	2, 3,11, 14
Donor	A person that gives sperm, eggs or other organs for the benefit of others	161
Drag	Friction when moving through a fluid such as air or water	112, 118, 119, 120
Drug	A chemical that can be man-made or natural that changes how the body works or reacts to disease	54, 55
Efficiency	Producing a lot of useful energy with little wasted energy	40, 41
Electrons	The tiny bits that make the outside of atoms	96, 97
Emphysema	An illness that prevents you from breathing properly	50, 51
Endothermic	A chemical change that takes in energy	100, 101
Environment	Where we live	66
Erosion	Breaking up rock and carrying it away	60, 61
Exothermic	A chemical change that gives out energy	100, 101
Extinct	When every animal of one particular type dies out it is said to be extinct	10, 166
Fertilisation	The joining of an egg cell and a sperm cell	2, 3
Fertiliser	Chemicals added to or spread onto soil to increase its ability to support plant growth	88, 89
Fibrous Root	Lots of thin branching roots that spread out wide	86
Filament	A very thin wire	34, 35
Fossil	The remains of plants and animals preserved in rocks millions of years old	10, 11
Fractional distillation	Process to separate liquids by boiling	104,105
Fraternal twins	Twins that develop from two separate eggs and two separate sperm	2, 3
Galvanising	Protecting steel metal with a thin layer of zinc metal	102
Generator	A device which transforms movement energy into electrical energy	38
Genes	Small bits of DNA that control how we look	2, 3

Geostationary	A satellite orbit that takes 24 hours, so stays above the same point on the Earth's surface	78, 79
Global warming	The average temperature of the Earth's surface is getting hotter	62, 63
Gradient	Slope or steepness	16, 117
Greenhouse effect	A greenhouse heats up because it lets light in and uses it to cause heating	2
Greenhouse gases	Some gases trap energy in the atmosphere like the glass of a greenhouse traps energy	62, 63
Halogens	A family of similar elements – very reactive non-metals	106, 107, 151, 154
Hardness	Sugar is hard but not strong, it crushes easily	16, 17
Harvest	A crop, like corn or potatoes that is gathered or ripens during a particular season	88
Hexamethylene diamine	Chemical used to make nylon	109
Hinge joint	The type of joint found in your elbows and knees	48
Hormones	Chemicals that make plants grow, produce fruit or roots	8, 9
Humus	Dead plant remains, adds nutrients to the soil	60
Hydraulic	Transferring force by liquid pressure	128
Hydroelectric	Using flowing water as an energy source	38, 39
Hydrogen peroxide	A substance used to make pure oxygen in the lab	22
Identical twins	Twins that develop from one egg splitting into two	2, 3
Illegal drugs	Harmful drugs that cannot be bought or used legally	54, 55
In Vitro Fertilisation (IVF)	When an egg is fertilised outside a woman's body, normally in a glass dish. The word *vitro* means glass	160
Incompressible	Not able to be squeezed	128, 129
Infertility	The name given to a condition where a person cannot have a baby naturally	161
Input variable	A variable that we can control	141
Instantaneous speed	Speed at any one instant in time. The speedo on a car measures instantaneous speed	114, 115
Insulate	Slowing down the process of transferring energy	42, 43
Inverse relationship	A relationship where one variable gets larger as the other gets smaller	124
Ions	A particle in a salt, ions can be positively or negatively charged	18, 96, 97, 106, 107
Kinetic	About movement	36
Ligaments	An elastic tissue that stops joints moving too far	46, 47
Lime	This sort of lime is a white powder called calcium oxide	58
Mass	How much of an object there is	72, 73
Medicinal drug	Drugs taken to prevent or cure illness	54
Metal ore	Rocks containing metal compounds usually oxides	24
Methane	Natural gas	98
Microbes	Living organisms too small to see with the naked eye	158
Models	A way of thinking about how a scientific idea works. It is a similar thing that you can see in your imagination – like particles and Carnival People	148
Molecule	A little group of atoms held together	96, 97
Moment	Turning effect of a force	130, 131
Monomer	One unit of a polymer	104

Neutralisation	Acids and alkalis can cancel each other out to make new substances . . . 18
Newton metre	Unit of turning effect or moment . . . 130, 131
Nicotine	A harmful chemical found in tobacco . . . 50
Nitro-glycerine	Explosive in dynamite . . . 108
Non- metal	An element that does not have the properties of a metal . . . 16, 17, 22
Nutrient	A substance that provides nourishment, for example the minerals that a plant takes from the soil . . . 86, 87, 159
Oesophagus	The food pipe or gullet leading from the mouth to the stomach . . . 46
Organ Systems	Groups of organs that work together . . . 46, 47
Organic	Crops grown without using chemicals . . . 92
Output variable	This variable changes when we change the input variable. We have no direct control over it . . . 141
Ovule	The female sex cell in plants found in the ovary . . . 8
Oxidation	Reacting with oxygen . . . 22, 102
Oxide	Simple compounds made by oxygen . . . 20, 22, 23, 103
Oxygen	A very reactive non-metal . . . 22, 23, 99
Ozone layer	A layer of ozone gas high up in the atmosphere that absorbs harmful radiation . . . 64
Ozone	A particular type of oxygen molecule (O_3 instead of O_2) that is harmful to life at ground level . . . 64, 65
Pascal	Unit of pressure – 1 Newton per square metre . . . 126, 127
Passive heating	Collecting heat from the Sun . . . 42, 43
Passive smoking	Breathing in harmful tobacco smoke in the air, but not actually smoking . . . 50, 51
Pasteurised	A process of heating foods to a high temperature for a short time to kill off any microbes . . . 158
Pest	A living organism that can destroy crops . . . 92
Pesticide	A chemical that kills pests . . . 92
pH scale	Number scale to measure acidity, neutral is 7 . . . 58, 59
Photosynthesis	The process that plants use to produce food using energy from sunlight, water and carbon dioxide . . . 82, 83, 84, 85, 165
Pitted	Little dents in the surface of a metal caused by corrosion . . . 26
Pivot	The point around which a force turns . . . 130
Pneumatics	Transferring force by air pressure . . . 127, 129
Pollen	The male sex cell in plants, found in the anthers . . . 8
Pollen tube	A tube that delivers the nucleus from a pollen grain to an ovule . . . 8
Pollution	Waste materials in the wrong place . . . 58, 59, 61, 66, 67, 68
Polymer	A long molecule made from many units . . . 104
Potential	About position . . . 36
Potential difference	Voltage . . . 36, 37
Power rating	The rate at which an appliance transfers energy . . . 40, 41
Precision	Accuracy. In sporting events we measure to one hundredth of a second. If we want a higher precision we measure to a thousandth of a second . . . 114
Pressure	Force per unit area . . . 124, 125, 126, 127, 128, 129
Principle of moments	Total clockwise moments = total anticlockwise moments . . . 130, 131, 132

Pumped storage	A power station which uses the potential energy of water stored in an upper reservoir. At times of peak demand water flows from the upper reservoir into a lower one generating electricity. When electricity demand is low, the water is pumped back to the upper reservoir	38, 39
Reactive	Combines easily with other elements to make compounds	20, 21, 150
Reactivity series	League table for which metal reacts fastest	26, 27, 28, 30, 31
Recreational drug	Drugs taken for pleasure and that can be bought legally (or because you are addicted to them)	54
Renewable energy	An energy source that will never run out	42, 43
Rhizome	An underground stem	8, 9
Salt	Formed by the spectator ions left over after neutralisation	18, 19
Satellite	An object that orbits a planet	78, 79
Smelting	Heating metal ore with charcoal to get the metal from it	24, 25
Soot	Tiny particles of carbon	98
Sour	Nasty tasting like bad milk	102
Species	All the animals of one type that can breed and produce offspring that can breed	10, 66, 67
Spectator ions	The part of the acid or alkali that just looks on	18, 19
Stalactites	These are rock points hanging from the roofs of caves. They are made when a slow drip leaves minerals behind	60
States of matter	Solid, liquid or gas	96
Stomata	Small holes on the underside of a leaf through which gases move in and out of the plant	82
Streamlined	Shaped to have a smooth air flow over its surface	120
Subliming	Turning from solid to gas with no liquid state, melting and boiling at the same temperature	151
Substitute	To take the place of	109
Sustainable development	Human activity that does not harm the environment	66, 67
Synthetic (rubber)	Man-made, not the natural product	109
Tap root	A long thick root that can grow deep in the soil	86
Tar	A chemical found in tobacco	50
Tarnish	Dull oxide layer that forms on the surface of a metal	26, 27
Taxidermist	A person that stuffs animals for display	10
Temperature	A hot temperature is to do with faster moving particles	96, 153
Tendons	Tissue that attaches a muscle to a bone	46, 47
Terminal velocity	Constant speed of a falling object	70
Terminals	The ends of a battery or power supply	34
Textiles	Cloth	109
Thermit	Reaction used by rail workers to join steel rails	30, 31
Thrust	A forwards force	112, 118, 119, 120
Titanium	A very strong light metal	28
Trachea	The wind pipe leading from the mouth and nose into the lungs	46
Traits	Features or behaviour (shown by animals)	4
Transpiration	The process where plants lose water from their leaves	86, 87
Turbulence	The breaking up of streamlines; unsmooth air flow over a surface	120
Units of alcohol	A useful way of measuring how much alcohol you drink	52

Unreactive	A very stable element that needs lots of energy put in before it will form compounds 150
Variable	Something which can change 139
Voltmeter	Instrument to measure the voltage or strength of an electrical supply 34
Watt	The unit of measuring power. One watt is the transfer of one joule of energy per second. 1 kilowatt = 1000 watts 40, 41
Weedkiller	A chemical that poisons unwanted plants 90, 91
Weight	The force of gravity acting on the mass of an object 72, 73
Wilderness	Out in the wilds a long way from any towns 30